THE FAITH
OF AN HISTORIAN
AND
OTHER ESSAYS

Books by JAMES T. SHOTWELL

Blackstone Studios, Inc.

James Thomson Shotwell at his desk in the Carnegie
Endowment for International Peace, New York, 1960

THE FAITH
OF AN HISTORIAN
AND
OTHER ESSAYS

by
JAMES T. SHOTWELL

AN ANTHOLOGY

Foreword by Adolf A. Berle

Introduction by Norman Cousins

Selected and Arranged by
LEO PERLA *and* HELEN H. SHOTWELL

WALKER AND COMPANY, NEW YORK

PUBLISHED IN ASSOCIATION WITH INTER-ALLIED PUBLICATIONS

COPYRIGHT © 1964 BY JAMES T. SHOTWELL

PRINTED BY THE AMERICAN BOOK-STRATFORD PRESS, INC.,

IN THE UNITED STATES OF AMERICA

FIRST PRINTING

LIBRARY OF CONGRESS CATALOG CARD NUMBER: 64-25613

908
S559

To MARGARET
      GRACE and
            HELEN

61897

CONTENTS

vii

PREFACE

This book is in the nature of a testament, the fruit of a search for the meaning of History. It is the story of an historian's journey into the fascinating bypaths of scholarship out of which came *The Discovery of Time* and the philosophy of history as registered in my studies on which these chapters are based.

It is hoped that by bringing them together their fuller meaning may be realized. It has been a joint enterprise with old-time companions on other journeys, Norman Cousins and Adolf Berle, to whom I render warm tribute here.

I am also deeply indebted to my daughter Helen for her invaluable help in the shaping of the text, and to my friend Leo Perla for his enthusiastic editorial collaboration.

I owe much to my old friend Nicholas G. Balint for his editorial experience and technical advice in preparing the text for publication.

JAMES T. SHOTWELL

NOT IN WORDS ONLY

Not in words only is God glorified.
The beauty that lies hid in everything
Awaits the eye and ear for capturing
From darkness and the silence. Open wide
The portals of the senses to the tide
Of light and sound racing from stars to fling
The sparkle of their javelins on the wing,
And the music of the spheres to which they ride.

Like brooding Saul within the shadowy tent
We let these splendors pass, until we hear
The glory of beaten strings; then is unfurled
The miracle of beauty in sacrament
Like sudden burst of sunlight shining clear
Through the cathedral windows of the world.

Reprinted from POEMS, by James T. Shotwell
SIMON AND SCHUSTER, *New York, 1953*

FOREWORD

James Shotwell, historian, philosopher, poet, occasionally a diplomat and always a teacher, will reach his ninetieth birthday on August 6, 1964. Publication of his collected essays, presented in this volume, is the only adequate commemoration. Here he speaks for himself. He proves the truth of his own words "Time is not a thing to be measured out, but an everlasting flux . . . moving through the very heart of things."

Professor Shotwell (to give him a beloved but unnecessary title) has achieved that greatest of accomplishments—he has lived in his time. Pitting head, heart and pen against the greatest enemies of man —war, tyranny and hatred—he became a creative intellectual force and presently an international influence. Therewith he helped to be born the still rudimentary but growing instruments of international and world organization, whose present institutions are in appreciable part monuments to his dream and his thought.

As a very young man, I met him when the Paris Peace Conference convened to end World War I. He was then Chief of the Division of History of the American delegation. A generation and a half later, all of us can see, as can he, how the combined failures and successes of that period in which he played a splendid part laid the foundations for the reasoned and realistic hopes we have today.

All Professor Shotwell's friends, known and unknown to him, salute him now in affection, respect and solid admiration for his classic personal achievement. In his lifetime he has joined the company described by the prophet Daniel—

"They that be wise shall shine as the brightness of the firmament; and they that turn many to righteousness as the stars."

ADOLF A. BERLE

Columbia University,
May, 1964.

INTRODUCTION

When thirty years ago, I first came across a book by James T. Shotwell, I was struck not just by its penetrating scrutiny into history but by the presence of a profound moral sense. It was not intrusive; it was not hortatory. It was nothing more than a mood perhaps; but it was a magnificent mood nonetheless—one that was produced by a combination of historical knowledge and profound insight into the effect on history of man's response to questions of right and wrong. The writing of history is supposed to be aseptic. This is as it should be. But there is also a tendency among historians to avoid the highly intangible forces affecting history that are represented by man's response to moral issues. Professor Shotwell has a supreme awareness of this response; in dealing with it, he maintains complete balance and vital proportion.

A second point of distinction in the work of James Shotwell is his ability to see not just the main lines of history but the connecting joints. He knows that no period in history stands alone; it runs out of the past and it runs into the future. Contemporary events are interrelated—however separated they may appear to be by geography or circumstance. Dr. Shotwell knows how to preside over the observation of the interrelationships of events.

Still another important characteristic of James Shotwell's writings is his sensitivity to the vital fractions of history—those small turnings that open out into major change. He knows how to deal with cause and effect; but he also knows the hazards of assigning too much weight to historical determinism. So long as history is made by man; so long as men are mobile and creative and capable of aspiration or indignation, their world will be a stage for change. While paying proper attention to the historical flow, Dr. Shotwell is also on the alert for rapid turnings in the river produced by the small but potent bank or dam.

A fourth item of special distinction in his work: Some historians find a home for themselves in a fixed and limited period of history and dwell therein for the whole of their academic and professional lives. Dr. Shotwell is a historian who has developed the kind of skills that enable him to venture into almost any period of history and feel at home. It is the historical method that counts heavily with him. He is not so much an annotator of events as a trained observer and analyst. To be sure, he has a field in which he has achieved special eminence; his works on the First World War, on the architecture of peace, and on the history of recent diplomacy represent the particularized contributions by which he is most readily identified in the craft. But what is most significant about the full body of his work is the absence of confinement and the presence of a universal sense and capacity.

Few things are more satisfying to a student than to be able to pay tribute to a great teacher. This tribute I now proudly offer.

NORMAN COUSINS

THE FAITH
OF AN HISTORIAN
AND
OTHER ESSAYS

CHAPTER I

❧❧

THE FAITH OF AN HISTORIAN

WHEN I COMPARE the world of today—its desperate confusion, the fears that mock its hopes, its sense of powerlessness in the possession of power—with the quiet, isolated world of the nineteenth century in which I grew up, the perspective of the years takes on incredible dimensions of distance. Although the signs of coming change were all about us, most of our lives still followed the pattern set for us by the past. Progress was made with increasing tempo in the arts and sciences, but only at such speed as to enrich without unduly disrupting the heritage of the past. Life was still dominated, as it had been from the beginning, by the iron law of repetition forced upon it by the tyranny of the calendar, so long as each one had to meet his recurrent needs by his own effort. Life on the farm still followed the routine of ancient times as set forth in Hesiod's "Works and Days" or Cato's directions for good farming. Town life, except in the few big cities, responded to much the same rhythm and kept largely to old, established ways.

It was a world of familiar things; upon the whole a friendly one, in spite of the fact that most people worked hard and long. For church and school taught that the pursuit of happiness lay in the performance of duty, a comfortable doctrine as long as duty consisted in doing the things that brought immediate rewards in the good opinion of one's neighbors. When the whistle blew at six

Reprinted from the Saturday Review of Literature, December 29, 1951.

o'clock for the twelve-hour day at the mill, the workman knew that the farmer was already at his chores, and the level of life was kept even for town and farm. The accepted things were done in the accepted way.

We are now so far from that repetitive, static world that it is almost impossible to realize how near in time to it we still are—not merely where time has stood still in isolated, backward parts of the country, but where it has moved most swiftly. My own grandparents hewed their farms from the wilderness. Every hundred acres, the unit of pioneer farming, was a self-contained economy, using the word as Aristotle used it, to describe household management. Only, Aristotle had in mind a much more complicated, more highly developed society than that of this simple way of living—the kind of estate, for example, that George Washington owned at Mount Vernon, with all the complications of slavery and access to more than local markets. The range of market towns for the early settlers was not over a dozen miles, and each settlement lived a life apart. Politics intruded only a little into it, because it dealt only with a limited range of questions, leaving the most pressing ones to the local community. Party loyalties were inherited, embodying past outlooks or prejudices and only changing when the structure of society was shaken by crises. The Founding Fathers held a place alongside the Major Prophets; there could be differences in interpreting them but no difference in attitude towards them, for orthodoxy was sound politics.

The remainder of these things, so near and yet so far off, is not a mere excursion from realities today, however it may stir nostalgic memories. For it is against that background that the central fact in contemporary civilization becomes clear, the change from a static to a dynamic world. Greater than all the achievements of science in discovery and invention are the differences in the nature of its processes from those of the pre-scientific ages. They have broken in upon the endless rhythm that repeated age-old ways of doing things, and created a world that is forever new. For every advance in science causes a displacement in society, which in turn calls for new inventions and discoveries with further displacements. The process is one of geometric progression. This is the fundamental nature of the revolution caused by modern science, the greatest happening in all history.

Now what contribution can the historian offer to the understanding of such an event, which has no parallel in the past? There would be none at all if history were what most people think it to be, a museum of antiquities, or a branch of literature. The discipline of the historian lies more in the field of science than in that of the arts. Meticulous scholarship is as necessary for establishing truth in the confused and contradictory annals of the past as mathematics for measuring the elusive data of science. And scholarship means criticism, not only of the facts but of their interrelations—which is the only way the records acquire meaning. Antiquarianism is a pleasant pastime, but history has a sterner purpose.

That history began as a declaration of freedom of thought, as a denial of accepted belief rather than a repository of it, should not be lost sight of today. If it is to serve as a glass and compass by which to take our bearings on the vast and turbulent tide of current happenings, we cannot accept the past on its own terms, for it did not have the problems which now confront us. Disaster lurks for those who look behind while moving forward. On the other hand, we cannot chart a course for ourselves and those who follow after unless we know how we got where we are.

Now, viewed in the long perspectives of history, the most significant thing about this culmination of all revolutions, which science has brought about, is not that it has opened up the universe to knowledge and power, but that it is so late in coming. Time stood still for the men of the ice ages. There are two stone axes on my desk, which serve for paper weights on documents of the United Nations, one of chipped stone and the other rubbed to more even shape. Between these two techniques lay some ten or twenty thousand years. Yet both were used for cutting or smashing things long centuries before the first trickle of molten copper and tin furnished tools to build the pyramids. The obstacle to progress was not a lack in the capacity of primitive man for that faculty which leads to discovery, curiosity, for that is an instinct older than man himself; it was because the two techniques which governed actions outside of the range of habitual routine led into blind alleys instead of toward the freedom of the mind—which is the one essential for progress. They were the techniques of safety against the dangers due to the nature of man himself, those of the taboos and of war. The long delay in human development was chiefly due to the fact, still dominant today, that protection in time of crises may become oppression in the normal course of daily life.

The specialists in the taboo—medicine men, magicians, and priests—were the only ones who knew how to deal with that deadly potency residing in new, strange things and revealing itself in the crises of life. The cults and codes over which they presided were not for the purpose of escape from the orthodoxy of superstition, but gave it expression in ways that held awed and submissive minds in unprotesting bondage. Civilization, as the name implies, was the taking over of these processes by secular powers. This did not mean a lessening of the spiritual life, so blindly fumbling in primitive man, but a clarification of it. Its place in the dynamic world of today is not that of a technique of safety to meet the psychic terrors of change, as in taboo, but in the recognition of the limitations of the mind in its exploration of the mystery of life and the world. That exploration is left for science, the only valid interpreter of change.

In the vast horizon which this opens up, two qualifications must not be lost sight of. The primitive mind lives on in all of us; and it dominates in all the backward areas where the conditions of living have only now begun to feel the touch of progress. In all of us reason is still only a covering for a mile-deep reservoir of instinctive sentiments and emotions. This persistence of the primitive in our minds was the chief theme of one of the most intellectual historians of our time, James Harvey Robinson; but his illuminating surveys of "the ice-age mind" should not blind us to the fact that the rate of our escape to a more rational world has speeded up incredibly, even in our own lifetime. That puzzle of the philosophers, which so intrigued the sages of China, as to which has primacy, thought or action, is being solved before our eyes by the way the conquest of time and space is made possible by instruments that reach beyond the limited capacity of our senses. In these last few years we have left Newton's solid universe almost as far behind as that of Ptolemy, and the tracers that have replaced the microscope have only just begun the exploration of the solar system of the atom. Knowledge has become a temporary lodging place in a mysterious universe, which we shall never wholly understand. But the mystery is now a challenge to advance, not an impediment. The obstacles are only stepping stones along the way.

The lesson of history in the great area once dominated by the taboo is therefore, upon the whole, reasonably reassuring. But what of that other technique of emergencies, war? Does it offer any promise of a parallel development toward control and ultimate disappearance? If the answer to this question is sought in a survey of purely contemporary events, it is an emphatic "no." Never have war and the threat of it more dominated human affairs the world over than in these last years. But in the perspectives of history this tragic era presents another aspect than that of helpless involvement in an ever mounting danger. For that very danger has for the first time made the problem of peace the supreme issue of politics. The fact that the solution has not yet been found, or at least not yet accepted, should not blind one to the epochal fact that never before our time was *peace as such*, as against *war as such*, considered by practical statesmen or by realistic nations as a political possibility.

Again, as in the case of the taboo, the full significance of the place of war in the world today can best be seen by going back to the beginnings. More constant than the psychic dangers that confronted primitive man were the physical ones, especially from beasts of prey, of whom he was one. By stratagem and by the use of weapons he not only survived as a fighter, but proved his superiority over all the animal world. More dangerous, however, than any other animal was man himself. The interplay of hunt and war was natural, and perhaps inevitable, when scarcity of game led to expeditions on the ranges of other tribes. The needs of war in turn brought about a rudimentary organization. It was not enough to be the wiliest fighter with the best weapons. The horde had to work together under the guidance of the most experienced leader, and a warrior class developed with a privileged place among those who depended upon it for safety. Society was given its first secular organization within the framework of the war system.

The beginning of politics, in Greece and Rome, was due to the needs of war, when citizens were organized not according to their place in tribal or family cults as in patriarchal society, but according to the weapons they could bring for defense or for expeditions against their neighbors. Within this framework the arts of peace developed, but we should not forget that even the Parthenon was built from a war-chest and by slave labor. No one was then aware of the inherent weakness of such a society. The fall of the Roman Empire was outwardly due to the barbarian invasion, but its collapse really came from the fact that the wars on which Rome grew great sapped the life of the State economically, as well as politically. All antique history is a lesson in the fallacy of militarism.

Now we are at the point where the same judgment can be passed on the nation-state system, which is the modern parallel to the city-state system of antiquity. Although throughout the centuries of its formation the Church as the symbol of peace stood out in contrast to feudal violence and brutal war, it had to admit that wars were sometimes justified, for otherwise it would not have been on the side of law and order against anarchy and violence. St. Augustine faced the dilemma by admitting that it was the Christian's duty to aid in "just wars," meaning those in support of the established authority. But when, even in Augustine's day, the unity of the Empire was broken, this distinction between just and unjust wars became meaningless. When in the seventeenth and eighteenth centuries Grotius and the other founders of international law tried to revitalize this moral distinction of the theologians a new formula replaced it.

In the process of the upbuilding of nation-states war had been "the final argument of kings." Now, following Machiavelli, it became a recognized "instrument of politics." The phrase apparently goes no further back than Clausewitz in the early nineteenth century, but it describes the whole process of European state-making for a thousand years. Now that process is being ended by modern science, by a revolution in warfare, which fully parallels that in the processes of peace. In the first days of August 1914 Walter Rathenau, the industrialist, tried, with only partial success, to get the German War Department to see that war had become an industry under the conditions of the Industrial Revolution, and that its impact extended in other directions than those of marching troops. By 1917 this fact was clear to all the belligerents. War, in the scientific era, could no longer be held to the limited purposes for which it had formerly been fought. It had become a catastrophe for victor and victim, a contagion attacking neutrals as well as belligerents. But the weight of the centuries lay behind its use, and the efforts made at Geneva to curb or eliminate it failed as much from half-hearted support as from the frank militarism of the Axis powers. Only the absolute proof of the changed nature of war could prevent it in nations conscious of both grievances unlistened to and power to strike. This proof came in World War II and in the subsequent development of weapons of mass destruction.

It must be admitted that this view of the changed place of war in European history is not shared by many of my historical colleagues, who, having traversed the weary centuries, feel only the weight of the past upon their minds. But these "realists" in history do not come to grips with the fundamentals of the problem: what is the nature of war and the nature of science. It is a strange fact that, although war has been the dominant theme in most historical narratives, it was not until the First World War that any effort commensurate with the task was ever made to analyze the nature of its impact on the life of nations. The pioneering study was the "Economic and Social History of the First World War" of the Carnegie Endowment for International Peace, on which I mobilized over two hundred experts, including some thirty-five wartime cabinet ministers. Out of the vast assemblage of the data in this survey the one conclusion which finally became clear was that just outlined above: that for nations living under the regime of science, with their world-wide interplay of interests, war is no longer a valid "instrument of policy," not only because of its vastly increased capacity for destruction, but also because it can no longer be held to the purposes for which it is fought. It was this reasoning which induced M. Briand to propose that resort to war of this kind should be "outlawed," and at the same time to warn that such a declaration should be implemented by sanctions "as in the Covenant of the League of Nations or the Treaties of Locarno."

Thus, to summarize much history in a few words, the Charter of the United Nations rests on the lessons of two world wars. It differed from the Covenant in providing stronger measures of defense against an aggressor nation engaged in an unwarranted attack upon a sovereign state. The old kind of war was to be suppressed by a new, more vigorous form of collective security.

Then, just as it seemed as though the long road to peace were almost reaching its goal, it was suddenly enveloped in the shadow cast by the Kremlin, and to most people it has seemed that we must start all over again. The peace of nations is challenged in the name of social and economic justice. The challenger claims to be the champion of the new world of science, armed with its dynamism against the forces of capitalism, held to the past by their very nature as the guardians of vested interests. It is impossible to overestimate the strength of the appeal of this doctrine of revolutionary Communism, with its confidence of ultimate victory based upon an interpretation of history which views the capitalist state as the result of class struggle and the continuing embodiment of war. Peace— Communist peace—can come only when the last war is fought and won, that which is to rid the world of its whole barbaric past— meaning our past as well as that of the uncivilized. Applied in the first place to Europe and still urged there with revolutionary zeal, this theory is now directed chiefly by the masters of propaganda in Moscow to stir the sleeping giants of Asia and Africa against the economic imperialism of the capitalist countries. Thus the Cold War became world-wide.

In the light of these movements what is left of the hope for world peace? This question is generally thrown out as a challenge by those who think there is no answer to it. But such a negative would be a surrender to the Communist conception of the inability of the capitalist nations to achieve their purposes by peaceful means. Why not meet the Communists on their own terms? There should be no doubt as to what they are. The task is to check Communist aggression in the present and to develop social and political justice under the regime of freedom in the future.

Finally, we come to the problem of social justice. The Communist emphasis upon it as the one firm basis of enduring peace is certainly justified by history. But history is equally clear that Communism cannot provide it a fitting embodiment. For only in freedom can it discover and protect the fundamental human rights of those who need its protection most. For these coincide with the interests of the subject masses, and there is no guarantee that this condition will not continue. On the contrary, all history points in the other direction.

The Marxian theory of the Communist revolution looked forward to the "dwindling away" of the state into a world of peace and justice. But Marx, living in the *laissez-faire* England of the mid-nineteenth century, never tried to think through the final problem of just how this classless world would be governed. Lenin and Stalin found their answer in despotism, which, by its very nature, must continue the use of terror until all opposition is so crushed that it cannot rise again. The state, far from "withering away," became more and more tyrannical, and the interests of the ruled must be measured by those of the ruler.

This situation can be partly remedied by enlightened despotism— witness not only Oriental empires but eighteenth-century Europe. Even at best, however, it blocks the pathway to the full attainment of social and political justice. For it runs counter to the fundamental fact that what is right is not necessarily what each claimant individual or government thinks it to be, but the equilibrium of their conflicting "rights" in free interplay with those of others. For justice, as defined in the precepts of Confucius and in Roman law, is merely the "fixed and constant" application of the Golden Rule.

One dare not avoid or minimize the issue of communism. The supreme need in the world today is the prevention of the exploitation of honest, decent people by those in positions of power or economic advantages and their oppression by the cunning or the strong. It is but natural that the communists should attempt to solve this problem by resort to force, for that is the way most revolutions have been carried through in the past. But the communists would maintain their revolution by a continuing denial of individual freedom, a tyranny designed to check or undo that long process of emancipation of intelligence so slowly and painfully gained in the course of the centuries. Civilization is not a mechanism, but a vital principle, or rather an embodiment of many varied principles of life, which have their roots in diverse soils and their expression in diverse cultures. It cannot flourish, it cannot even survive, if those in the seats of power deny it the fundamental freedoms of life itself. All history shows that tyranny must govern by bureaucracies, which in the end fasten their dead weight on society, stifling initiative and progress. The cause of the decline and fall of the Roman Empire was not the irruption of barbarians but the fact that from the days of Diocletian, the organizer of empire, it was ruled by bureaucracy and lost its vitality. Without straining the historical parallel too much, we can at least expect that what Djilas called "the new governing class" growing up within the Soviet empire will either hold it down to the routine of bureaucracy or, in course of time yield to new forces in a changing world. It seems likely, in my opinion, that the world of the future will be neither that of the doctrinaire communist nor that of capitalism as it developed in the nineteenth century. The doctrines will remain for those interested in them, but, just as Catholicism and Protestantism, two of the most rigid doctrines in history, three centuries ago, ceased their cold and hot wars under the impact of new interests and new conceptions of the world, so the present doctrinal dispute will change its nature in an ever changing world.

And so we conclude that *the way to meet the challenge of Communism is not to resort to war, which would only create conditions favorable to it, but the elimination of exploitation the world over.*

The instrument to hold the divided world to this dual ideal of peace and justice is at hand in the United Nations. Its inadequacies are apparent, but still more apparent is the need of it. Even its failures clarify its problems. They should be a challenge to courage, not a source of disillusionment. The greatest of all political creations cannot be made in a day or generation. After all, Magna Carta is still violated even where accepted, although it established the bases of law and order more than seven centuries ago.

Certainly one cannot be sanguine or over-optimistic in our world of today. The drama of history is still enacted on the ill-lighted stage where the animal in man has so long stalked its prey. But even while trite force acquires the most deadly power of mass destruction, the theme of the conflict is changing to the realm of the spirit. The principles of secular society, which each nation accepted for itself but denied in its relations with others, are now being forged in the white heat of controversy into universal concepts of right and wrong, applying everywhere, to everyone.

CHAPTER II

⤞⤝

THE CITY OF MAN

THE UNIVERSITY

NOWHERE ELSE in the world is there such a community of understanding as in a great university. In this respect a mirror of the whole civilized world, it is a sort of synthesis of that joint endeavor in which past and future give meaning to the present. This is the chief purpose of its existence. Not merely preserving but reinterpreting the heritage of culture and adapting it to continually changing minds, it coordinates the splendor of the past—in art or science or philosophy—with the adventure of those who explore the uncharted frontiers of our thought and extend the symbols of human control still farther into the encircling mystery.

The fellowship of minds in such a community is the very condition of its existence. There is in every institution which persists through successive generations something of this solidarity of interest and outlook, which carries on the ideas and purposes of men and gives their activities continued play, long after the initial impulses have ceased. In every society the individual must surrender something of his individuality in order that it may be incorporated into that of the group itself. But in a university this sacrament of life holds true to a supreme degree. Here it may truthfully be said that he who loses his life shall find it in the lives of those who are

---

Taken from a commemoration address delivered at St. Paul's Chapel of Columbia University.

11

already partly won to ways of thinking and doing which accord with the sacrifice itself. The university permits no one-sided, partial interpretation of the paradox of Christianity; he who loses himself in its great fellowship of service also finds himself again, here and now. The gift is not left upon an altar like an offertory but, like the sacrament it really is, strengthens, develops and matures the giver who is at the same time the chief recipient.

Here we reach depths too profound for casual consideration. That there should be a purely human sacrament may seem to some of us a misleading parallel, a figure of speech not wholly appropriate to a secular community and its ideals. It may be objected that the analogy between the university and the church should not be carried to the point of employing the formulae of religion for merely human relationships; and it may be properly recalled that the very text in question was originally applicable only to the setting of life with reference to the Deity, the sacrifice of the Human to the Divine. But any such narrow construction of the frontiers of religion is as false to religion as it is to the truest appreciation of the meaning of life. A religion that does not include the highest capacities, the most unselfish purposes of the intellectual life is inadequate as a guide for humanity.

Let it be frankly stated, not as a challenge but as a fact of history, that any form of religion which tends to deny the essentially spiritual quality in the best achievement of the best minds, when questing along the frontiers of the surrounding mystery, is by its very nature destined to be passed by and discarded as the quest proceeds. Creeds can maintain themselves by force of repetition for long stretches of time, but not forever. The condition of their existence is in the long run the same as that of the rest of our heritage. In so far as belief rejects that sceptical process of inquiry which is the scientific method, it seems to erect for itself safeguards against attack. But this appearance of safety is delusive; for, the creed that lives by isolating itself from the essential condition of the intellectual life loses its own vitality and ceases to offer any effective help to square the ideal it cherishes with the reality which it ignores. History, as we have just said, bears constant witness to this law of the adaptation of creed to experience. The old saying that the heterodoxy of one age becomes the orthodoxy of the next, may be extended to a wider horizon still. For it is equally true that the major superstitions are the dislocated or fragmentary remnants of religion no longer adjustable to rational terms. There is, therefore, a pragmatic test for even those beliefs which grapple with mystery and so transcend experience. The ideals they interpret must harmonize with the understanding of things gained by intelligence.

If this be so, then the work of a university, in which intelligence is directed to the fundamental problems of life, is itself religious, not figuratively but intrinsically. It is surely an artificial frontier which theology erects between the creed that embodies belief and the processes of thought which condition its interpretation—processes which may even determine our acceptance or rejection of it.

Much more valid is the distinction which has been drawn between the attitude of mind in each case. Religion exalts the mind by the contemplation of mystery; it apprehends truth in reverence and awe. Science and reason move in the more open light of day. But here again the moving frontier shifts as we examine it. What higher mood can creeds compel than that which inspires the creative mind in the hour of its creation? Exultant in the power to mould the stubborn elements of thought into new forms for the use or contemplation of mankind, it is at the same time held in check by a sense of its own limitations. For, the knowledge gained never reaches beyond the manipulation of these elements, never unlocks their inner mystery. The case for and against us was never better stated than years ago by one now dead, that all we ever can hope to do is to build up alongside the world we cannot understand, whose mystery eternally escapes us, a parallel structure resembling those aspects of it which lend themselves most readily to our observation. Knowledge, in short, is merely a human parallel to mystery; and truth merely the harmony within this structure which we erect to fit alongside those fragments of the unknown which eternally confront us with their question. The attitude of mind of all those who really explore the mystery of life and the world is substantially the same; it is only the trifler and the dilettante who miss the religious implication in phenomena. For the mystery sobers all thoughtful men who come in contact with it.

But is this really all that knowledge is, all that truth implies? These are not the definitions of the fathers of the church. Theology, it would seem, conceived the world in less mystical terms than science. For the orthodox conceptions of sacred knowledge assert an actual penetration of mystery.

It was but natural, perhaps inevitable, that the early Fathers should draw rigid lines of distinction between the sacred and the secular. Historically it was the perpetuation of primitive attitudes; for this fundamental antithesis goes back to the dawn of reason. Its roots lie in the sensing of things beyond control which nevertheless affect or may affect human life. Such things are marked out by common consent; society is warned that they have the power to bless or curse; and, once the warning is given, the automatic action of the taboo perpetuates it. Thus the sacred acquires a separate technique. Recognized formulae must be used in speaking of it; definite and traditional ceremonies precede approach to it. The ceremonial of religion today is largely derived from such far origins; sacrifice and sacrament go farther back in human experience than any other conscious fact of social life.

Now, when the Christian Church developed its own worship, it naturally protected itself, as other religions had done, against the profane world outside. The revolutionary nature of Christianity emphasized—as revolutions do—the contrast between its beliefs and those it rejected. No other revolution in the Western World was ever so thoroughgoing in its challenge to the existing order of thought and society as Christianity; hence the tremendous strength of its denial of the legitimacy of pagan conceptions or of pagan aspirations, even when they sought the same ideal by different ways. Against such seductions—which were really the heritage of most of human achievement—the early Church set up the walls of doctrine of the City of God, the *Civitas Dei*, which reached its classic form in the theology of Augustine. Within those walls the doctors of the Church built that marvellous architecture of philosophic thought which is the Christian parallel to the city-state of the antique world. Fortunately, by the time of Augustine the model for his scheme of theology was no longer the exclusive, narrowly jealous, political structure of ancient Greece, but that one city-state whose walls had grown from seven hills to encompass all civilization. Like Rome, the City of God would one day be universal—once the pagan gods yielded before the triumph of the Church militant. But unlike Rome, this city would be eternal; built as it was—in Augustine's conception—of the unchanging and unchangeable truth of a Divine revelation, as unalterable as the Rock upon which it was based. This was a supreme challenge to history. At a time when Alaric had just stormed and taken the most enduring human city—a city that had believed itself eternal—when the world-empire was falling to pieces before the onslaught of barbarians, the Church of Christ was proclaimed the successor of the antique State—not merely as a refuge from the world, it offered that as well—but as a substitute for it. The sacred was to triumph over the secular. This was the supreme purpose of the Church; not reconciliation but conquest. The impulses to enjoyment were seduction; and enjoyment of the material world a denial of the privileges of citizenship in the Divine city. The sacred was something not to be profaned by pagan culture; it was enshrined in the gospel of the new faith, the ceremonial of the new cult. It was true that the City of God preserved many an edifice of pagan thought, just as the ancient cities preserved through successive ages the splendor of their monuments. But the contributions of philosopher or poet were reinterpreted and dedicated to the service of faith—faith in dogma foreign to their origin.

For over a thousand years the bulwarks of this mighty city of the soul withstood the shock of temporal onslaught. Against it the powers and principalities of this world raged in vain. It was the ideal and the inspiration of thoughtful men—even for those poetic minds who, like St. Francis, knew and celebrated the eighth sacrament of beauty in the world around. But during most of that time its defenders—so it seems to us—made the mistake of continuing to repeat that emphasis upon the conflict between the sacred and the secular which had been the slogan of the revolutionary era in which the early Church had won its liberty and established its institutions. Then the profane might really have profaned. Read Augustine's graphic pages to see what a grotesque conception of life and reality gave way to the new scheme of a Divine governance in and over all things.

But after the Church had been established and its doctrine had won an almost unquestioned allegiance, then the walls of the City of God could no longer remain closed to the movement of inquiring minds. Out and in its gates began a movement of exploration, and from that early tentative beginning in the closing centuries of the Middle Ages has grown the chief interest of the modern era, critical thought and scientific discovery. So large is this movement now, so different in its outer aspects from the guardianship of ancient dogma, that many have been struck by this external contrast and failed to see its real meaning. They have failed to take account of the changes wrought by history and judge it now as the Fathers of the early Church would have judged a similar movement in their day, as a revolt against the Divine government of the world, or an attempt to escape the responsibilities of its citizenship.

But that is a complete misunderstanding of the nature of modern thought. What has really happened is that the narrow confines of theology remain upon their seven hills, while the city-state—become the empire of the world—includes all valid, reverent search for truth, all sacrifice of self for high ideal in the realm of thought or social service. It reaches through the entire field of daily experience. The process which made the whole world Roman is today making of the *Civitas Dei* a *Civitas hominum*. The City of God extends its bounds to include the farthest conquests of the human mind, and its citizenship implies service for humanity. It is in this setting that we claim the validity of the sacrament of fellowship.

In every sacrament there is a benediction. The petty round receives new meaning from the contemplation of its great and lasting mission, that of the City of Truth which is the City of Mankind.

CHAPTER III

❧

SOCRATES WAS WRONG

SOCRATES, ACCORDING TO PLATO, lamented the passing of that time in Greece when the only known facts about the past were those treasured in the memory of the tribal bard, and the coming of that degenerate age when people no longer would bother remembering things they could read in books. He deprecated the invention of writing. Yet it was by the written page of his pupil Plato that the conversations in the cool gardens on the outskirts of Athens have survived, to secure his own immortality.

This objection of Socrates to the invention of an alphabet was something more than the proposition of a philosopher in need of an argument. It was a protest against mechanism. Making black marks on Egyptian papyri or skins from Asia—those skins the merchants of Pergamum later made into parchments (pergamenta)—compares with reciting an epic as the use of machinery compares with hand labor. Socrates, we suppose, would have preferred telling the time by a guess at the lengthening shadow on the square rather than by the use of such an instrument as a watch. By ignoring inventions one kept "close to nature."

This is an attitude to be found throughout the whole history of culture. Its most earnest advocates have been the artists, impatient of anything interposed between nature and the individual. But ideal-

Reprinted from "Mechanism and Culture," in The Historical Outlook, Vol. XVI, No. 1 (January, 1925), pp. 7-11. It was first given as an address at the 57th Annual Commencement of Stevens Institute of Technology, Hoboken, N. J.

ists generally have joined in the denunciation or shared the contempt for mechanism, no matter what their field. Literature has held aloof, except in patronizing, romantic moods, until the present. History has ignored the very implements of progress—the tools of work, the mechanism of effort—even while recording the results. There has, therefore, developed a gulf between "culture" and achievement which has widened with each new invention.

There have been, in recent years, some signs of a revolt against the conspiracy of the poetically-minded to ignore the creations of the practically-minded, but unless the revolt becomes a revolution we shall never square ourselves with reality. If we are to make anything intelligent out of the world we live in, we must free ourselves from this romantic sentimentality, which goes back to Socrates and beyond. Idealism, left to itself, is futility. There is no sadder fact in the tragic circumstances of the present than that idealism failed to avert the desolation of Europe. It will always fail, so long as it holds itself aloof from the grimy facts of daily life.

Like the forces of nature, ideas must be harnessed and set to work, or things will remain exactly as they were before. One cannot weave cloth with an idea, but embody the idea in wood and iron and it will replace all the hand-loom workers in the world. Wherever a locomotive sends its puff of steam through the smoke-stack, the idea of George Stephenson is at work—an idea that a forced draught on the fire would give the engine enough power to pull its load. There are spindle whorls in the Grimaldi caves along the slopes of Menton, used by the fingers of spinning women of the late stone age, over 10,000 years ago. How often in all that stretch of years have spinners dreamed of something to carry on the motion of the whorl besides the arm and hand! Out of such longings came—no one knows from where—the simple spinning wheels of the late middle ages. Yet it was only in the eighteenth century that a tinkering watchmaker helped Arkwright to get his roller-frame to work, and the work of spinning passed forever from the fireside to the mill. New cities arose by the marshy waste of Lancashire, and the shipping of Britain, carrying its goods overseas, made possible a new world empire—not created in a fit of absent-mindedness, as an idealist historian declared, but through the might of the Industrial Revolution.

Few students of literature stop to think that its existence depends upon paper and ink as well as thought! The records of history depend upon the cutting of the chisel in the stone, the sharp impress of the scratching stick, on clay or on wax tablet, the scrawl of charcoal or ink on leaves of trees, papyri wrappings, or leather. Before these devices were used lie the unnumbered centuries of that period we call the prehistoric; this side of it, is the world of history. History begins with writing; the prehistoric, as we use the term, is a synonym for the preliterate. History depends upon that mechanism which transfers thought from brains to material substances, and so enables thought to endure while the thinkers come and go.

It is strange that the extent to which thought depends upon mechanism for its preservation seldom occurs to us except when the mechanism fails. We know that the burning of the library at Alexandria blotted out for all time much of the culture of the distant antiquity which it had gathered in the papyri on its shelves. We know as well that the last classics of Greece and Rome perished in the mouldy rolls of papyri which could not last in the climate of the northern Mediterranean as they do in Egypt. The book trade of the ancients was careless of the future,—as ours is today. But had it not been for papyri rolls dealt in by those astute traders who brought their goods to the wharves of Athens and Ostia, it is doubtful if the literature of classic Greece and Rome would have been produced at all. Had there been nothing better than clay tablets to scratch, how would the Augustan age have achieved what it did? Imagine Dante in his exile, accumulating the mud cylinders necessary for the Divine Comedy. Or, to bring the matter down to our own time, what would our modern literature and journalism amount to if the Arabs had not invented paper? A printing press without paper is unthinkable; and literature cannot exist without them both. We need a *Sartor Resartus* in the history of literature to show us how naked and helplessly limited is thought except when provided with mechanism.

There have been two great creative epochs in the history of our civilization; that of ancient Greece and that of today. The one produced critical thought; the other applied it to produce machines. Besides these two contributions to secular society, all others rank as minor. The one stirred into activity that critical intelligence, upon which rests our whole apparatus of knowledge; the other made nature our ally not merely by applying its power to do our work, but also by supplying the means for extending knowledge itself, almost to the infinite. Seen in this light the protest of our modern humanists against mechanism has little of that insight into reality which was the characteristic note of Socrates.

What is needed in both humanists and scientists is the Hellenic sense of just proportion, so that neither thought nor machines shall become master of life. For thought turned upon itself, divorced from the setting in a real world, becomes as idle as the speculations of the schoolmen; and machines become, not instruments for human liberation, but the dominant element in society. Education in a modern world must respond to both these demands. It cannot be purely literary or idealistic without losing touch with the spirit of the age in which we live; it cannot be purely technical and remain education.

How many of us realize that a steam engine is as genuinely an historic product, as fittingly the symbol of an age, as the feudal castle or the medieval cathedral? that a modern factory is as much the center of historical forces as the ancient city?

We shall never see the true perspective of history so long as we accept unquestioned the mediocre outlook of those we call common-sense people. We need imagination and insight even more than judgment, for otherwise our judgments simply circumscribe and limit our activities. If there were only one factory in the world, if the power that Watt released from the coal mines were so concentrated that instead of invading every hamlet of the civilized world it was confined to the single valley of the Clyde and drew to it there the work of the world, we should have some feeling for the importance in history of one of the great inventions. But instead, its effects penetrate the environment of common life everywhere, and so we miss its meaning.

Invention is an art. It is the projection into matter itself of the conscious will. It makes matter a part of the agency of control, and also a part of intelligence. Loose grains of muddy ore, lying in the bosom of the hills, become iron axes. They have nothing in themselves to indicate axes. They might, if placed too close to a fire, under certain circumstances become hardened into a mass. But while the ore is merely matter, the axe is matter plus mind. It bears the impress of intelligence, and that to so great a degree that the anthropologists passing before the rows of axes in the cases at a museum can reconstruct from their form and composition the state of culture of the makers, like a pianist whose symphonies arise from the keys of his piano. The axe implies both consciousness and purpose; it means cutting. The same is even true of a forked stick which the savage uses as a spade, though here the injection of the human element into the material is less obvious, because the object has not been refashioned. The fork was a result of its nature as a branch; that is, a part of a vegetable mechanism for catching air in leaves and conveying nitrogen to the trunk. It was not produced by nature to dig potatoes. Nature leaves the branch in the air and the potato in the ground. But in the hands of man the fibres of wood, like the particles of iron, are turned into something else, they become part of conscious action, a continuation of muscle and an agency of mind. The potentialities of the tool are those of the brain that conceived it and controlled the fashioning hand, as much as they are those of matter. Invention is a projection of consciousness into the unconscious; a creation.

If this can be said at the dawn of invention, and of a tool like a digging stick, which itself embodies no thought, which is not a tool except when so regarded or used, the utility of which is accidental, it is abundantly evident when invention produces not a tool but a machine. The difference between a tool and a machine is that the tool helps a man to do his work, but the machine does the work itself. The man changes his position entirely with reference to it. His business with the machine is simply to make it work. The factory operative does no spinning; he mends threads and makes the spindles spin, forces the steam to move the iron and the iron to transmit its energy to the whirling spools, and they in turn to gather up that energy and imprison it in the spirals of thread or yarn, where our fingers later may find it stored up—a source of strength against strains and pulls. The factory spinner merely assists at this transformation like the impressario at a theatre. Steam and iron and fibre dance before him into new combinations, like a dream from the Arabian Nights.

The machines that do these things are the perpetuation of the initial energy of their inventors. In the steam engine, for instance, Papin, Newcomen and Watt have found an immortality larger than we have yet realized. In its gliding rods and noiseless wheels the brain of the inventor lives as that of Virgil in the *Aeneid*. But while the art of the one is cast cathedral-like, in static mould, to resist the forces of time by its perfection and its strength, that of the other—the invention—is thrown, as it were, into the crucible of change, and creates itself the forces that reveal its imperfections and weakness. The engine develops the speed that breaks it down. Yet the immortality of the invention is perhaps the surer of the two, for it enlists its destroyer as its ally. It becomes part of change itself, and so gains some control over it. It sets going the irrecoverable march of events, which make up what we call time, and becomes an integral part of the ever-fleeting present. For its immortality lies in its use. By the work it does it disturbs the poise of phenomena so that once started it creates the demand for its own continuance. It contains its own stimulation, for its imperfections call as much for further invention as its successes encourage to new ones. So it is a social phenomenon of the most complex nature. If it immortalizes the Watts and Arkwrights, it is only by merging their creations into that of a vast composite whole. The original engine of Watts and spinning frame of Arkwright are in museums; but both machines are also preserved wherever engines are at work or cotton is being spun. The original inventors have become contributors to a more august creation than they guessed. The brain of the individual scientist or mechanic fuses its creation (steam valve, automatic brake) into those of all society and all future time. It will live only so long as it can be adjusted to the changing machine. Each bolt and bar, each wheel or crank is the crystallized thought of some nameless engineer. When they fit and go, the structure lives, and each part is instinct with life. Apart or unfitted they die. The cylinder that might hold the power to drive ocean-liners is good only for the scrapheap unless the pistons fit and the gearings work. And so, if one could imagine the whole dynamic force of the Industrial Revolution gathered together and concentrated in a single cylinder, with a power to which that of Niagara would be like that of a rivulet, it would be as useless as the energy of ocean tides today, unless there were the nicest adjustment in the parts of the machine. Machinery is a social creation and is itself a sort of society!

Thus, in the social preservation of inventive thought, by a strange paradox, this individualistic age is the annihilation of the individual. Its greatest art-creation, machinery, it maintains and treasures only so long as the individual contributions are in tune with the whole.

There are two kinds of immortality: the immortality of monuments,—of things to look at and recall; and the immortality of use,—of things which surrender their identity but continue to live, things forgotten but treasured, and incorporated in the vital forces of society. Thought can achieve both kinds. It embodies itself in forms,—like epics, cathedrals, and even engines,—where the endurance depends upon the nature of the stuff used, the perfection of the workmanship and the fortunes of time. But it also embodies itself in use; that is, it can continue to work, enter into other thought, and continue to emit its energy even when its original mould is broken up.

It is the first kind of immortality—the monumental kind—which has mainly drawn our attention, for it is clearer, if not larger, in our consciousness. Use, on the other hand, obliterates outlines so that the things used most are often least seen. So in keeping with our natural tendency to visualize our thought even in the things of use, as if to make up for this indistinctness, we encourage the perpetuation of form,—in institutions and traditions,—and enshrine it in art.

Let us be clear about this monumental side. Poems live in themselves and not simply as stimulations to deeds or other thoughts. Form imposes itself on thought and preserves by means of its external beauty, even though it is often only a successful distortion of the thought with which it started. Cathedrals stand before us out of the Middle Ages which created them, defying time in their own right, by the double strength of poise and beauty in stately columns and towering walls. These formal perpetuations of thought in its own expression are the most appreciated, as they are the most obvious. They require no penetrating analysis to detect; they are matters of pure observation. Thought grips materials without effort, but hesitates to tackle thought; so the concrete world lodges in the memory while the abstractions slip by unnoticed.

So important is this formal apprehension of things, that it has been taken at its face value by society, as society takes things at their face value (which includes of course the value of the face not simply its looks), and made synonymous with art; as if there were not a greater art in the mastery of those intangible, elusive forces which have escaped from their mould and penetrate wherever thought can go, the art of mathematics, science, and invention. Indeed, the same tendency which makes us see the obvious first and prize it most carries us still further. It tends to become a sort of sacramental attitude, consecrating not only the form in which the thought is cast, but the material embodied in it and the environment which moulded it. The tongue of Dante, of Luther, and of the King James Bible are monuments of such consecration. We even carry this sacramentalism to its primitive conclusion. Although we know better, a strain of fetish worship runs through us all. The bones of men receive our reverence, as if in them resided—or resides—the efficacy of their thought and action. Placards are posted where thinkers have lived and died, as if their thought belonged like some haunting spirit to walls and garden walks.

Now all of this is legitimate enough so long as much of our thought is sacramental and our feelings stir with fetishistic suggestions at historic sites or relics. But it obscures the larger life and the truer immortality of thought, the immortality of use. Dante's vision has entered into many a scheme of the world besides that into which he wove the picture of the Florence of his day. In fact, for centuries it moulded the cosmology of all Christendom and it still colors the common dream of immortality. It is this larger vision, built of the universal hope and fear, that is the real *Divina Commedia*, not the epic locked in its stubborn Tuscan rhymes. No form of art, however perfect, can imprison or contain all of a living thought. If thought is alive it is more than its form. It will escape and live. Often it carries with it in its new use broken fragments of its form, and so may still be recognized at sight, as the architecture which produced the medieval cathedral breaks up into the buttressed piles of a modern city, a dome here, flying arch there, walls soaring for the light, towers that carry forever the memories of Italy, but all disparate and merged into a new creation. This new creation, however, is no massive, self-contained whole, it is instinct with life and change. It is not static like the old, but eternally recreating itself, replacing arches and domes by girders, and leaving the old architecture behind with the problems it faced and the material it faced them with. The one imperishable thing is the science of which these are the fleeting traces.

It is the same with history as with art. At first glance what one sees in it is the formal event, the embodied institution, the externals of things. But when we look deeper we find that what happens in a given time and place is only a part of the real event. The cause and results are also parts of it. The result is merely the prolongation of the event in other circumstances, the releasing or the destruction of its potentialities. Battles are more than charging cavalry and riddled squares; they are not over when the firing ceases. They still continue in the hatreds and enthusiasms they arouse, in politics of state, in armaments, in nations themselves. The German Empire was Sedan crystallized—Sedan and other things. The battle itself is only the most concentrated form of an event, just as a poem is the most perfect expression of an idea. But the real significance, the essence of both is something larger than the form, however concentrated or complete it seems.

Now, it is in the same way that the cylinder syringe and separate condensers of Watt's first engine are curiosities for the historian, but the idea, the creative power, of that invention is moving on with all the forces of the Industrial Revolution. It was born of an application of Scottish ingenuity to Scottish thrift, for all that Watt had in mind when he set to work was to save coal by making an engine that did not have to heat a cool cylinder at every stroke. But the engine that was invented to save coal, in its generation of power has eaten into the heart of every coal deposit of Britain, while the power it releases has not merely changed the material environment of civilization, but actually brought millions of human beings into existence—each with his and her own world of thought and work—in the stimulation of population through the production of wealth.

Indeed in a sense one may say that machines—the product and embodiment of invention—attain a sort of life of their own. They enter the field of industry to play their own role, always incalculable, often achieving what their creators never dreamed of and the opposite of what they intended. They are not simply aids to labor, doing more things than the hand-worker, producing more and more things of the same kind, in an endless addition to the stock of goods. They are changing the mental and moral outlook of society as well as its physical basis. To what extent they do this must be left to a consideration of the economic interpretation of history. But when even philosophy (in the metaphysics of Bergson), recognizes that the machine steps, as it were, into the main problem of life, adjustment and adaptation—and so becomes an element, and the largest element—in this present phase of our biological evolution, it is time for history to wake up to this tremendous fact. It is not a fact for economists or philosophers alone. Not only is it, in itself, an *event* of keen human interest, clear definition and notable prominence, but it underlies every other event of large importance in the political history of the last half-century. The Industrial Revolution and the machine will inevitably furnish the central text of those histories of the future which deal with our era, as Bergson says. It is our privilege even now to see how magnificent the text will be.

Compare the transport of the eighteenth century with that under the control of the engineers of the twentieth. The overland trade in the goods of the world was carried or drawn by horse. Now there is more horsepower dragging the freight trains of this country than all the horsepower of all the ages put together. Even in the city which we can see across this river, at this moment there is more horsepower driving the irresistless freight along the chasm in the rock which we call our subway than is needed to move all the goods on the roads of England at the present time.

Go down to the great power-house where the force is generated to drive these trains and see what degree of control over nature has been reached with reference to the needs of civilization. There the power is generated from the coals of Pennsylvania. The heat stored up from suns of geologic ages is released once more under the exacting control of an engineer and adjusted by automatic devices to correspond with the weight upon the floors of the cars, so that it is hardly a figure of speech to say that as you step upon the train a few more leaves of prehistoric forests crackle away in the energy of heat, and that energy becomes a substitute for the human energy of the traveler.

Talk of miracles, with such an annihilation of time and control of power! One can imagine that, if Aristotle or Dante were back in the world today, they would be found exploring such mysteries as these and finding in them their inspiration, rather than in outworn philosophies or metaphysical speculation.

No writer that I know has ever expressed so well the full significance of the inventive art as the man who protested most against the changes which it wrought in the society of the nineteenth century. Let me close by quoting this extract tucked away in a hidden corner of the works of John Ruskin:

"What may be the real dignity of the mechanical art itself? I cannot express the amazed awe, the crushed humility, with which

I sometimes watch a locomotive take its breath at a railway station, and think what work there is in its bars and wheels, and what manner of men they must be who dig brown iron-stone out of the ground and forge it into that. What assemblage of accurate and mighty faculties in them, more than fleshly power over melting crag and coiling fire, fettered and finessed at last into the precision of watch-making; Titanian hammer-strokes beating out of lava these glittering cylinders and timely respondent valves, and fine ribbed rods, which touch each other as a serpent writhes in noiseless gliding, and omnipotence of grasp, infinite complex anatomy of active steel, compared with which the skeleton of a living creature would seem, to the careless observer, clumsy and vile. What would the men who thought out this, who beat it out, who touched it with its polished calm of power, and who set it to its appointed task, and triumphantly saw it fulfill the task to the utmost of their will, feel or think about this weak hand of mine, timidly leading a little stain of water color which I cannot manage, into the imperfect shadow of something else . . . mere failure in every motion and endless disappointment; what I repeat would these iron-dominant genii think of me? And what ought I to think of them?"

CHAPTER IV

❦

THE DISCOVERY OF TIME

I. THE APPRECIATION OF TIME

THE HISTORY of civilization ordinarily omits one half of the narrative. We live in a world of time as well as of space, in which our yesterdays, to-days, and to-morrows are as essential for us as land and sea. The process of social evolution has been one of temporal as well as of spatial mastery, for without a chart of our yesterdays we could never have mapped out the fields and built the cities or planned the empires which mark the stages of our advance. Indeed, not only has the conquest of time been as real as that of the material world, but the two have marched side by side,—from nomads careless of all but the moment's satisfaction, to the world of business and of politics, calculating in the present for the future on the basis of the past. And yet, while we are glad to hear and proud to tell the story of the triumph of mankind over material conditions, the other half of the story remains untold, except as it lies in the manuals of astronomers and chronologers, where its meaning as history is seldom seen.

To be sure one does not have to go far to find the reason. The world that endures has this great disadvantage over the world that expands; we have no sense by which to apprehend it. Yesterday and

Reprinted from The Journal of Philosophy, Psychology and Scientific Methods, Vol. XII, Nos. 8 (April 15, 1915), pp. 197-206; 10 (May 13, 1915), pp. 253-269; and 12 (June 10, 1915), pp. 309-317.

to-morrow lie beyond hearing or sight. We talk of a "sense of Time," but the phrase is misleading. No subtle distillation of animal instinct can give us a "sense" of that mysterious process in which the flow of a "future" into a "past" acquires meaning, and whose "present" invites analysis only to elude it by dissolving continually before our eyes. The sense of Time is really a sense of times, and that is not a sense at all, but the slow product of developing intelligence. A sense of time means a knowledge of happenings. It is to be found only where a memory has been keenly disciplined to its task of knowing the world that was by a mind keenly aware of a world that is; where the historical sense has been called into being, with its consciousness of the past clarified by an analysis of the present. It is no neglected inheritance from primitives, but the slow and still most imperfect acquisition of culture.

Neither calendar nor chronology was worked out in the first place to discover Time or keep track of it. They have to do with events and the problem of tracing their relationships, not with what lies between them. The one deals with recurring events, the other with those which occur but once. As the number of these increases, however, the individual events tend to lose their individuality and attention is diverted more and more to the general statement of their relationships. So, by way of mathematics we pass to the world of abstractions.

Our knowledge of "the past" is, therefore, really a knowledge of things in the past. It seems at first glance as though, by giving each day and year a number, we bring them all within the field of knowledge. But the numbers mean nothing by themselves. Only those dates upon which memorable things have taken place really stand for anything. Our dates are like the numbers on city houses; they stand for something other than a stretch of street or of time. The numbered periods which intervene serve little but to insure that dates worth remembering, that is, events of men worth knowing, shall be properly placed. The units between might as well be zeroes for all that we care about them. In other words, though we cover all Time with numbers, we do so only in order to find things in it, and to know where we are when we find them, how far we have traveled from to-day or from other points already familiar. In short, we mark Time by events rather than events by Time.

It is claimed now by philosophers that all of this mathematics of

dates, whether of calendar or of chronology, only misleads us as to
the real nature of Time, which is not a thing to be measured out,
but an everlasting flux moving in mysterious, non-spatial currents
through the very heart of things; that the events themselves are not
so much set in Time, as a part of it, not simply serving to mark it,
but making it, in a very real sense. Moreover, since the relationships
between events are in ceaseless readjustment, the more important
ones are often obscured by forcing all to conform to external standards on static bases, and so the real nature of Time escapes analysis.
We shall come to these considerations in due course. But for the
historian all such recent speculations do not affect the fundamental
point that, however distorted our appreciation of Time has been,
mathematics has made the use of Time possible, and so, ultimately,
even the metaphysics which criticizes it. For here, as in the world
of space, measurement is the sign of occupation and control. The
history of Time begins in numbers.

Dates do not matter in primitive stories. Myths need no arithmetic. All the child's story requires for a proper beginning is "once
upon a time." So with the childhood of the race. Poetry, the universal vehicle for the saga, can not well risk marking its mervelous
events with exact days and years. There is a sense of mystery in the

> Old, forgotten, far-off things
> And battles long ago,

which must not be disturbed by too precise information. In fact the
early narrative loses much of its charm if it is set too accurately in
this prosy world. Dates would break that spell which imparts to
vague, half-real events of legend and tradition the spirit of romance.
The poet knows the size of his hero's shield, the length of his spear,
the numbers of his men,—but these are details which he can clothe
as well with unreality and manipulate to suit the situation. On the
other hand, one date is like another. Contrast this "once upon a
time" with a date. "Once upon a time, there was a man named
Napoleon." How romantic that sounds compared with the prose
of history: "In 1799 Napoleon obtained control of France!" The
dated history is much less interesting. There is no such dangerous
venture facing you as in the legend. You know that the historian
will not try his imagination, he will not sail off into uncharted seas,
but follow his dates in their sad succession in dreary prose. What

else can he do? He is trying to be accurate; and accuracy is dull, because it is calculable.

This is one reason for the dislike of history so largely prevalent in our schools,—although the situation is now improving rapidly. It is certainly a healthy discipline for the imagination to be called back from its excursions into the land of romance, where things may happen any way one wills, and forced to follow real roads to Rome. But the discipline becomes affliction when the young traveler is kept so busily reciting the time-table that he never sees the pageant of the past through which he is journeying. When the race as a whole, with all its sophistication, has found it so hard to acquire a passion for dates, how can one expect it of a child? We are apt to forget that the high culture of antiquity did not evolve a satisfactory method for keeping track of time, that even the keen old Greeks never learned—outside of scientific circles—to count the years accurately. Beginners in history might find consolation for their frailties, if they only knew that the greatest historian of antiquity, Thucydides, avoided dates as far as he could, and made his years consist merely of a long summer and a short winter.

And yet the situation is not so bad as it might seem. For, aside from the fact that our text books in history are no longer monkish chronicles, any one who teaches the subject knows from experience that there are few students—even in colleges—whose dates are more accurate than "once upon a time." Indeed, that is about all even the best of us commonly can do. What do dates amount to in our own lives? How many of us, for instance, can recall at once, without a moment's hesitancy, the date of the war with Spain? Tests of dates like these in large classes show ordinarily that not five per cent have any tendency to associate mathematics with the happenings of their lives, except in the matter of recurring dates, which have to do with the calendar and not with chronology.

We must not be misled, however, by any infirmities on our part. The calendar, and the chronology which the calendar made possible, are not only the basis of scientific history, but of far more than we suspect in the structure of civilization. Try to think what it would be like if we had no dates for our business world, where "time is money" in the most real sense of the word; where every letter bears its date, every paper is issued with it on the title-page; where laws, treaties, the world's affairs as well as its history, depend so largely upon the relation of one date to another. However much we may still appreciate the vagueness of poetry and romance, we have erected a civilization based on dates, in which the mathematics of Time is as fundamental to human relationships as that of Space is in the conquest of the material world.

II. THE NATURAL CALENDAR

Now, imagine that, instead of the great City of the Past, of which we of the twentieth century have been given the freedom and the rights of citizenship, we have only a little village. Instead of vast horizons charted to the day and the vista of centuries stretching toward the dawn-ages of geology imagine that we know only what we ourselves can find out and can remember of what other people found out or remembered,—and so through the endless, but misleading tale of barbarian tradition. Imagine that we have no books or implements for measurement, that we can hardly count beyond our fingers or a few notches on a stick,—and then let us try to settle down in the world of Time and Space, as our forefathers had to do, and see how much—or rather how little—of either we could appropriate. A little exercise in such imaginative ignorance (not hard exercise for most of us), will enable us to deal sympathetically with our ancestors, to understand both their age-long apathy about things outside their immediate experience, and so to deal historically with the slow beginnings of the historical sense.

A surprise awaits us upon the threshold of our survey. For, viewing the process from the primitive world to our own, it is apparently a sense of the future rather than of the past which has been most important in the evolution of our civilization. That which has never been, which exists, seemingly, only in our imaginations, turns out to be the very basis upon which we have erected the world of intelligence and activity.

Our commerce, manufactures, education, culture,—everything is for the satisfaction of future needs. It is this sense of tomorrow which stings us to work. The haunting specter of possible want, even when we are needing nothing, the hope of future rewards, the confidence of success or fear of failure, these are the stimuli which carry us along from savagery to civilization. The savage at first has no sense of them,—or at least but very little. He satiates his hunger by gorging to the full, even when he does not know where his next meal will come from. Why worry about tomorrow; it has not yet come to worry him. This is the attitude of all races in savagery; anthropological books are full of instances of it, from Australia and Borneo to Arabian Bedouins and American Indians. Livingstone calls Africa "the blissful region where time is absolutely of no account and where men may sit down and rest themselves when tired." [1] The Negro "dreams away the day in laziness and idleness, although he knows quite well that for the night he needs his draught of water and his log of wood; nevertheless, until sundown he will certainly not disturb himself, and only then, or perhaps not before dark, will he finally procure himself the necessaries." [2] The nomad hunter lays nothing by for the next meal—unless he has more than he can manage to eat at the time; and having nothing laid by, he must hunt for his next meal as he did for his last. His savagery means improvidence, and his improvidence keeps him a savage.

The first steps of progress come when the hunter lets the small animal grow bigger with an eye to future eating, or when his women-folk scratch the ground with their forked sticks for the rudiments of a garden. Even then the progress is slow. When, for instance, the Hottentots acquired a rude agriculture, the disgusted missionaries found that at harvest time they ate, "almost night and day," until the little they had was devoured.[3] When the hunter emerges into the pastoral nomad, however, and keeps his meat alive along with him in his flocks and herds, his sense of property and of the future develop side by side. Then the more cattle and goods he has, the harder it is to wander far; and the more he tends to settle, the more he must make sure that the local supply of food will not run out. So the scratching of the soil for a few chance roots develops into agriculture, and he ploughs and sows for a year ahead and eats of the fruits of last year's labor.

The future, then, far from being the unreality it seems to us, upon first glance at the problem, is rather the determining factor in developing an appreciation of the present. The imagination is no idle plaything for the children of the race, but the engine by which the paths of progress were opened up. But, at the same time, we must not forget that the imagination is built up out of experience, that it embodies the memories of the past, and does not exist except by reason of them. As we can not imagine what lies beyond the reach of our experience, the imagination only arranges the data of the past in new combinations. We are aware of the past, therefore, before we can imagine the future at all. There would be no stimulus to prepare for tomorrow's meal if one could forget the hunger of yesterday, and no knowledge of how to prepare without the experience of such other situations. In short, if imagination carves out for us the possibilities of advance, it does so only because it has been stirred to its task and given the material for its tools by the memory.

Memory and imagination, reaching out into past and future, furnish us with our appreciation of Time. But their interworking in all-important enterprise depends upon one fundamental fact: the future must repeat some of the data of the past. If it did not, memory would bear no relation to present experiences and imagination could not even attain the vaguest outlines of surmise. Some of the data of experience must repeat themselves in order that mankind may be able to deal with the rest. Repetition, routine, enables us to calculate, and classify in terms of the old and known, the new phenomena which are set alongside them, as the moving present eternally varies our experiences. But since the data of life do not repeat themselves, but only those of its environment, the necessary framework for history must be furnished by the physical sciences, or their pre-scientific forerunners. In other words, the origins of the calendar precede the origins of chronology.

Strangely enough, although it lies in the prehistoric world, we know under what circumstances the calendar was first worked out. It began when men settled on the soil and began to farm it. The wandering savage may have a crude sense of time-periods; but, as we have seen above, his mind does not play on into the future in such a way as to modify his present by the calculation for its needs. Once entered upon the agricultural stage, however, the conditions of life demand more thought and foresight, more planning and work for tomorrow, and the day after. Henceforth, it is impossible to live entirely in the momentary present, to eat when hungry, chase where the game may lead, and in general follow the fortunes of nature, as was the case with the ancient hunter. There is surely a significance, hitherto unguessed, in the fact that Time and Space were appropriated jointly, and that the farmer who settled down in them, was the first to demand the measurement of each. His stretch of Time, like his stretch of field, lies out before him, marked by duties and rewards, needs and their satisfaction, from one horizon to the other. The horizons of Time are still confined to a season or two, as those of Space are limited to the village fields, except as the elders tell of adventures beyond the run of daily memory. But just as it is only the cleared fields, cultivated in yearly rotation, which are really the village property, whatever rights of chase or pasture there are in the dark woods beyond, so it is that narrow stretch of time which is covered by routine, and not the half-known past where myth and fancy make excursions, which is really taken over and made a working possession. Only recurring dates furnish a basis for measurement; and so the farmer's calendar is the first survey of Time as his fields are the first survey of Space.

Simple observations of nature supplied the first basis for the calendar.[4] Naturally this varies according to land and climate. Where the monsoon blows from the southwest from May to November, and from the northeast from November to May, as in Nicobar, even low-grade savages have a loose sense of the year or the half-year, which the changing moons can make still more definite. The floods of the Nile stimulated in Egypt its extraordinary progress in time-reckoning, as the cloudless skies of Babylonia called out its progress in astronomy. But where nature is less calculable, where the sky is largely overcast with clouds, storms are sudden, winds variable, harvests precarious—as in most of Europe—the reckoning of calendar in terms of the weather or of the common phenomena of nature is much more difficult. There are some world-old signs of the seasons,—lore which goes back to the ancient hunters before the days of agriculture, and is still in use. For instance, the flight or flocking of birds presaging winter was already an old sign in ancient Greece. Hesiod warns the Boeotian farmer to "take heed what time thou hearest the cry of the crane from the high clouds uttering her yearly cry, which bringeth the sign for (the late autumn) plowing and showeth forth the season of rainy weather, and biteth the heart of him that hath no oxen." [5]

Similarly Jeremiah, in ancient Palestine, remarks that: "The stork in heaven knoweth her appointed time; and the turtle and the crane and the swallow observe the time of their coming." [6] As far back as the records of mankind can go, the return of the cuckoo and the "twittering swallow" [7] have been the harbingers of spring. But however much the farmer might gain from observing the migration of birds, the habits of animals or plants, he could hardly have got beyond a few signs of weather-forecasting if he had not had more stable and more frequently recurring data to fall back upon. These were furnished by sun, moon, and stars.

As for the sun, while it furnished the divisions of day and night, it offered no ready multiple for their grouping. Its yearly circuit served for no more than the framework of the calendar; in a sense, it merely offered the cycle that needed calendaring. And yet, in those parts of the world where the seasons are marked off from each other with any degree of distinctness, a rough solar year could be appreciated without any detailed divisions by stellar or lunar periods. This is especially true outside the tropics, in the northern or southern temperate zones, where the farmer can grow but one crop of grain in the year, so that from a practical standpoint, he divides his time into two main seasons, winter and summer.[8] This has always been, and still is, the essential basis of the farmer's calendar in Europe and America. One may, as in Homer, divide the longer season into summer and harvest-time; but autumn and spring seem even to us now like transition periods between the two fundamental seasons of heat and cold. Of the two again, the warm season is, of course, the all-important one. Indeed, winter seems rather like an interval between summers than a legitimate time in itself. We should realize this even more if we had to face the weather in the scanty clothes of a primitive farmer. It is not a time for enterprise. One huddles close at home, and the pursuits of war as well as of peace are at a standstill. The literatures of the world, if not the almanacs, present this point of view in never-ending variety. From Hesiod's haunting picture of the cold north wind that "bloweth with chill breath" through the hide of an ox and "shaggy breasted" beasts, and drives "the horned and hornless creatures of the woods, with piteous chattering teeth to seek shelter in glens and caves," to the weary misery of a Walter von der Vogelweide, in the musty cold of a medieval castle, with his very wits frozen until the spring comes again, and the politely heroic rhetoric of a James Thomson, braving in hexameters the "oppressive gloom" of a season which is the very symbol of death,—throughout all the world's poetry there is but one feeling about winter.

The real beginning of the farmer's year, then, at least in a temperate climate, is not a winter solstice, in the very heart of this dead season, although that may be noted expectantly, with reference to the slowly lengthening days. The new year of the seasons naturally comes in the spring. The old Romans and the early Germans (at least the Franks) dated it from the month of March.[9] Through most of the middle ages, and in England until 1752, the year began on the twenty-fifth of March—Annunciation Day. But whatever the exact date, whether according to the official calendar or not, the starting-point for the new year is when the first wild-flowers come again, and, in the joint phrase of Hesiod and Browning:

> "The lark's on the wing,
> The snail's on the thorn,"

if not March, then April, the "opening month" as the name itself tells, "when longen folk to go on pilgrimages" and all the world is astir with the new activities.

From March to November is the usable part of the solar year for war as well as for farming. The campaign can begin when winter is over; and the priests of Mars shake their spears to rouse him. In the Autumn they hang them up again in his temple. So the farmer's year, calendared in large by the seasons, is suited for the politics of the city state. In Greece, a country of commerce as well as farming, a more complicated system took its place; but in Rome the simple farmers of the Latin plain took over the Hesiodic calendar which Greece had grown out of, and kept it as the basis of their year until the great reform of Julius Caesar,—at least so it seems from the fragmentary sources which have come down to us. Even in Greece, however, the vague old calendar of the seasons was not entirely lost. Thucydides chose to keep to it, instead of reckoning by the complicated official calendar, for the campaigns of the Peloponnesian war. Spring, summer, and autumn count together, in his history, as one long half of the year.

The solar year of the seasons was more, however, than a vague and more or less uncertain calendar based upon homely observations of weather forecasting.[10] It was universally a stellar year as well. The moon, of course, did not fit in, since its periods shift annually with reference to the sun; but the motions of the stars more nearly coincide, and from earliest times their rising and setting furnished the most definite and surest dates for all the seasonal occupations.[11] The opening lines of Hesiod's "Days" mark out the two chief moments of the farmer's calendar, ploughing and sowing, by the rising and setting of the Pleiades; and that faintly glittering constellation has been a farmer's guide through many centuries.[12] Arcturus, "rising in his radiance at eventide" just sixty days after the winter solstice, was a more final sign of spring than the "twittering swallow," and the dog star was as much a symbol of summer as the sun itself. Vergil's farmer knows the "twelve constellations of the world" through which the sun passes in order that he "may foretell the storms in the doubtful sky, the day of harvest and the time of sowing," and when to risk one's self by sea, for "not in vain," he says, "do we watch the settings and risings of the constellations." [13] All antique literature is full of such references to the connection of the stars with the seasons—a connection which religion was still further to enhance. In fact, so important was the observation of the stars, and so closely did their phases seem to fit the changes of the weather, that they seem to have furnished the basis of the practical farming calendar to both Greece and Rome, in spite of the rivalry which came from the beliefs about the moon.

III. The Supernatural Calendar

The practical needs of farming have, therefore, taken us a little distance toward astronomy; but yet not far. It is doubtful if that alone would have ever produced the mathematical calendar, for a day more or less one way or another is seldom a matter of much importance in such operations. But there was another element in the situation, more important than practical needs or the homely observation of nature, that of religion. For the early farmer was surrounded by more than merely natural phenomena. Spirits, presences, gods, and demons, shared his world with him on rather more than equal terms; and his *luck* in farming—as in everything else—depended upon keeping on good terms with them. Hence his anxiety (the Romans called it *religio* or *religion*) to know exactly what to do and when to do it. For evidently the gods of the harvest are about when the grain is ripening, mildew and frost, rain and drought, are due to the spirits of soil and weather, and one never can tell what may happen. One must, then, placate the gods; that is as much a business as to plough or fight; and the gods will not be placated unless one sacrifices to them in seemly fashion, taking a day off, now and then, to do it. They are not satisfied with casual attentions; they insist that the whole society, family, village, city, or state, shall worship at one and the same time.[1] It does not do to worship when you feel like it; to arrange the ceremonies to suit your own convenience. You must suit the convenience of the gods. They have, themselves, indicated in some way or other what times should be devoted to them.[2] And they are exceedingly particular and liable to take offense. One need not care whether the grain is sown on the afternoon of one day or on the morning of the next so far as mere farming goes. But if the morrow be a Sabbath, pagan, Jew, or Christian is likely to suffer the consequences of some divine displeasure. And so, in a world inhabited jointly, even worked in common by men and supernatural beings, it was necessary for the junior partners to adjust themselves to the ways of their uncanny but powerful colleagues. It was, therefore, not by chance that the formal reckoning of time [3] grew up in the hands of those first specialists of the great science of living, the priests.

Religion, then, combined with the observation of nature, presided over the origins of the calendar. The simple lore of the weather remained, as we have seen, like a persistent vernacular alongside the formal arrangements of priestcraft; but the anxiety to be in right relations with the uncanny powers which dispense the good and bad things of life was bound to force a more careful observation of the calendar than the return of the cuckoo or the rising of the Pleiades. So the calendar began everywhere, the world over, as a cycle of religious feasts. It was the gods, not man, for whom and by whom the days to count were first marked out. A part of the time became definitely the property of the gods. It was henceforth a violation of divine law to work or transact business on the days thus set apart. Holidays were at first genuinely holy days, and the calendar grew up around them. They were and are taboo; not to observe them with proper ceremonies was to bring down upon one the power of the curse which is the awe-inspiring element in the early idea of the sacred. One needs no stimulus to the imagination from anthropology to realize the force of this, for out of the background of our minds there are few of us who can not still, by slightly straining our ears, hear the thunders of Sinai if we play a game of golf on Sunday. If that is the case in this highly secularized twentieth century, we can imagine what the taboo on time meant— and means—to those whose world had been so largely shared with these mysterious presences. It was necessary to find some way by which the festival, the *dies nefastus,* or the day on which business was sacrilege,[4] should not be violated. It had to be kept track of in order to insure that the proper festival should be celebrated upon it. Hence the elaboration of that succession of religious feasts and fasts, such as still persists in our church calendar. The idea would not naturally occur to one that the lists of saints' days and holy days which preface our liturgies are the historic remnants of the first definite marking of time.

This is carrying us a long way back; but there are other traces which open up even dimmer antiquities. For in the practically universal superstitions about planting crops, gathering herbs, or doing almost anything in the dark or the full of the moon, we have a clue to something infinitely older than any sacred dates commemorating miracles, that first vague fear of the uncanny and sense of its possibilities for good or ill out of which theologies as well as calendars have been born. The key-note to the whole story lies in the word "luck." To us, now, rather colorless and incidental, a thing to joke about, "luck" stands throughout the ages as the unsolved in the stern problem of life, the element which lies beyond control. It is no trifling matter; life and death depend upon it, the life and death of nations as well as of individuals.[5] It plays even athwart the will of gods, and so, paradoxically, justifies their ways to men by offering an explanation of their failures. Elusive, never fully revealing its presence until the damage or the benefit has been wrought, it yet stimulates the mind to be up and after it, to apprehend it beforehand, if possible; and the response to that stimulus has led to the larger part of the evolution of the human intellect. For the apprehension [6] passes from nerves and sense to the processes of observation which lead to intelligence, or else concentrates in the emotions and so opens up the responses of fear and awe. On the one hand lies science; on the other, religion.

There is no sure way of dealing with luck. The fact lies in its very nature. But one thing is agreed the world over: it is associated with the uncanny, the queer, the unaccountable, the un-understood. Things that force themselves upon one's attention and yet remain unexplained or unappropriated, are especially known to be full of the mysterious potency. If things are weird and awesome, they will "get you" if you don't watch out. If they are fair and seem promising—like a waxing moon—they will likely bring good luck. But there is no logic in the matter. It is a jumble of outlandish beliefs, intermixed with some genuine observation of nature. However, the very obscurity of the lines of thought upon which these magical-religious ideas rest furnishes us with one clue for their apprehension. The things of luck are not closely defined and distinct; they fuse together. One thing passes along its luck to another. This is what anthropologists call the principle of contagion.[7] On a night when the moon is in eclipse, the dangerous power is there—dangerous if you deal with it the wrong way. The primitive can not quite tell you whether the power is in the moon or in the shadow or in the night; but on that night he knows that it is there. And so a time when such weird, unaccountable phenomena occur is so closely associated with the phenomena as to absorb into itself the very luck of the things with which it was connected. The principle involved in this is capable of the widest application. Give a day a name, and, like a man, it absorbs the luck of the name. Since certain numbers are as lucky as names, if not more so, numbered days are just as subject to the contagion. Hence we find that, quite apart from festivals to the gods, days differ in their virtues. The belief is, we surmise, as old as the discovery of time; it still persists, hardly yet degraded to the rank of superstition, in the attitude toward Friday and the thirteenth.

This excursion into primitive psychology has really, then, brought us into the heart of our subject. For we have the calendar now opening up before us.[8] Time was not discovered by counting days, like knots on a string, but by observing their virtues. We have already seen this in the practical farming calendar, where the signs of the seasons are observed to make sure that the right thing shall be done in its time, that the vintage be begun under the star that is associated with it, and the like. To plough out of the ploughing season is to invite failure; the very fact that one talks of the "ploughing season" shows that time is described rather than counted. The same is true, much more obviously, of the calendar of luck and of mythology. Days differ in their virtues so much that one of the main problems of life is to find out which is which. The old belief

runs like a persistent theme through the Old Testament, and perhaps never had a fuller statement than in the third chapter of Ecclesiastes: "To everything there is a season, and a time to every
purpose under heaven; a time to be born and a time to die; a time
to plant and a time to pluck up that which is planted." Here, however, we run over from the waywardness of luck as chance into the
iron grasp of Fate [9]—a transition not difficult to make.

Now, if there is a time for everything; if some days are lucky and
some are unlucky, it is highly important to keep track of them, and
there is only one way to do so,—by watching the heavens. Sun,
moon, and stars, by their recurring movements, furnished a basis
for reckoning, indeed the only basis either for primitive or civilized;
for the most perfect of mechanical chronometers today must be
continually verified by the sun. But we must be careful in our survey of the origins of the calendar not to put the cart before the
horse. Sun, moon, and stars were invested with the miracle of luck
untold millenniums before their cycles were reckoned into calendars. The step between the observation of nature, stimulated by
supernatural fears, and the development of mathematics is one which
only a relatively small portion of the race has been able to take
until the very present. The stars that shone over Babylon, in all the
brilliance of the oriental night, offered themselves first to the imagination of the ancient Chaldaeans as objects of superstition, as the
living counterpart of living things below, and not as a procession
of units in a mathematical table. But, fortunately for the future of
history of the race—for civilization rests largely upon the fact—this
was one part of religion where the supernatural was calculable.[10]
The gods of rivers or storms and all the variable phenomena of nature leave man always uncertain of their caprice. The same is true
of the gods or demons of disease or health, of property and the like.
Primitive theology tends to become less sure of its efficacy the more
it deals with such wilful Powers. But the gods of the sky are in
another class. They come and go with majesty; their motions, once
observed, are so exact as to furnish the mind with its one real picture of regularity in a universe where everything else is in a jumble
and seems to be run utterly haphazard. The stars of Babylon are
still shining.

Hence here, and here alone, in the history of religion, there
opened up before men's eyes the prospect of actually penetrating
the mysteries of the future with purely human intellect. The god

would come again, the cycles would be repeated, and the luck which would be discharged upon the earth from their astral bodies would be what it had been when experienced before. So superstition developed the rudiments of astronomy, and the study of astronomy strengthened the superstition. The "virtue" in the stars started people counting their revolutions or measuring their positions; in short, "religion" called out science. It was to be many a century before science had matured sufficiently to assume that cold, ungrateful attitude toward its progenitor which led it to deny the very existence of the "virtue," and ridicule the attempt to learn that part of time which the stars were first supposed especially to reveal—the future.

Astrology, the parent of astronomy, was more a religion than a science. It was a science of priestcraft; its principles were worked out by a great cooperative effort directed for the service of religion. Mathematics was largely begun under its auspices, and so appropriated to the mysteries that the astrologers were ordinarily known in Roman law simply as "the mathematicians." Mapping the universe with the care of professional observers, they tried to measure not only the position of the stars—and so to tell the time by the clock of the universe—but also the force of that mysterious power of luck which the stars cast, stronger than their rays, upon the earth. Like Newtons of the pre-scientific world, they dealt with a force of attraction which bound the stars together—spiritually. This is more than a chapter from the history of delusion. The best, rather than the poorest, minds of antiquity were adherents of astrology, and in its lap was nursed that genuine science which at last enabled men to measure accurately both space and time, and so to pass from the rude guesses of trial and error to the settled conquest of our whole environment. Egypt and Babylon offered Greece the basis of its reckoning, and the science of measurement—not of motion, but of things at rest—was the fundamental intellectual contribution of antiquity. If the stars had not been worshipped and their virtues regarded as decisive in the realm of Fate, all this could hardly have been.

iv. From Luck to Mathematics

Months, Weeks, and Years [11]

When we come to look with scientific eyes, however, at the data of the heavens which were gathered for the service of religion, we see how poor and insufficient they must have been. The recurring heavens are an almost inextricable tangle. There are no satisfactory units. The day, the most obvious astronomical measurement, is too short to serve as anything but the counter for longer periods. It has to be fitted into a calendar instead of furnishing one.[12] The solar year and its accompanying stars may supply a framework for the calendar, but, as we have pointed out, their intervals are, on the other hand, too long to be of much service in actually reckoning or dating events. The moon seems at first to meet the situation, and this is the setting for its prodigious role in the history of both religion and the reckoning of Time. Waxing and waning in periods not too long for even low-grade intelligences to follow, sufficiently later each night to mark its new position, and sufficiently changed in form in the course of a short interval to show a different aspect, dominating the sky when full, and mysteriously but faintly shining in its last phase, after the sun has effaced the stars, the moon attracts attention above all else in the heavens. There is a fund of primitive philosophy in the claim of the old Negro, in the story of the debate as to which was the more important, the sun or the moon, that the moon was the more important because it shone by night when it was needed, while the sun came only in the daylight. The prominence of the moon was further enhanced by its relatively common practice to enter into an eclipse. All these practices seemed to witness to an unusual amount of uncanny power in it, or associated with it. Whatever god or goddess it might be termed, it was *par excellence* the dispenser of luck. Its very motions made a "luck calendar" which has lasted from prehistoric ages till today.

The month, then, as the most natural, was the most important unit of time for religious observance, and the importance of religion made it the dominant factor in the antique reckoning of time. But, as we remarked at the opening of our study, it is a unit which fits nothing else; neither days nor years coincide with its cycles. When we try to divide it up, we find that the astronomical (synodical) months contain 29 days, 12 hours, 44 minutes, 2.9 seconds,—which is 53059/100000 of a day more than the even 29 days.[13] When we try to fit the lunar year with the solar cycle, upon which the practical business of settled life depends, we find the same ragged fraction of time that will not fit; for the lunar year is 354 days, 8 hours, 48 minutes, and 36 seconds. So that if we follow the moon we go astray in both days and years. There could hardly be a better proof of the power of religion in the pre-scientific world than in the fact that this inadequate lunar period held its own as the unit of time-reckoning down to the climax of antique culture; for the festivals of the gods, based upon it, were more vital than the business affairs of men.

As for the measure of time within the month, no one but an astronomer would think of any unit but the day—which has, of course, nothing to do with the moon. The period between moon-rise and moonset is unknown to most of us even now. It is an item to be looked up in an almanac, not a fact of practical experience. Yet the days and nights need not be counted straight through the month, from one new moon to another. For the phases of the moon offer an easy means of division. The full moon on the fifteenth is as important as the new moon on the first, in some ways more so. There are festivals to be kept on both dates the world over. Moreover, the first half of the month, while the moon is waxing, occupies a different place in the dynamics of luck from that of the last half, while the moon is on the wane. It stands to reason—primitive reason—that the luck of the moon is good while the moon is growing, bad while it is losing its strength and size. For if the moon can impart its virtue, it must impart the kind of virtue which it itself possesses at the time. Moreover, this idea links itself up with all those vague, but convincing analogies and ideas of contagion which underlie the practises of what we call sympathetic magic. Similar things are associated with similar results; things once in contact with other things absorb their qualities, and the like. In this way the moon—or rather the potency in it—practically dictates the time for enterprises. Bad luck, sickness, sterility, and the like, attend the waning moon; one must not plant crops or undertake business at such an unpropitious time. It is doubtful if mankind has ever had any other single belief, according to which it adjusts its action, so widespread and so ancient as this old superstition of the moon. To judge from anthropology, it is rooted in an antiquity so vast as to make the years between Babylon and now seem like a day; and it is as firmly held by many a farmer in our enlightened twentieth century as it was by the savage whom he has replaced.

When we pass from such general principles, however, to definite days, from rude observation to accurate counting, and try to reduce the periods of the moon's phases to so many days and nights, we come upon something more curious and less explicable than the religious beliefs about the moon or stars. For the numbers by which the days are counted are themselves charged with luck! Just why, no one knows; but this, too, is a fact the world over. Primitive man does not count with mere units; the numbers vary in power or prominence; some are unimportant, some are sacred, charged with that same pervading, mysterious luck, which we have seen to reside in every peculiar, uncanny, or striking phenomenon of nature.[14] The sacred numbers differ in different parts of the world; yet, the same general principles seem to apply everywhere. The Australians have a world in which even human relationships, such as the classifications for marriage relationships, are largely dominated by the simple parallel in two, in which connection one should recall that the Romans went to the extreme of regarding all even numbers as unlucky, with the result that their calendar is unusually hard to straighten out. The number three may owe its sacred qualities to some such suggestion of completeness as one gets from the idea of beginning, middle and end, or perhaps, to the vaguer suggestiveness of finality in rhythm. In any case the triads of the gods, as in Egypt and Babylon, long precede the development of the Christian Trinity. The number four, which lost its religious potency in the Christian world,—possibly because of its place between three and seven, in which it was obscured by the latter,—was the object of a wider primitive cult than any other. It was the number of the four directions and as such one sees traces of its mysterious power in the all but universal sign of the cross.[15] Moreover, as the symbol of the dimensions of space, it was accepted by the Pythagoreans as the most perfect number, and so exerted its spell upon that mystic trend of thought which passed from Greek philosophy along the borderline of medieval magic. But no other number has had such a tremendous history in European civilization as the sacred number seven,[16] sacred or accursed, as in early Babylon, for the curse and the blessing are all in one category for untrained minds. To it is due the whole Sabbatical system of Jewish and Christian law, into which we have had to fit the mechanism of our civilization. The week of seven days cast its shadow backwards as well, along Jewish history, and in the hands of priestly theologians it became the basis for the framework of the story of creation as recorded in Genesis.

To the work of the Creator was assigned six days and thus was secured an ultimate authority, in the revised mythology, for the Sabbath of the seventh—henceforth devoted to Jahve.

The week of seven days, although falling within the month, had, therefore, another origin than as a mere division of it, corresponding to the phases of the moon.[17] In the first place it does not correspond. The four weeks are out at the end of the fourth phase, or last "quarter" of the moon, by a day and a half. The luck of numbers, which seems to us so fanciful and unreal, was strong enough to give the seven-day period an existence of its own, making a purely conventional cycle which cuts its way through years as well as months and corresponds with nothing in the whole range of nature. Perhaps its very singularity had something to do in securing for it the acceptance of those credulous civilizations of antiquity to whom we owe both our mathematics and our reckoning of time; but whatever justification we can find for it in primitive psychology, it rather complicated than helped the development of a rational calendar.

The week does not owe all of its vitality, however, to the mystic power of a sacred number. It has been, as well, a cycle of religious feasts in which each day is dedicated to a deity.[18] This was already the case in Babylon, where each day was linked with the worship of the major divinities of the astral religion—the sun, moon, and the five planets. The order of their succession seems to have varied in the records of the Babylonians,[19] but after the later paganism had properly translated the deities into the Greco-Roman pantheon,[20] a Christian world finally accepted Sun, Moon, Mars, Mercury, Jupiter, Venus, and Saturn as the proper names in the proper order.[21] Thus the week remains in form, though not in substance, the most perfect remnant of the ancient, religious cycles. The use of names for days, instead of numbers, has proved too useful a device ever to be discarded by a race that still finds arithmetic less interesting than description.

The only people of antiquity who numbered the days of the week, instead of naming them, were the Jews.[22] The "Sabbath," sacred to Jahve, was the one day with a name, the rest were reckoned up to it.[23] The week was a cycle concentrated upon its closing day. The Bible is full of the precepts of law and prophets concerning it, and the whole national life and thought were deeply colored by it, as we have intimated above. But modern criticism is inclined to state that this coloring was a relatively late operation, the work of the Jahve priests after the captivity. The natural conclusion, then, would seem to be that the Jews took the seven-day week from Babylon, and such is the statement generally to be found in popular treatments of the subjects. But careful scholarship is not so sure; for, so far, in all the cuneiform inscriptions there is no trace of a Babylonian week, which, like that of the Jews, cut its way as a cycle completely independent of the moon, undisturbed by the boundaries of months or years.[24] Wherever and whatever its origin, however, the Jews were mainly responsible for its adoption by the western world, though we have taken it over in a perverted form in which the first, instead of the seventh, day becomes the pivot upon which the cycle turns. The law of Constantine which definitely established the "Day of the Victorious Sun" as the religious holiday, while opening the door for the ever-living influence of Babylon by way of the Persian sun-god, allowed the Christians the chance to appropriate for the church a cycle which harmonized with its own. For from early days the Christian festival, the Day of the Lord (*Dies Dominicus*),[25] had been the first day of the week. The day of Mithra and of Jesus was henceforth to outshine new moons. The sacred number seven, crowned with myth and historic associations, carried the day over the luck of monthly periods; orthodoxy triumphed over superstition!

The week of seven days was an invention of the Semites. The Egyptians used a "decade" of ten days, and owing to their early adoption of the solar year, they made no effort to fit it to a lunar month, but counted 36 weeks one year and 37 the next to round out a two-year period of 365 days each. The Greeks, also, used the period of ten days as the basis of their "week," but tried as well to fit it to the month which, of course, could not be done, since their alternate months were 30 and 29 days. The result was that the last decade of a "hollow" or short month was a bothersome irregularity.[26] The Romans used, upon the whole, the most complicated and difficult calendar with which history deals. "Every school boy" is supposed to know its devious turnings and its ungrammatical grammar. But however much one learns it, only the teacher is likely to remember it beyond next day's recitation. The month was divided in the middle by the *Idus*, which fell on the fifteenth or the thirteenth day, and then the time between it and the first of the month (the Calends) was divided by the *Nones*, which thus fell on the seventh day of a thirty-one day month and on the fifth of the others. This back-handed way of counting was complicated by the twisted arithmetic which always seemed a day out in its reckoning. Only some mystery of the religion of luck [27] can account for such a calendar.

Looking back over the path we have just been following, we can see, as perhaps in no other way, what a prodigious role has been played by the moon in the origins of society. No wonder that its magical power lasts in the modern world, when it so largely ruled the fate and regulated the actions of mankind for untold millenniums. Try to imagine what primitive mankind would have done had there been no moon to mark the time! The moon supplied more than luck to early societies; it made possible cooperative effort and homogeneous action by enabling men to calculate for a given time and plan ahead so as to bring in line, for common purposes, such as hunt or war, the divergent interests of individuals.[28] But what was a blessing to the primitive became a handicap as society developed. For the moon, as we have pointed out, does not fit with anything else in the heavens and a month based upon it was bound to run foul of any other system of time-reckoning. We have already seen how the weeks—probably at first just fractions of the month based on a loose reckoning of the moon's phases—broke loose and ran away, as it were, setting up a career for themselves on the luck of the number. But that was a relatively slight matter. The lunar month still remained as important as before; the very Semites who invented the week being the strongest supporters of the cycle of the moon. The real trouble with the month was not so much to fit the days into it as to fit it into the year. When we come upon this problem, and realize that it is insoluble—at least without the aid of higher mathematics—that moon periods and sun periods do not coincide and that, therefore, we must choose between them, we realize how the moon became a bother rather than a help, by retarding the use of solar time. For, after all, in spite of our Negro logic quoted above, the sun is more important than the moon! And it, too, has its cycle, that of the seasons, or the year. We have already seen how the primitive farmer tried to fit his work within this cycle, without actually counting the days or at best counting them in a vague, uncertain fashion. The nomad can gauge his time—and even his distances—by the moon, for he is not planning a sowing-time in order to reap "in due season." His future is as vague as the horizons of the plains over which he wanders. This is especially true of the desert-dwellers of hot countries, like Arabia, who ordinarily move around and do much of their work by night, in order to avoid the heat of the day; so, as might be expected, we find that even to this day the Bedouins reckon time by the moon, and the Mohammedan calendars [29] bear still this reflex of the desert origins of the thought of the Prophet—to their own disadvantage. The moon is an adequate guide so long as the society has not progressed beyond the pastoral and stock-breeding stage.[30] But, when the nomad settles down, and ploughs and sows for the future he must turn to the sun. His society reflects his environment; his social and political arrangements must also in course of time fit the sun as well. And then the moon, which is the outward and visible sign of that inward and invisible Luck of his primitive universe, bars the way! It barred it through all antiquity. Even the keen, bold temper of the Greek was halted here, thwarted by the weight of superstition and of antique custom. So that it was not until the days of Julius Caesar that the great reform was put through for the Mediterranean world and the moon definitely dismissed from its official position as chronometer. From the standpoint of its own history, this reform was also a desecration, as most reforms are. But it was just the final chapter in a process begun when settled life succeeded to that of the ancient hunters, and routine, urged by need, wore through the haze of memory a sense of the extent of the solar cycle. Between a sense of its extent and the exact measurement lay practically the whole history of civilization, for the most learned astronomers of antiquity never knew it exactly; and Caesar less. Even today only astronomers can tell its precise length. Nevertheless, the adoption of the solar year was a part of that great process of secularization which is the major theme of social evolution, that process of the development of rational control in which time, like space, is being won over from the realm of imagination and feeling into that of intelligence—by way of use.

But the adoption of the solar year was not the work of any single epoch. The solar year was not a sudden innovation like the age of steam; nor was it a purely secular period winning its way over the lunar, merely in order to sow wheat on time. It was also a religious cycle, with its festivals of the seasons as well as its dates for plough-ing, and the gods and their grace held men to the almanac here as in the case of the moon. We have already spoken of these in dealing with the farmer's calendar; but the fact is too important for us to pass it by in this connection,—since, to emphasize solely the prac-tical advantages of the solar year over the lunar as the reason for its adoption would be an unhistorical injection of the modern point of view into antiquity. We must never forget that luck is the most practical thing in the world—if one believes in it. Hence the reck-oning of solar years was also largely a religious matter. The one advantage it had was that it coincided as well with the laws of work as with those of belief.

The one country which led all the others in the adoption of the solar year was Egypt. And it was incomparably in the lead. Already in the fourth or fifth millennium B.C. the year in Egypt consisted of 365 days, and the months ceased to correspond with the movements of the moon and became divisions of solar time—or what the Egyp-tians imagined was solar time. Twelve months of thirty days each, with five days added at the end, made up the year. Some traces of the old moon cults were left in the calendar, as, for example, the festival on the first and the fifteenth, which apparently corresponded with the old, new, and full-moon festivals. But these indications of the universal primitive outlook were in Egypt quite overshadowed by the cycle of the great Sun-god, the king of heaven, known to the Egyptians as Re, Atum or Horus, with whom the River-god, the life-giving Osiris, was indissolubly bound by the tangle of mythol-ogy. But the supernatural calendar really depended, in the most transparent way, upon the natural.[31]

v. THE EGYPTIAN CALENDAR

We have seen, in our general survey, how the reckoning of time reflects everywhere the outlook and habits of society, as these in turn reflect the environment and conditions of life of early peoples. In no other country is this more evident than in ancient Egypt. There it was almost inevitable that the solar year should triumph, for the land itself forced along the adjustment. Nowhere else does nature provide such a chronometer as in the valley of the Nile. The long, rock-bound river basin, like a vast but narrow-throated water-glass, holds and slowly passes along the periodic floods. There was no such instrument as this at hand for the farmers of Boeotia or Italy to measure by. For four out of twelve months the water-glass fills and empties, leaving an interval of only eight months which it requires no great ingenuity to divide into two seasons of four months each, the first being that of the growth of the crops and the second rounding out the easy symmetry of the year.[1] For the flood returns at such regular periods that it is possible for even fairly simple people to calculate against the time of its coming, especially since the interval is not too long. Moreover, by a strange coincidence, priestly observers, watching the heavens at the critical time when the flood was due, could see the bright dogstar, Sirius, just rising then at dawn. This "heliacal rising" of the star, so strangely fitting in with the coming of the flood, furnished, therefore, a genuine date for a New Year,—and the river itself swelling out before one's eyes, announced the fact to the whole country. The coming and going of moons—while still a matter of some importance—was bound to be subordinated to such a system, where the major gods of a religion, the constant stars and the demands of business all fitted into a common scheme. Moons would do for reckoning time in Babylonia, where the floods of the Euphrates were less exact, and less important. But in Egypt, where the whole country was a clock, how could one miss the time?

Yet that is just what the Egyptians did! They never reckoned the time correctly. Three hundred and sixty-five days do not make a solar year, but only a rough guess at one; they are over six hours short. However, the Egyptians let it go at that and held to their venerable error through all the long centuries of their history. It was not until the year 238 B.C. that the simple device of a leap-year of 366 days once every four years was decreed, in order to keep the civil year in correspondence with the stars.[2] But even this was not obeyed nor followed up, and it was left for Augustus to end the age-long blunder by imposing upon Egypt that revised calendar of 365¼ days which Julius had himself received from an Egyptian astronomer.[3]

Although Egyptologists are all agreed that the Egyptian year was thus inaccurate, they are by no means united upon what was done by the Egyptians to make such an inadequate calendar work. It is claimed by one group of Egyptologists that nothing was done to check the error, that the short calendar year went on for centuries, gaining days and years over the solar year without any one ever bothering about it. This is as flatly denied by other scholars, basing their argument upon both inscriptions and probabilities. It is a controversy in which only the trained Egyptologists have the right to speak; although even they have hardly the right to speak with dogmatic assurance. For the mere existence of such divergent views shows upon how slight grounds some of them must rest.

The foremost exponents of the former view are Eduard Meyer in Germany and J. H. Breasted in America, both illustrious names in the science of Egyptology. According to them the calendar year, running ahead a little over one day in four years, had gained a whole year in 1460 (4 × 365) years, without priests or pharaohs intervening to stop the process. The gain was very slow, almost imperceptible, only a week in a generation, or about a month in a lifetime,—too little to bother about. Any reform would disturb business and religion even more than the retention of the old misleading cycle. Hence, they claim, the Egyptian year revolved through the solar once in every 1,460-year period. A text in Censorinus, the astronomical writer of the days of the Antonines,[4] states that the opening of the calendar year coincided with the heliacal rising of Sirius in the year 139 A.D.; i.e., that in that year the star rose at sunrise on the old first day of the Egyptian year, our 19th of July. With this as a starting point our historians reckon back "Sothic cycles"[5] of 1,460 years to 1321, 2781 and 4241 B.C. on which years the star Sirius rose at dawn on the 19th of July. This leads to the statement that in the year 4241 B.C. the calendar year of 365 days was inaugurated, since 1,460 years before that date would be too early and 1,460 later would be too late.[6] If this theory could be accepted, then, we have an exact date, and one of the oldest in the world, for the beginning of an astronomical measure of time. Unfortunately, there seems to be little to support it. There is no mention of the "Sothic cycle" until late in the Roman period. The ancient monuments are silent upon it. So the first obvious conclusion seems to be that it was a creation of the late astronomers, calculating backwards in the way just indicated, and that it never existed as a matter of history at all. In fact, when it is used for chronology its critics claim that it leads to some impossible dates and direct contradictions with some of the monuments.[7] These facts, combined with the silence of Herodotus, seem to the critics of the Meyer hypothesis sufficient ground for consigning the "Sothic cycle" to the realm of historical myth. And yet when the critics come to offer the alternative hypothesis, i.e., that the year was lengthened from time to time to bring the festivals' stars together, the data in the texts are just as lacking. Moreover, the Decree of Conapus assures us that in 239 B.C. the calendar year was 10 months out, and as the reform of that decree was not carried out we see how the short year was apparently allowed to go on completing its cycle then.

It is unnecessary here to follow further the details of a controversy which still divides Egyptologists and can only be settled by the discovery of new data. But it is important for us to realize how either hypothesis detracts from the achievement of the ancient Egyptians, as set forth in some enthusiastic histories. Either they rested content with a revolving year which corresponded with nothing in nature, except once in almost 1,500 years or they intercalated days at odd intervals, without the regularity necessary for accurate records of time. The year of 360 days with 5 extra ones thrown in was apparently in use in Egypt long before the fifth millennium; but the science of Egypt never, until the close of its history, and then under foreign auspices, broke loose from the bonds of its own forging. It left the field of astronomy and accurate chronology for the Greeks in Alexandria to discover in a later era.[8]

VI. THE BABYLONIAN CALENDAR

From Egypt we turn to Babylon—known almost from the dawn of history as the mother of astronomy. But again we find that what has passed the careless scrutiny of most historians for scientific achievement is a poor and disappointing thing. Contrary to common belief, ancient Babylon and Assyria contributed almost nothing to any real science of astronomy until almost the close of Assyrian history. This fact, which is now established by ample evidence from the inscriptions, is one of the most important in the intellectual history of mankind. It shows again with clear and crushing force what lasting barriers superstition can erect on the road toward science.

The earliest chapter of Babylonian—or, more correctly, Sumerian—history reveals the common outlook of any semi-savage people, sunk in that crude animism which fills the world with supernatural powers. Every living or moving thing had its *zi*, or spirit, every uncanny spot was haunted by the ghost-demon, *lil*, and fetish cults and magic rites extended the imagery of fear. Over and above this low grade superstition there was a worship of local and tribal divinities and of those mysterious forces of nature which are to be found in every pantheon of advancing cultures.

We cannot attempt here to disentangle the complicated mythology, in which these divinities interfuse and interwork. How, for instance, Ea, the god of Eridu, the city on the gulf, was as well the god of water, or Enlil, of Nippur, the god of the underworld and the life-giving earth remained a sort of second personality for Marduk,[9] the great god of fertile Babylon, and how these two formed with the sky god, Anu, of the city Erech, the Sumerian triad, to be invoked together for so many centuries. A new situation was created, however, when—still long before the great days of Babylon—the Semites swept in upon Sumeria, bringing with them, so it seems, that devotion to the supreme moon-god, Sin, and developing that accompanying worship of the sun, Shamash, and of Venus (Ishtar) of which the records now yield increasing evidence.[10] At first this triad differs in no way from the other. It was undoubtedly just part and parcel of the great pre-religion of luck, muddled in with the luxuriant beliefs of animism, an extension, if anything, of primitive superstitions. Nevertheless it contained—as we see it now—the possibilities of a new intellectual outlook. The haphazard, unaccountable world, where spirits and demons and all the fantastic embodiments of the uncanny might cut athwart the natural movement of cause and effect, could in future be organized into a pattern of vast and regular form,—could, that is, if the priests would merely watch the movements of their deities. In the normal run of things it would seem that, when religion fastened the hopes and fears of men to the stars, a science of astronomy would inevitably follow, that the attention bestowed upon Powers at once supreme and visible, would result in definite and careful observation and a body of knowledge of lasting value. But such was not the case. The pattern of the universe was not accurately mapped out, the motion of the stars was not correctly calculated until thousands of years after the moon-god began his reign in Babylon. Fetishism, magic, incantation, rites of sacrifice and augury maintained their hold. If religion directed attention to the clock of the universe, it also drew across its face the veil of mystery and diverted the observer by its fantastic myths, so that even astrology made little progress until the closing period of Assyrian-Babylonian history. Egypt reveals the benumbing influence of custom and habit; Babylon the blight of credulity. Social convention in the one and religion in the other barred for many centuries the path of scientific inquiry.

Yet the work of the priests of Babylonia was destined, in a strange and tortuous way, to furnish the basis for the scientific advance. For untold ages they applied themselves to the futile task of mastering the data of luck, by observing portents and recording omens. Libraries were filled with tablets preserving the directions for charms in magic and the rules for taking the auspices. In the same way they noted the stars that "presided" over crises in life and interpreted their coincidences in terms of that universal law of similarity which, as we have seen, so largely explains the world to the primitive. The blood-red planet Mars (Ninib) would somehow coincide with something in the story of war; Ishtar (Venus) would somehow be connected with the story of love. The connection might seem, to any chance doubter, had there been one, often farfetched and distorted, but the codification of all this mass of conflicting material fell to the hands of men highly gifted in the art of codifying. The code of Hammurabi, the oldest systematic and comprehensive body of law in the world's history, the discovery and publication of which thrilled with surprise even the blasé dawn of our twentieth century, was but one of many such compilations in Babylonia. The task of codification was forced upon the inhabitants of a country of shifting races and empires, of continual intercourse through commerce with the outside world, if the heritage of the past were to be made to fit with the contributions of the present; and the priests of Mesopotamia met the task nobly, in the spirit of scholarship. The libraries of the Assyrians bear witness to an activity such as that which codified the Roman law or harmonized the theology of the Middle Ages.[11] Had a science of luck been possible, the long and careful labors of the Babylonians surely would have discovered it. As it was, the study of the conditions in the universe under which things happened, in order to learn the forces of luck involved in them, would seem at least to have held the promise of eventual discovery of the conditions in and for themselves, and so instead of a science of luck there would have been a science of nature. It was a promise, however, which the Babylonians themselves never really fulfilled. They furnished the basis for the scientific advance, but were never able to win sufficient emancipation from the primitive superstitions to make the advance themselves. They did succeed, finally, in the seventh, sixth, and fifth centuries B.C. in supplanting the crude old myths by a mathematical statement of the movements of the stars.[12] But astrology, the last phase of Babylonian priestly lore, was still rather a religion than a science. Its calculations and observations were, as in the earlier cults, for the purpose of discovering the properties of the stars, and the very numbers in which the astral movements were reckoned were the mystical embodiments of fate. It was reserved for another and more gifted people to transform astrology into astronomy; and even the Greeks were not quite emancipated from the age-long curse of the religion of luck.

The main reason why this mass of priestly lore was not more useful for science, was, as has just been hinted, the weakness of its mathematics. And this was due in turn—apart from the eternal stumbling block of the mystery and sacredness of numbers, of the luck embodied in the sixes, sevens, and their multiples, and all the persistent jumble of accompanying superstitions—to the lack of an accurate base of reckoning. The first essential for the study of recurring phenomena of the heavens is a reliable measurement of the intervals at which they recur, and this, in turn, is impossible so long as time is measured by the moon.

We have seen how the moon-god gained ascendency in Babylon in the days of the first Semitic kingdom. Dominating the religion, it dominated the cosmology. In the earliest Semitic records, Sin, the moon-god, is so lofty a deity that the sun-god, Shamash, is referred to as his "servitor." [13] The "victorious sun" won his supreme place in Mesopotamia only in later ages, and not until the Semite had yielded before the Aryan Persians was his triumph assured. So long as the Semites ruled, the moon blocked both his path and that of a rational cosmology. Why this was so—that Babylon should cling so persistently to the moon, when Egypt so many centuries earlier turned to the sun as the center of its cosmology—is not a fact to be explained away on any easygoing materialistic basis. But, on the other hand, the materialist data need not be neglected, and a little consideration shows us that although nature was perhaps more kindly disposed to Babylonia than to Egypt in the fertility of farms, it was, by this very fact, less propitious in the arrangement of the seasons. Pliny tells us how wheat grew there twice a year,[14] which would disorganize any farmer's calendar that was trying to follow the sun. Under such circumstances, we can see how the invading Semites, coming from the desert where they had imbibed so deeply the nomad feeling for the moon, would not be obliged, when settling on the soil, to lay aside that deep-seated, primitive sense of its dominating luck over the nights and days, for another calendar run by the sun. Whatever the reason,[15] the moon ruled in Babylon, and the calendar bore the marks of it.

We shall leave aside the question of the exact way in which the Babylonian calendar grew up.[16] It is a matter concerning which Assyriologists are still not agreed, and new inscriptions may at any day recast the story in a different setting. But, whatever primitive measures of time they started with—different in different cities—the priests of Babylonia had their lunar calendar in operation as long ago as 2500 B.C. The month, which began with the first appearance of the new moon, in the evening sky, was reckoned with fair exactness as 29½ days,[17] but as this was an impossible measure, two lengths of months were employed, 29 days for a "hollow" month and 30 days for a "full" month. In the early calendars it was, therefore, customary and necessary to indicate along with the name of the month what number of days it contained. Twelve of these months made a year of 354 days. As this was over 11 days short of the solar year, the next calendar year would be quite out of reckoning with the sun, the seasons, and such festivals as they involved. As this kept getting worse instead of better, an additional month had to be intercalated—making the year 384 days—at the command of the priests, whenever they decided that the festivals needed readjustment. The priests seem to have worked out no unchanging system of intercalation until the close of Babylonian history, when in the Persian period regularity was definitely assured.[18] The query comes to even the superficial student whether the "victorious sun" of the Persian heavens was not in some way responsible for this rectification.

So far, the survey of the ancient Babylonian history has been disappointing. But a new era began in the seventh and sixth centuries B.C., in which the age-long groping of the priests, their uncertain dating and ineffective observations were changed into accurate and scientific calculations. This was one of the most important events in all the world's history, one of the major epochs in the history of intellectual emancipation, perhaps hardly less decisive than the age of Copernicus and of Newton. For to it we can trace the first accurate orientations of mankind in time and of the world in space. To it go back all lines of scientific advance in chronology and astronomy. The story of this achievement, however, carries us from the consideration of calendars to that of chronology, from the reckoning of time by days to that of years and then of non-recurring periods. In the chapters which follow we have, therefore, the setting for the dawn of history.

NOTES

II. THE NATURAL CALENDAR

1. David Livingstone, "Narrative of an Expedition to the Zambesi," 1866, page 104.
2. W. Junker, "Travels in Africa," Eng. Trans. II., page 168. Cf. Carl Bucher, "Evolution of Industry" (Tr. Wickett), page 19.
3. Quoted by H. L. Roth, *Journal of Anthropological Institute*, 16 (1886), page 116. Cf. W. I. Thomas, "Source Book for Social Origins," pages 98-112.
4. Cf. F. K. Ginzel, "Handbuch der Mathematischen und Technischen Chronologie" (1906), I., pages 58 ff. The progress of anthropology has opened up many a field of study in this realm. Already at the opening of the nineteenth century, Ludwig Ideler,—whose "Handbuch der Mathematischen und Technischen Chronologie" has been and still is unsurpassed as a manual of historical chronology—stated with wistful sense of the limitations of his texts (Vol. I., p. 64): "It would be interesting to be able to follow the history of any reckoning of Time from the first rude beginning through all its phases to its completion; ordinarily we know the time-reckoning of a people only in the most perfect form which it reached with them." Comparative study of similar cultures helps us in some degree to make good the lacunae. But, as the chapters show, the full history of the appropriation of Time can never be written except in the broadest outlines.
5. Hesiod "Works and Days," Tr. A. W. Mair, 1908. Page 448.
6. Jeremiah, viii, 7.
7. Hesiod, *op. cit.*, page 486.
8. As in the old Norwegian year for example. One might also recall the poetic terseness of the text given in Genesis, viii, 22, of the covenant of God with man after the flood: "While the earth remaineth, seed-time,

and harvest, and cold and heat, and summer and winter, and day and night shall not cease."

9. Hence September, October, November, and December, the seventh, eighth, ninth and tenth months in the old Roman year.

10. Cf. Vergil's "Georgics," Bk. I., for an insistence upon the importance of weather forecasting.

11. Cf. Vergil's "Georgics," I., 230 ff. Columella, "De Re Rustica," Preface: "Let the farmer keep in mind the rising and setting of the stars, lest he begin his work when rains and winds are menacing and so his labor be in vain."

12. Cf. Mair's note, pages 136 ff. Vergil, "Georgics," I., pages 205, 229; Columella, loc. cit., II., page 80.

13. "Georgics," I., pages 250 ff.

III. THE SUPERNATURAL CALENDAR

1. A singular indication of the social origin of religious belief. Cf. H. Hubert, "La Representation du Temps" in "Melanges d'Histoire des Religions" by H. Hubert and M. Mauss (1909) pages 219 ff.

2. The best example of this "revealed" character of the religious calendar is, of course, in the Mosaic code.

3. Or, to be more exact, of times.

4. The Romans, characteristically viewing things from the practical point of view, had the terms inverted: the dies fasti were those on which business was permitted. Business, not religion, was the criterion.

5. Cf. Polybius or Caesar or any other antique observer of the power of Fortuna.

6. The word "apprehension" fortunately has both these meanings.

7. Of course this applies to the whole sphere of religion, more especially to the sacramental or sacrificial aspects. Robertson Smith's phrase "the contagion of holiness" seemed to many sacrilegious thirty years ago. It is a commonplace now in comparative religion.

8. The calendar is thus obviously rather an expression of the variety and value of times than a mere counting of units.

9. Fate may be regarded as the luck in essentials, i.e., in matters of life and death; it can not be escaped, and so we are impressed mainly with its irrevocable character, but in essence it is like the luck of lesser happenings, which may be avoided and so seem wayward. Chance is uncertain as fate is certain.

10. So here the data of religion become also the data of science.

IV. FROM LUCK TO MATHEMATICS

11. Perhaps the best single survey of the various calendars of different peoples is the article, "Calendar" in Hastings's Encyclopaedia of Religion and Ethics.

12. It is possible that in what follows, as we trace the growth of the larger time—framework of months, years, centuries, etc.—we may lose sight of this fundamental importance of the day, which after all is the main time unit. In this connection the story of Creation, as told in Genesis, keeps recurring to our memory as we move along this border-land of poetry and religion: "Evening came and morning came, a first day."

The separation of light from darkness marked the first act of creation: and the result was—Time! Such is the common impression of the implications of that text. Behind it lay eternity. As a matter of fact, all that happened was the appearance of a time-schedule. The clock of the universe was set going.

13. The tropical month, i.e., the mean period taken by the moon in passing through 360° longitude, as from one vernal equinox to another, is 27 days, 7 hours, 43 minutes, 4.7 seconds, which is 6.8 seconds less than the sidereal month, the difference being due to the precession of the equinox.

14. This opens up a field as yet but little explored, that of the mystical, religious, pre-history of mathematics. A short, but most suggestive survey of the field is given by W. J. McGee in his article on "Primitive Numbers" in the *Nineteenth Annual Report of the American Bureau of Ethnology*, II., 821-852 (J 900). Cf. also J. H. Graf, "Ueber Zahlenaberglauben."

15. This question of orientation, as for example, in the placing of the temples of antiquity—or for that matter any definite boundaries—is a wide and alluring field. It corresponds, relative to space, with the questions treated here, relative to Time. The starting point for reesarch in the antique field still remains the old work of Heinrich Nissen, *Das Templum* (1869).

16. The sacred power of seven is recognized all over the world. Everyone knows of the uncanny power of the seventh son. In China we are told that the emperor was wont to sacrifice on seven altars to seven groups of spirits; that he was placed in his coffin on the seventh day after death, and was buried in the seventh month. In India and Persia, in early Teutonic and Celtic religions, the system of seven constantly occurs, as also in Greece and Rome, where the seven hills form an obviously artificial grouping on a religious basis. There were in reality more or less than seven hills in Rome; it all depended on how one wished to count them. Such references are compactly grouped by O. Zockler, in the article *Siebenzahl* in Harch-Herzog, *Realenencyclopadie*. (Abbreviated but with good bibliography in the new Schaff-Herzog, *Encyclopaedia of Religious Knowledge*, article "Seven.") Cf. also the article *Zahlen* (Kautsch) for Biblical citations of sacred numbers. The Sumerian word for seven was translated by the Semitic Babylonians by a word meaning completeness, which carries us back beyond all Babylonian history.

17. Hehn, *Siebenzahl und Sabbat* in Leipzinger Semitische Studien, II., 1907, attributes it to the phases of the moon, while refuting its derivation from the seven planets. Against his view, see Ed. Meyer's *Geschichte des Altertums*, pp. 578-588, Meyer holds that the sacredness of seven is due to its being prime and difficult to reckon.

18. Except, of course, in the Jewish religion, where monotheism concentrated its taboos upon the Sabbath.

19. Cf. Ginzel, "Handbuch," I., pages 120, 121.

20. The week was adopted in the Roman Empire largely through the influence of the Persian religion of the sun-god Mithras, in which there was a special liturgy for each day's star, as in the case of the Chaldaeans. Cf. Cumont, "Astrology," page 164. There are few more interesting

sources in this connection than the eighteenth chapter of the thirty-seventh book of Dio Cassius, in which he attempts to enlighten his age on the origin of the names of the days of the week. It is a good example of the misinformation of an antique rationalizer. He attributes their origin to the Egyptians, who, so far as we know, did not have the seven-day period, except as they may have been familiar with the astrological lore of Babylonia. Then he has two theories to advance, one of which suffices here: "If one apply the so-called principle of the tetra-chord (i.e., skipping two stars in the count every time one goes over the list)—which is believed to constitute the bases of music—to these stars in order (of their distance from the earth) . . . and beginning at the outer orbit assigned to Saturn, then, omitting the next two, name the master of the fourth, and after him, passing over two others, reach the seventh, and so on the return . . . in this same way, calling them by the names of the days, one will find all the days to be in a kind of musical connection with the arrangement of heavens. . . ." The other account of Dio need not be taken any more seriously than this one. One sees, however, the artistic possibilities of the world of time.

21. For the transmission of this astralization of the gods from Babylon to Hellas see the short, clear account in Cumont's "Astrology and Religion among the Greeks and Romans," Lec. II. In Homer the planets are named from their qualities. "Herald of the Dawn" (Venus), "Twinkling Star" (Mercury), "Fiery Star" (Mars), "Luminous Star" (Jupiter), "Brilliant Star" (Saturn). After the fourth century these became Aphrodite, Hermes, Ares, Zeus, Kronos, corresponding both to their qualities and to the Babylonian parallels of Ishtar, Nebo, Nergal, Marduk, and Ninib. "Thus the names of the planets we employ to-day, are an English translation of a Latin translation of a Greek translation of a Babylonian nomenclature." French and Italian perpetuate the Roman day-names: Lune-di or Lundi, Marte-di or Mardi, Mercoledi or Mercredi, Giove-di or Jeudi, Vener-di or Vendredi. In Sabbato and Semedi, however, the Jewish Sabbath triumphed over Saturn, just as Domenica or Dimanche is the purely Christian *Dies Dominicus* or Lord's day. Of the Teutonic counterparts, "Tiu" seems to have been a somewhat obscure parallel of Mars, as the nominative form is not found and the genitive "Tiues" is found only in the name of the day. Woden, Thor, and Freja are, of course, recognizable. Thor's day seems to have been the most important day in the Scandinavian world, as it was upon that day that the assemblies met.

22. To-day perhaps the only religious sect to protest against the pagan days of our calendar is that of the Friends, or Quakers, but from a different motive from that of the Jew. For the Quaker makes it a rule of faith to deny that one day is more sacred than another, and to carry this theory over into practise goes to "meeting" on "Fourth Day" as well as "First Day."

23. To be sure, in one sense, the naming of the Sabbath named the other days as well. They were parts of the Sabbatical cycle.

24. The origin of the week of seven days has been generally ascribed to Babylon. The Hebrew "Sabbath" has been held to connect with the Babylonian "sabattu," which was used to denote days of penitence. But

no inscription so far has revealed the use of "sabattu" for the seventh day, although the number seven was a sacred—or fateful—number. The seventh, fourteenth, twenty-first, and twenty-eighth days of the month were "evil days,"—a fact apparently connected with the four quarters of the moon. But that is quite a different thing from a week which breaks through the months altogether and continues its way undisturbed by phases of the moon. Of this there is as yet no trace in Babylonian inscriptions. Moreover, the fifteenth, the full moon, seems as well to have been "sabattu." This leads to a recent conjecture that "Sabbath" is to be derived rather from sabbat, to be complete, i.e., the day when the moon has completed its phase and is full. The transference of the periods from lunar to purely numerical would have been the work of the priesthood after the return from the captivity. The role of the Israelites in the adoption and spread of the week is beyond question, but that they invented it instead of working it over from Babylon, is a point as yet unsettled. On all this see the summary in Ginzel, I., 118 ff., 5 ff., and authorities there cited.

25. The origins of the Christian's celebration of the first day are obscure. They were apparently observing it already in the time of Justin Martyr by the middle of the second century. Perhaps it was partly due to the observance of the day of the resurrection. Cf. I. Cor., xvi, 12; Acts, xx, 7; John, xx, 26. But there is no command to observe the Lord's day in apostolic literature. The Didache emphasizes the significance of "The Lord's day of the Lord" by an unconscious pleonasm, but makes Wednesdays and Fridays memorial days as well as fast days in commemoration of the betrayal and crucifixion (c. viii.). Ignatius, however, shows the distinct advance. Sunday is to him "the festival, the queen and the chief of all the days of the week" (Magn. IX.). The earliest apologies, therefore, seek to explain that the first-day is to be substituted for the seventh of the old dispensation; cf. Epistle of Barnabas, XV. Justin is the first to mention it as "the day called Sunday" (Apol I., 67). Two centuries later Sunday legislation begins by the constitution of Constantine of the year 321. The distinction it draws between the practical and the religious calendar is curious. "All judges and city folk and all craftsmen shall rest on the venerated day of the sun. But country folk may freely . . . attend to the cultivation of their land, since it often happens that no other day is so opportune for sowing the grain in the furrows or setting out the vines in the ditches; so that the advantage of a favorable moment granted by providence may not be lost." Cod. Just. III., tit. 12, 1, 3. Cf. M. A. Huttmann, "The Establishment of Christianity," etc., page 158. This was the old Roman customary treatment of agricultural work on holidays; cf. Vergil, Georg. I., 268 ff., Cato, De Re Rustica, c. 2. A long series of imperial constitutions followed, most of them gathered up in this same title (De Feriis) of the Code of Justinian.

26. This is, of course, for business and state purposes. The month was also observed in the farmer's calendar, and it had its lucky and unlucky days, just as in Babylon—or any place else the world over. Hesiod's farming calendar ends with a list of them. The luckiest time is about the eleventh and twelfth, just as the moon is reaching the full; the sec-

ond half of the month, including the fifteenth, is, upon the whole, unpropitious, although with some peculiar exceptions. This, however, was rather folk-lore than calendar. Mr. Mair, in his edition of Hesiod, has arranged the month "according to what appears the most probable interpretation," as follows:

1. A holy day.
4. A holy day. Propitious for marriage, for commencing to build ships; a day on which sorrow is to be avoided.
5. An unpropitious day. On this day the Erinyes attended the birth of Oath (Horkos), whom Strife bare to punish perjurers.
6. Unpropitious for the birth of females; propitious for the birth of males: only such a child will be prone to mockery and lies and crooked words and secret talk; propitious for gelding kids and lambs and for penning sheep.
7. A holy day. Birthday of Apollo.
8. Geld boar and bull.
9. Altogether propitious; to beget or to be born, for man or woman.
10. Propitious for the birth of males.
{11. Most excellent for mortal works: for reaping and for shearing
{12. sheep. Yet the twelfth is even better than the eleventh. On the twelfth, when the spider spins its web in full day, and the ant gathers her store, a woman should set up her loom and begin her work. On the twelfth also geld mules.
13. Bad day for sowing: good for planting.
14. Good for the birth of females, for taming sheep, cattle, mules, dog. This day broach the cask. Above all a holy day.
15. Unpropitious.
16. Bad day for planting: good for birth of males: not good for girl to be born or to marry.
17. Good for threshing and for cutting timber.
19. Better in the afternoon.
20. On the Great 20th at noon is propitious for birth of a wise man.
24. Best in the morning, worse toward afternoon. A day on which to avoid sorrow.
25. Unpropitious.
{27. On one of these (edd. differ as to which) broach cask; yoke oxen,
{29. mules, horses; launch ship.
30. Inspect works and distribute rations to servants.

27. That of the *Idus* is clear. The word itself may be connected with the Sanscrit *indu*, "the moon," or the root *idh*, "to lighten."
28. It also enabled the savage to reckon distance with the primitive counterpart of the modern time-table. The land of the traveler lies so many "moons" away—a form of expression used by nomads in wide range.
29. Mohammed definitely ordained the lunar unit of time-measurement in the Koran, Sura II., 214. "Concerning the phases of the moon shall they ask thee, so tell them they serve to mark out time to men and the pilgrimage to Mecca." Sura X., 5: "God has set the sun to shine by day and the moon by night, and his ordinances have so arranged it that you by this can know the number of the year and the reckoning of time."

30. Easter, for instance, seems to have developed out of a nomadic feast at the time of the birth of the lambs.
31. Cf. J. H. Breasted, "The Development of Religion and Thought in Ancient Egypt" (1912), Lecture I. This was the first attempt to apply the Pyramid Texts to the understanding of Egyptian religion.

V. THE EGYPTIAN CALENDAR

1. For details on the three seasons, Cf. Ginzel, I., page 159. On the artificial character of the four-month season of harvest, see Foucart in Hastings's *Encyclopaedia of Religion and Ethics*, article "Calendar." The Egyptian farmer's calendar was, from the peculiar conditions of the Nile, life, a complete variation from that indicated above as the basis of European farming calendars.
2. The Decree of Canopus, under Ptolemy III, Euergetes, dated its reform from the 7th of March, 238 B.C. The inscription was found in 1866. German translation in Ginzel, "Handbuch," Vol. I., page 197.
3. The exact date of the introduction of the Julian year in Egypt—known as the Alexandrine era—is a matter of dispute. For discussion see Ginzel, "Handbuch," Vol. I., pages 224-228, who inclined to the view that the first leap-year was 26 B.C., but that the epoch was carried back to 30 B.C. E. Meyer, "Geschichte des Altertums," Vol. I., page 29, dates it from the twenty-ninth of August, 25 B.C.
4. *De die natali*, c. 18; written 239 A.D.
5. *Sothic* from *Sothis* the Hellenized form of *Sopdu*, the Egyptian name for Sirius.
6. Cf. Ed. Meyer, "Aegyptische Chronologie" in *Abhandlungen der Berliner Akademie der Wissenschaften*, 1904, 1907, and his "Geschichte des Altertums," Vol. I., page 30. Brested, "Ancient Records," Vol. I., pages 25, *et seq.*
7. Cf. summary by G. Foucart, in article "Calendar" (Egyptian) in Hastings's *Encyclopaedia of Religion and Ethics*, page 95.
8. Ginzel, Vol. I., page 152, points out the relatively slight progress made in astronomy by the ancient Egyptians. They knew the Zodiac, the most important constellations; they had distinguished planets from the fixed stars, had observed the heliacal rising of Sirius, etc.; and yet the results of their observations were very crude. The monuments do not show whether they knew the relations between the movements of the planets or not. The development of astrology in Egypt came in its later period. There is nothing in the sources on the observation of eclipses,— the very thing which furnished the Babylonians with the means for determining the movements of sun and moon. Ptolemy, the great astronomer, had to turn to Babylonian and Greek forerunners, apparently, in view of the lack of Egyptian material. In any case, in the material found so far, there is absolutely no trace of that systematic activity in the taking of observations, without which no certain progress can be made in astronomical science.

VI. THE BABYLONIAN CALENDAR

9. Marduk absorbed the powers of Enlil just as later the Hebrews attributed to their Jahve powers which the Babylonians had attributed

to Marduk. Cf. R. W. Rogers, "Religion of Babylonia and Assyria," page 134.

10. Sin had been as well the local deity of the city of Ur, and Shamash of Larsa and Sippar, but the gods share the fortunes of their worshippers, and apparently it was the Semite conquest which was responsible for the dominance of the moon over the affairs of Babylonia.

11. Codification involves a historical operation in its discriminating analysis and careful synthesis, whenever it deals with data of social evolution. There is a sense in which the code of the Roman law would fit very well with the conception of history in antiquity, particularly that expounded by Polybius. In it the experience of the past is teaching the inexperienced present; it is a preservation of those elements of the past which can apply to the complications of other times. The rest may be discarded; what is kept is the useful, the real fruit of all past activity. But the more historical the codifer is, the less his work is likely to be of value. For when the sense of the past is strong—as is surely to be the case in all religious compilations, owing to the sacredness of origins—the result is a failure to meet the changed conditions of the present. The result is stagnation. Boldness in the intellectual quest is sacrificed in order to secure results which harmonize with those already attained, and no matter what wealth and variety of phenomena the present offers, what chances of intellectual and social advance it opens up, the mind or the society which is bound to the wheel of antique premises or authority revolves, but does not progress. It is from this angle that one comes upon that antagonism between antiquarian scholarship and radicalism which has been so marked in the last two centuries.

12. The achievements of the ancient Babylonians in astronomy have been much over-stated by a group of scholars, of whom the chief is Hugo Winckler—the pan-Babylonians—whose main tendency has been to trace everything back to the early age of Babylon. The recent works of Strassmaier and Kugler, based upon the deciphering of Assyrian astrological tables, have quite disproved this proud claim of extreme antiquity for Babylonian astral science. Eduard Meyer ("Geschichte des Altertums," page 458) points out the striking fact that Orion seems to have been unknown to the ancient Babylonians, while it appears that in the oldest periods of Egyptian history, along with Sirius, and plays a great role in the hieroglyphs. It was also known very early to the Greeks (cf. Hesiod as above). The same is true of the Great Bear. From dim antiquity the Babylonians had known the movements of Venus—the brilliant star which rose on winter mornings and set on summer evenings, and already in the twentieth century B.C. they had measured its heliacal cycle of 21 years (from 1977-1957 B.C. See Kugler on Table 63). They also easily distinguished the four other planets of that group which, as we have seen, gave us the names for the days of the week: Ninib (Mars), Nibo (Mercury), Marduk (Jupiter), and Nergal (Saturn). Eclipses were also kept track of, but not with sufficient accuracy to yield any scientific results until in the late Babylonian period.

13. Cf. M. Jastrow, "Babylonian and Assyrian Religion," pages 68 ff. It is interesting to note that the name, "Sin," occurs in "Sinai," showing some definite south-Arabian affiliations. The early custom of reckoning the

day from the evening is of interest in this connection. Later, the Assyrians began it at daybreak. Compare the North American Indian's reckoning by so many "nights" or "sleeps."

14. "Natural History," Vol. XVIII., page 17.

15. The greater ease of observing the moon with the naked eye as compared with the sun is also a factor.

16. The exact origins of the Babylonian calendar are as obscure as those of the Egyptian. The hypothesis of an original year of 360 days with 5¼ added, which was advanced by H. Winckler and those of the "old Babylonian school," has, apparently, no data in its favor. Every city seems to have had a different calendar at first, and the unification to have come only very slowly, after the first dynasty of Babylon. Cf. Ed. Meyer, "Geschichte d. Altertums," pages 365 ff.

17. The length of the astronomical month, it may be recalled, was 29.530589 days.

18. Cf. Ginzel's "Handbuch," Vol. I., pages 132 ff., for lists of the years of intercalation.

CHAPTER V

⚜

THE INTERPRETATION OF HISTORY

TWO GREAT QUESTIONS front all students of the social sciences: What happened? Why? History attempts to deal mainly with the first. It gathers the scattered traces of events and fills the archives of civilization with their records. Its science sifts the evidence and prepares the story. Its art recreates the image of what has been, and "old, unhappy, far-off things" become once more the heritage of the present. Though no magic can wholly restore the dead past, history satisfies in considerable part the curiosity which asks, "What happened?" But "Why?" What forces have been at work to move the latent energies of nations, to set going the march of events? What makes our revolutions or our tory reactions? Why did Rome fall, Christianity triumph, feudalism arise, the Inquisition flourish, monarchy become absolute and of divine right, Spain decline, England emerge, democracy awaken and grow potent? Why did these things happen when or where they did? Was it the direct intervention of an overruling Providence, for Whose purposes the largest battalions were always on the move? Or are the ways past finding out? Do the events themselves reveal a meaning?

These are not simply questions for philosophers. Children insist upon them most. He is a lucky storyteller whose Jack the Giant Killer or Robin Hood is not cut through, time and again, by unsat-

This chapter is the reprint of an article in The American Historical Review, Vol. XVIII, No. 4 (July, 1913), pp. 692-709. It was first given as a lecture in the University of Illinois in that year.

isfied curiosity as to *why* the beanstalk grew so high, *why* Jack wanted to climb, *why* Robin Hood lived under a greenwood tree. Many a parental Herodotus has been wrecked on just such grounds. The problem of the philosopher or the scientist is the same as that brought forward by the child. The drama of history unrolls before our eyes in more sober form: our Robin Hood becomes a Garibaldi, our Jack the Giant Killer a Napoleon, but we still have to ask how fortune and genius so combined as to place southern Italy in the hands of the one, Europe at the feet of the other. Not only is the problem the same, but we answer it in the same way. Here, at once, we have a clue to the nature of interpretation. For any one knows that you answer the child's "Why?" by telling another story. Each story is, in short, an explanation, and each explanation a story. The schoolboy's excuse for being late is that he couldn't find his cap. He couldn't find his cap *because* he was playing in the barn. Each incident was a cause and each cause an incident in his biography. In like manner most of the reasons we assign for our acts merely state an event or a condition of affairs which is in itself a further page of history. At last, however, there comes a point where the philosopher and the child part company. History is more than events. It is the manifestation of life, and behind each event is some effort of mind and will, while within each circumstance exists some power to stimulate or to obstruct. Hence psychology and economics are called upon to explain the events themselves. The child is satisfied if you account for the career of Napoleon by a word "genius," but that merely opens the problem to the psychologist. The child in us all attributes the overthrow to the hollow squares of Waterloo, but the economist reminds us of the Continental System and of the Industrial Revolution which made Waterloo possible.

The process of interpreting history, therefore, involves getting as much as possible out of history, psychology, and economics— using economics in the widest possible sense as the affective material background of life. This does not get to final causes, to be sure. It leaves the universe still a riddle. Theologians and metaphysicians are the only ones who attempt to deal with final causes as with final ends. Certainly historians cannot follow them in such speculations. The infinite lies outside experience, and experience is the sphere of history. When we talk of the interpretation of history, therefore, we do not mean its setting in the universe, but a knowledge of its own inner relationships. We confine ourselves to humanity and the theatre of its activities. But within this realm of mystery man exists, acts, and thinks—or thinks he thinks, which is all the same for historians—and these thoughts and deeds remain mostly un-understood, even by the actors themselves. Here is mystery enough, mystery which is not in itself unknowable but merely unknown. The social sciences do not invade the field of religion; they have nothing to do with the ultimate; their problems are those of the City of Man, not of the City of God. So the interpretation of history can leave theology aside, except where theology attempts to become historical. Then it must face the same criticism as all other histories. If the City of God is conceived of as a creation of the processes of civilization, it becomes as much a theme for scientific analysis as the Roman Empire or the Balkan Confederacy. If theology substitutes itself for science, it must expect the same treatment as science. But our search for historic "causes" is merely a search for other things of the same kind—natural phenomena of some sort —which lie in direct and apparently inevitable connection. We interpret history by knowing more of it, bringing to bear our psychology and every other auxiliary to open up each intricate relationship between men, situations, and events.

This is our first great principle. What do we mean by the "meaning" of anything but more knowledge of it? In physics or chemistry we enlarge our ideas of phenomena by observing how they work, what their affinities are, how they combine or react. But all these properties are merely different aspects of the same thing, and our knowledge of it is the sum total of our analysis. Its meaning has changed, as our knowledge enlarges, from a lump of dirt to a compound of elements. No one asks what an element is, because no one can tell—except in terms of other elements. The interpretation, therefore, of physical phenomena is a description of them in terms of their own properties. The same thing is true of history, but instead of description we have narrative. For history differs from the natural sciences in this fundamental fact, that while they consider phenomena from the standpoint of Space, history deals with them from the standpoint of Time. Its data are in eternal change, moving in endless succession. Time has no static relationships, not so much as for a second. One moment merges into the next, and another has begun before the last is ended. The old Greeks already pointed out that one could never put his foot twice into the same waters of a running stream, and never has philosophy insisted more eloquently upon this fluid nature of Time than in the writings of Professor Bergson. But, whatever Time may be in the last analysis, it is clear that whereas physics states the meaning of the phenomena with which it deals in descriptions, history must phrase its interpretations in narrative, the narrative which runs with passing time.

Hence history and its interpretation are essentially one, if we mean by history all that has happened, including mind and matter in so far as they relate to action. Any other kind of interpretation is unscientific; it eludes analysis because it does not itself analyze, and hence it eludes proof. So theological dogma, which may or may not be true, and speculation in metaphysics are alike outside our problem. Indeed, when we come down to it, there is little difference between "What has happened?" and "Why?" The "Why?" only opens up another "What?" Take for example a problem in present history: "Why has the price of living gone up?" The same question might be asked another way: "What has happened to raise prices?" The change in the form of sentence does not solve anything, for who knows what has happened? But it puts us upon a more definite track toward our solution. We test history by history.

The earliest historical narrative is the myth. It is at the same time an explanation. It is no mere product of imagination, of the play of art with the wayward fancies of childlike men. Myths—real, genuine myths, not Homeric epics composed for sophisticated, critical audiences—are statements of "facts" to the believer. They are social outputs, built up out of experience and fitted to new experiences. The long canoes are swept to sea by the northeast hurricane, and year by year in the winter nights at the campfires of those who go by long canoes the story is repeated, over and over again, until the sea is left behind or a new race brings triremes with machinery in the inside. So long as the old society exists under the old conditions the myth perpetuates itself; but it also gathers into itself the reflex of the changing history. It therefore embodies the belief of the tribe, and this gives it an authority beyond the reach of any primitive higher criticism. Appealed to as the "wisdom of our fathers," as the universally accepted and therefore true—*quod semper quod ab omnibus*—it becomes a sort of creed for its people. More than a creed, it is as unquestioned as the world around and as life itself. The eagle of Prometheus or of the Zuñi myths is as much a part of the world to Greeks and Zuñis as the eagle seen yonder on the desert rim. The whole force of society is on the side of myth. The unbeliever is ostracized or put to death. What would have happened to the man who had dared to question the literal narrative of Genesis in the thirteenth century has happened in some form in every society. The Inquisition, we are told, was merely a refinement of lynch law. In any case, it would never have been effective without popular support. The heretics of all ages suffer because the faith they challenge is the treasured possession of their society, a heritage in which resides the mysterious efficacy of immemorial things.

Now it is a strange fact that most of our beliefs begin in prior belief. It does not sound logical, but it remains true that we get to believing a thing from believing it. Belief is the basic element in thought. It starts with consciousness itself. Once started, there develops a tendency—"a will"—to keep on. Indeed it is almost the strongest tendency in the social mind. Only long scientific training can keep an individual alert with doubt, or, in other words, keep him from merging his own beliefs in those of his fellows. This is the reason that myth has so long played so momentuous a role in the history of the human intelligence—by far the largest of any one element in our whole history. Science was born but yesterday. Myths are millenniums old. And they are as young today as in the glacial period. Heroes and victims share the stage of the drama of history with those uncanny Powers that mock at effort or exalt the weak and trick with sudden turns the stately progress of society. Wherever the marvellous event is explained by causes more marvellous still, where the belief is heightened by basing it upon deeper mysteries, we are following the world-old method explaining by the inexplicable.

Myths are unsatisfactory as explanations for various reasons, but the main one is that human events are subordinated to the supernatural in which they are set. This means that normal events of daily life generally pass unnoticed and attention is concentrated upon the unusual and the abnormal. It is in these that the divine or the diabolic intervenes. They are preëminently—as we still say of railway accidents—acts of God. So the myth neither tells a full story, with all the human data involved, nor directs to any natural sequence of events. Sickness and consequent catastrophe are not attributed to malarial mosquitoes—such as filled the temples of Aesculapius with suppliants and depleted Greece of citizens. All misfortune is due to broken taboos. When Roman armies are defeated the question is, "Who has sinned and how?" When death comes to the Australian bushman, there is always black magic to account for it. And pontiffs and medicine men elaborate the mythology which explains and justifies the taboos.

That is not to say that myths are the creations of priests. The creation is the work of the society itself. The priest merely elaborates. The initial belief resides in the nerves of primitive men, the fear of the uncanny, the vague apprehension which still chills us in the presence of calamity. Social suggestion is responsible for much of it—we tremble when we see the rigid fear on the faces of those beside us. When someone whispers in the dark, "Isn't it awful?" "it" suddenly thrills into being, like a ghost. Voltaire was wrong to attribute the origin of these beliefs of superstition to priestcraft. The priest merely took hold of the universal beliefs of his people and gave them form and consistency, as the minstrel wove them into poetry. The scruple about entering the dark wooded slopes beyond the village grainfields is enough to people it, for most of us, with all uncanny things. If you are the kind of person to have scruples about entering a wood by night, you are the kind to appreciate the possibilities of lurking danger in its shadows and moving presences in its thickets. So on a night when the moon is high and the wind is still you may hear the hounds and the wolf packs of the wild hunters—of Diana and Mars. It needs no priestly college to convince us of that. The wood and the wolves and our own nerves are enough. But the priestly college develops the things of night into the stuff of history, and centuries after the howling wolves have disappeared from the marshes around Rome the city cherishes, to the close of its history, the myth of its founding.

Men first tell stories. Then they think about them. So from mythology the ancients proceeded to philosophy. Now philosophy is a wide word. For some of us it means keen criticism of fundamental things. For others it seems a befuddled consideration of unrealities. But whatever it may be now, philosophy came into the antique world as science, critical analysis, and history was but another name for it. The "inquiry" of those Ionian *logographoi* who began to question Homer in the sixth century before Christ challenged and interpreted myth. So, all through its history, history has demanded of its students denial rather than acceptance, skepticism rather than belief, in order that the story of men and empires be more than myth. But the tendency to believe and accept is so strongly impressed upon us from immemorial social pressures that few have risen to the height of independent judgment which was the Greek ideal.

One may distinguish two phases of philosophic interpretation of history, that in which the philosophy is in reality a theology and that in which it is natural science. In the first phase we are still close to myth. Myth places the cause of events in mystery of some sort—deities, demons, the Fates or Fortune. Early philosophy proceeds upon these assumptions, which also penetrate most antique histories. Even Polybius, hard-headed, much-experienced man of the world, cannot quite attribute the rise of Rome to natural causes. Fortune, that wayward goddess of Caesar, had something to do with it—how much of it would be hard to say. Livy had this myth-philosophy to the full; every disaster had its portent, every triumph its omen. This was the practical philosophy of all but the few calm thinkers whose skepticism passed into the second phase, which reached all the way from an open question as to whether or not the gods interfered in human affairs to the positive denial of their influence. The great source book for such interpretations of history is Cicero's *On the Nature of the Gods,* where one may find in the guise of a theological discussion a résumé of the various pagan philosophies of history. For the philosophy of history was more frankly philosophy than history; the question at issue was the intruding mystery rather than the circumstances of the intrusion, and one denied or affirmed mainly on *a priori* grounds. The denial was not historical criticism and the philosophy of doubt hardly more genuine historical interpretation than the philosophy of belief. Its conclusions more nearly *coincide* with the demands of scientific research; that is all. But mythology was not lightly to be got rid of, even among philosophers; as for the populace, it merely exchanged one myth for another, until finally it could take refuge in theology. The bold infidelity of a Lucretius was too modern for the age which was to give birth to Christianity, and the Voltaires of antiquity were submerged in a rising sea of faith.

Moreover there were two reasons why antique philosophy could not accomplish much. It lacked the instruments by which to penetrate into the two centres of its problem: psychology, to analyze the mind, and experimental laboratories, to analyze the setting of life or life itself. It had some knowledge of psychology, to be sure, and some experimental science, but relatively little; and it never realized the necessity for developing them. It sharpened the reason to an almost uncanny degree, and played, like a grown athlete, with ideas. But it followed the ideas into their ideal world and left this world unaccounted for. Above all, it knew practically nothing of economic and material elements in history. Even a Thucydides has no glimpse of the intimate connection between the forces of economics and politics. History for him is made by *men*, not by grainfields and metals. It was not until the nineteenth century—just the other day—that economic factors in historical causation were emphasized as playing a role comparable to that of man himself. Thucydides did not realize how commercial and industrial competition could rouse the rivals of Athens to seek her overthrow. Polybius felt that Fortune was a weak excuse to offer for Rome's miraculous rise and fell back upon the peculiar excellence of her constitution. Both were rationalists of a high order, but they never extended their history—and therefore their interpretation—beyond politics. The gods tend to disappear, and mankind to take their place. But it is an incomplete mankind, rational beings moved by ideas and principles, not economic animals moved by blind wants and fettered by the basest limitations. In short, a political man is the farthest analysis one gets. But even Aristotle never knew how many things there were in politics besides politics. The extent of the interplay of material forces upon psychological lay outside his ken.

Upon the whole, then, there is almost nothing to learn from antique interpretations of history. They interest us because of their antiquity and their drift from the supernatural to the natural. But they did not achieve a method which would open up the natural and let us see its working. They are of no service to us in our own interpretations.

Christianity dropped all this rationalist tone of the Greeks and turned the keen edge of Greek philosophy to hew a structure so vast in design, so simple in outline, that the whole world could understand. History was but the realization of religion—not of various religions, but of one, the working out of one divine plan. It was a vast, supernatural process, more God's than man's. It was no longer a play of rival forces, the gods of Rome against those of Veii or the Baalim against Jahveh. But from all eternity the drama had been determined by the Wisdom that was infinite, and it was being wrought out by an almighty arm. Baal and Jupiter are creatures and puppets, like mere men. History has only one interpretation. Rome— city and empire—is the spoil of the barbarian, the antique world is going to pieces, all its long heritage of culture, its millenniums of progress, its arts and sciences are perishing in the vast, barbaric anarchy: why? There is one answer, sufficient, final—God wills it. No uncertain guesses as to the virtue of peoples, weights of battalions, resources of countries, pressures of populations, wasteful administrations, Black Deaths, impoverished provinces. There is sin to be punished. The pagan temples of the ancient world, with their glories of art shining on every acropolis, are blasphemy and invite destruction. Philosophers and poets whose inspiration had once seemed divine now seem diabolic. Those who catch the vision of the new faith, shake off the old world as one shakes off a dream. Talk of revolutions! No doctrines of the rights of man have caught the imagination with such terrific force as these doctrines of the rights of God, which from Paul to Augustine were clothed with all the convincing logic of Hellenic genius and Roman realism. It is hard for us Christians to realize the amount of religion which Christianity injected into the world; not merely among the credulous populace, on the religious *qui vive*, but among thinking men. It saturated philosophy with dogma and turned speculation from nature to the supernatural.

The earliest Christians cherished the belief that the world was soon to end, and lived under the shadow of the day of doom. As time went on, this millennial hope seemed to grow fainter; but in reality it merely took a more rigid form. It became the structural heart of the new theology. The pageant of history, which had seemed so gloriously wonderful, so inspiring to a Polybius back in the old heroic days, was now a worn and sorry thing. It had no glory nor even any meaning except in the light of the new dispensation. On the other hand the new *patria*, the *Civitas Dei*, transcending all earthly splendor, was absorbing not merely the present and the future, but the past as well. For all the tragic lines of war and suffering were now converging. All the aimless struggling was now to show its hidden purpose. In Christianity, the story of nations, of politics, economics, art, war, law—in short of civilization—culminated, and ceased!

Such was the thought which underlay all Christian apologetic theology from the first. But it received its classic statement in the *City of God* by Augustine, written when the city of Rome had fallen, and—if it were not for the heretics and the barbarians—the claims of theology seemed almost realizable. For a thousand years and more it was the unquestioned interpretation of the meaning of history, easily adaptable to any circumstance because it covered all. It still is found wherever pure theology satisfies historical curiosity. That includes—or has included—not merely theologians but most other people, for, however slight has been the interest in theology, it has been greater than the interest in scientific history, at least until recent times. Religion has supplied the framework of our thought and the picture of our evolution. The most influential historians of Europe have been the parish priests. In every hamlet, however remote, for the lowly as for those of high degree, they have repeated the story week after week, century after century. Greek writers and thinkers, mediaeval minstrels and modern journalists can hardly match the influence of those priests upon the mind of the mass of men. The tale itself was an unrivalled epic, dark with the supreme central tragedy upon which Christendom itself rested, rising to the keenest voicing of the hopes of life. Its very essence was miracle. No fairy story could rival its devious turns, while at the same time the theme swept over the whole path of history—so far as they knew or cared. It was the story of a chosen people, of divine governance from Creation to the founding of their own church, guarded in a sacred book and interpreted from a sacred tongue.

Slowly, however, the setting of the Church had changed. The vision of the day of judgment died away almost altogether. Men who dared to dream apocalypses—like Joachim of Flora—or their followers were judged heretics by a church which had planted itself in *saeculo* and surrounded itself with all the pomp and circumstance of temporal power. There was still a lingering echo of the older faith, heard most often in the solemn service for the dead. So long as the universe was Ptolemaic—the world of Dante and of Milton—the heavy chord of *dies irae* would cut in upon the growing interest in the world itself. But once the crystalline sphere was shattered by Copernicus and Galileo, and the infinite spaces were strewn with stars like our own, the old idea of a world to "shrivel like a parched scroll" had to be revised and readjusted, and with it the simple conception of the divine purpose, centred upon the centre of things, and working by direct intervention through constant miracle. There was no sudden revolution; the old ideals were too firmly fixed for that. Moreover, science began to challenge the theological history of the universe before it challenged the theological history of man himself. But when geology began to bring in evidence of the age of our residence and physics achieved the incredible feat of weighing the forces and determining the conditions which held the worlds together, then the details of the scheme of Augustine had to be recast as well. From Augustine to Bossuet one may trace an almost unbroken line of theological interpretations. But some, at least, of the generation which listened to Bossuet were also to watch Bolingbroke and Voltaire whetting the weapons of rationalistic attack.

Now what is the weakness of the theological interpretation of history? It is of the same character as that which we have seen in the myth. The interpretation is outside history altogether. Grant all that theology claims, that Rome fell and England arose, that America was discovered, or was so long undiscovered, because "God wills it." That does not enlarge our knowledge of the process. It satisfies only those who believe in absolutely unqualified Calvinism—and they are becoming few and far between. If man is a free agent, even to a limited degree, he can find the meaning of his history in the history itself—the only meaning which is of any value as a guide to conduct or as throwing light upon his actions. Intelligent inquiry has free scope within a universe of ever-widening boundaries, where nature, and not supernature, presents its sober phenomena for patient study.

This patient study, however, had not yet been done when the eighteenth-century deists attacked the theological scheme, and their philosophy shares to some extent the weakness of the antique, in its ignorance of data. Natural law took the place of an intervening Providence; history was a process worked out by the forces of nature moving uniformly, restless but continuous, unchecked, inevitable. The process comprised all mankind; no chosen people, implying injustice to those not chosen; no miracles disturbing the regularity of nature. This was an advance toward future understanding because it concentrated attention upon nature and the method of evolution, yet in itself it cast but little light upon the problem, for it did not explain details. One sees its failure most where it risked hypotheses with most assurance, in its treatment of religion. It would not do for philosophers to admit that religion—at least of the old, historic type—was itself one of the laws of nature, implanted in humanity from the beginning. Consequently it was for them a creation of priestcraft. No dismissal of its claims could be more emphatic. Yet the old theologies have since proved that they have at least as many natural rights in society as the criticism of them; and now, with our new knowledge of primitive life, dominated by religion as we see it to be, we cast aside the rationalist conception as a distortion of history almost as misleading as those of the mythology it tried to dispose of.

But the work of Voltaire and his school in disrupting the old authority of Church and Bible—bitterly denounced and blackly maligned as it has been—is now recognized by all thinking minds, at least by all leaders of thought, to have been an essential service in the emancipation of the human intellect. The old sense of authority could never afterwards, as before, block the free path of inquiry; and the Era of Enlightenment, as it was fondly termed, did enlighten the path which history was to take if it was to know itself. The anticlerical bias of Hume and Gibbon is perhaps all that the casual reader perceives in them. But where among all previous historians does one find an attitude so genuinely historical? Moreover, in Hume we have the foundations of psychology and a criticism of causality which was of the first importance. It would be tempting to linger over these pioneers of the scientific spirit, who saw but could not realize the possibilities of naturalism. Their own achievement, however, was so faulty in just this matter of interpretation, that it was not difficult for the reaction of the early nineteenth century to poke holes in their theories, and so discredit—for the time being—their entire outlook.

Before Voltaire had learned in England the main lines of his philosophy, a German-Scottish boy Immanuel Kant had been born in Königsberg, in Prussia, who was destined to exercise as high if not as extended a sovereignty over the intellect of the nineteenth century. Kant was, however, of a different type. He fought no ringing fights with the old order. He simply created a new realm in metaphysics, where one could take refuge and have the world as his own. The *idea* dominates. Space and time, the *a priori* forms of all phenomena, lie within us. Mathematics is vindicated because the mind can really master relationships, and the reason emerges from its critique to grapple with the final problem of metaphysics. This at first sight has little to do with interpreting history, but it proved to have a great deal to do with it. The dominance of ideas became a fundamental doctrine among those who speculated concerning causation in history, and metaphysics all but replaced theology as an interpreter.

One sees this already in the work of the historian's historian of the nineteenth century, Leopold von Ranke. To him each age or country is explicable only if one approaches it from the standpoint of its own *Zeitgeist*. But the spirit of a time is more than the temporal environment in which events are set. It is a determining factor, clothed with the creative potency of mind. Ranke did not develop this philosophic background of history; he accepted it and worked from, rather than toward, it. His *Zeitgeist* was a thing for historians to portray, not to speculate about. History should concern itself with the preservation of phenomena as they had actually existed in their own time and place. It should recover the lost data of the past, not as detached specimens such as the antiquary places in his museum, but transplanted like living organisms for the preservation of the life as well as of the organs. Now, where should one look for the vital forces of history other than in the mind of the actors? So, if the historic imagination can restore events, not simply as they seem to us, but as they seemed to those who watched them taking place, we shall understand them in so far as history can contribute to their understanding. In any case, this is the field of the historian. If he injects his own theories into the operation, he merely falsifies what he has already got. Let the past stand forth once more, interpreted by itself, and we have the truth—incomplete, to be sure, but as perfect as we shall ever be able to attain. For, note the point, in that past the dominating thing was the *Zeitgeist* itself—a thing at once to be worked out and working out, a programme and a creative force. Why, therefore, should one turn aside to other devices to explain history, since it explained itself if once presented in its own light?

Ranke developed the implications of his theory no further than to ensure a reproduction of a living past, as perfect as with the sources at his disposal and the political instincts of his time it was possible to secure. But this high combination of science and art had its counterpart in the philosophy of Hegel. At first sight nothing could be more absurd than the comparison of these two men, the one concrete, definite, searching for minute details, maintaining his own objectivity by insisting upon the subjectivity of the materials he handles, the other theoretic, unhistorical, creating worlds from his inner consciousness, presenting as a scheme of historical inter-pretation a programme of ideals, unattained and, for all we know, unattainable. It would be difficult to imagine a philosophy of history more unhistorical than this of Hegel. Yet he but emphasized the Idea which Ranke implicitly accepted.

Hegel was a sort of philosophic Augustine, tracing through his-tory the development of the realm of the Spirit. The City of God is still the central theme, but the crude expectations of a miraculous advent are replaced by the conception of a slow realization of its spiritual power, rising through successive stages of civilization. So he traces, in broad philosophic outlines, the history of this revela-tion of the Spirit, from its dawn in the Orient, through its develop-ing childhood in Asia, its Egyptian period of awakening, its liberation in Greece, its maturity in the Roman balance of the in-dividual and the State, until finally Christianity, especially in the German world, carries the spirit life to its highest expression. In this process the Absolute reveals itself—that Absolute which had mocked the deists with its isolation and unconcern. And it reveals itself in the Idea which Kantian critique had placed in the forefront of reality and endowed with the creative force of an *élan vital*. So theology, skepticism, and metaphysics combined to explain the world and its history—as the working out of an ideal scheme.

As a series of successive ideals, the Hegelian scheme may offer some suggestions to those who wish to characterize the complex phenomena of any age or an empire in a single phrase. But it is no statement of any actual process. The ideals which it presents remain ideals, not realities. History written to fit the Hegelian metaphysics would be almost as vigorous a distortion as that which Orosius wrote to fit Augustinian theology. The history of practical Christianity, for instance, is vastly different from the history of its ideals. It is an open question whether the ideal could ever be deduced from the practice, and not less questionable whether we are any nearer realization than at the start. There has been little evidence in outward signs of any such determinant change in the nature of politics or in the stern enforcement of economic laws during the history of western Europe. We find ourselves repeating in many ways experiences of Rome and Greece—pagan experiences. Society is only partly religious and only slightly self-conscious. How, then, can it be merely the manifestation of a religious ideal? Surely other forces than ideals or ideas must be at work. The weakness of Hegel's interpretation of history is the history. He interprets it without knowing what it is. His interest was in the other side of his scheme, the Absolute which was revealing itself therein. The scheme was, indeed, a sort of afterthought. But before historians directed any sufficient criticism against his unhistoricity, skepticism in philosophy had already attacked his Absolute. It was the materialistic Feuerbach, with his thoroughgoing avowal that man is the creature of his appetite and not of his mind (*Der Mensch ist was er ist*), who furnished the transition to a new and absolutely radical line of historical interpretation—the materialistic and the economic.

Materialism has a bad name, partly earned, partly thrust upon it. But whatever one may think of its cruder dogmatic aspects, the fact remains that interpretation of history owes at least as much to it as to all the speculations which had preceded it. For it supplied one half of the data—the material half! Neither theology nor metaphysics had ever really got down to earth. They had proceeded upon the theory that the determination of history is from *above* and from *within* mankind and had been so absorbed with working out their scheme from these premises that the possibility of determination from *around* did not occur to them, until the physical and biological sciences and the new problems of economics pressed it upon their attention. To the old philosophies, this world was at best a theatre for divine or psychic forces; it contributed no part of the drama but the setting. Now came the claim that the environment itself entered into the play and that it even determined the character of the production. It was a claim based upon a study of the details from a new standpoint, that of the commonplace, of business, and of the affairs of daily life. The farmer's work depends upon his soil, the miner's upon the pumps which open up the lower levels. Cities grow where the forces of production concentrate, by harbors or coal fields. A study of plains, river valleys, or mountain ranges tends to show that societies match their environment; therefore the environment moulds them to itself.

This is innocent enough. One might have expected that philosophers would have welcomed the emphasis which the new thinkers placed upon the missing half of their speculations. For there was no getting around the fact that the influences of environment upon society had been largely or altogether ignored before the scientific era forced the world upon our view. But no. The dogmatic habits had got too firmly fixed. If one granted that the material environment might determine the character of the drama of history, why should it not determine whether there should be any drama at all? There were extremists on both sides, and it was battle royal—Realism and Nominalism over again. One was to be either a Hegelian, booted and spurred, sworn, cavalierlike, to the defense of the divine right of the Idea, or a regicide materialist with a Calvinistic creed of irreligion! The total result was that their opinion of each other brought *both* into ill repute. Philosophies of history became at least as discredited as the materialism they attacked.

Now the materialistic interpretation of history does not necessarily imply that there is nothing but materialism in the process, any more than theology implies that there is nothing but spirit. It will be news to some that such was the point of view of the most famous advocate of the materialistic interpretation of history, H.T. Buckle. His *History of Civilization in England* (1857-1861) was the first attempt to work out the influences of the material world upon the formation of societies. Every one has heard of how he developed, through a wealth of illustration, the supreme importance of food, soil, and the general aspect of nature. But few apparently have actually read what he says, or they would find that he assigns to these three factors an ever-lessening function as civilization advances, that he postulates mind as much as matter and, with almost Hegelian vision, indicates its ultimate control. He distinctly states that "the advance of European civilization is characterized by a diminishing influence of physical laws and an increasing influence of mental laws," and that "the measure of civilization is the triumph of the mind over external agents." If Buckle had presented his scheme politely, right side up, as it were, it could hardly have had a sermon preached at it! But he prefaced it with his opinion of theologians and historians—and few, apparently, have ever got beyond the preface. It was not encouraging reading for historians—a class of men who, in his opinion, are so marked out by "indolence of thought" or "natural incapacity" that they are fit for nothing better than writing monastic annals. There was, of course, a storm of aggrieved protest. But now that the controversy has cleared away, we can see that, in spite of his too confident formulation of laws, the work of Buckle remains as that of a worthy pioneer in a great, unworked field of science.

Ten years before Buckle published his *History of Civilization*, Karl Marx had already formulated the "economic theory of history." Accepting with reservations Feuerbach's materialist attack upon Hegel, Marx was led to the conclusion that the motive causes of history are to be found in the conditions of material existence. Already in 1845 he wrote, of the "young Hegelians," that to separate history from natural science and industry was like separating the soul from the body, and "finding the birthplace of history, not in the gross material production on earth, but in the misty cloud formation of heaven." In his *Misère de la philosophie* (1847) he lays down the principle that social relationships largely depend upon modes of production, and therefore the principles, ideas, and categories which are thus evolved are no more eternal than the relations they express but are historical and transitory products. From these grounds, Marx went on to socialism, which bases its militant philosophy upon this interpretation of history. But the truth or falsity of socialism does not affect his theory of history. In the famous manifesto of the Communist party (1848) the theory was applied to show how the Commercial and Industrial Revolutions, with the attendant growth of capital, had replaced feudal by modern conditions. This, like all history written to fit a theory, is inadequate history, although much nearer reality than Hegel ever got, because it dealt more with actualities. But we are not concerned here with Marx's own history writing any more than with his socialism. What we want to get at is the standpoint for interpretation. Marx himself, in the preface to the first edition of *Capital*, says that his standpoint is one "from which the evolution of the economic formation of society is viewed as a process of natural history." This sounds like the merest commonplace. Human history is thrown in line with that of the rest of nature. The scope is widened to include every factor, and the greatest one is that which deals with the maintenance of life and the attainment of comfort. So far so good. But Marx had not been a pupil of Hegel for nothing. He, too, went on to absolutes, simply turning Hegel's Absolute upside down. With him "the ideal is nothing else than the material world reflected by the human mind." The world is the thing, not the idea. So he goes on to make man, the modifier of nature with growing control over it, only a function of it—a tool of the tool, just when he has mastered it by new inventions.

But strange as it may seem, Marx's scheme, like Buckle's, culminates in mind, not in matter. The first part is purely economic. The industrial proletarians—"the workers," as socialism fondly terms them—are, like capitalism, the product of economic forces. The factory not only binds the shackles upon the wage slaves of today, it even fills the swarming city slums by the stimulation of child labor. So the process continues until the proletariat, as a last result of its economic situation, acquires a common consciousness. Then what happens? The future is not to be as the past. Consciousness means intelligence, and as soon as the proletariat *understands*, it can burst shackles, master economics, and so control, instead of blindly obeying, the movement of its creative energy. Whether socialism would achieve the object of its faith and hope is not for us to consider, but the point remains, that in the ultimate analysis even the economic interpretation of history ends uneconomically. It ends in directing intelligence, in ideals of justice, of social and moral order.

Where are we? We have passed in review the mythological, theological, philosophical, materialistic, and economic interpretations of history and have found that none of these, stated in its extreme form, meets the situation. Pure theology or metaphysics omits or distorts the history it is supposed to explain; history is not its proper business. Materialism and economics, while more promising because more earthly, cannot be pressed beyond a certain point. Life itself escapes their analysis. The conclusion is this: that we have two main elements in our problem which must be brought together— the psychic on the one hand, the material on the other. Not until psychology and the natural and economic sciences shall have been turned upon the problem, working in coöperation as allies, not as rivals, will history be able to give an intelligent account of itself.

They will need more data than we have at present. The only economics which can promise scientific results is that based upon the statistical method, for, in spite of Bergson, brilliant guesses can hardly satisfy unless they are verified. The natural sciences are only beginning to show the intimate relation of life to its environment, and psychology has hardly begun the study of the group.

Now the interpretation of history lies here with these coöperative workers upon the mystery of life and of its environment and their interplay. That does not mean that history is to be explained from the outside. More economics means more history—if it is good economics. Marx, for instance, attempted to state both facts and processes of industrial history, Malthus of population, Ricardo of wages, etc. Both facts and processes are the stuff of history. The statement of a process may be glorified into a "law," but a "law" merely means a general fact of history. It holds good under certain conditions, which are either historical or purely imaginary, and it is only in the latter case that it lies outside the field of history. It is the same with psychology as with economics. Psychology supplies an analysis of action, and action is history. Explanation is more knowledge of the same thing. All inductive study of society is historical.

The interpretations of history are historical in another sense. Looking back over the way we have come, from Greek philosophers to modern economists and psychologists, one can see in every case that the interpretation was but the reflex of the local environment, the expression of the dominant interest of the time. History became critical in that meeting place of East and West, the Ionian coast of Asia Minor, where divergent civilizations were opened up for contrast with each new arrival from the south and west and where travellers destroyed credulity. In the same way, as we have traced it, the isolated landed society of the Middle Ages, with its absence of business and its simple relationships, could rest complacent with an Augustinian world view. Nothing else demanded explanation. When business produced a Florence and Florence a Machiavelli, we have a gleam of newer things, just as when Voltaire and Hume mirrored the influences of Galileo and the voyages to China. With the nineteenth century the situation became more complicated, and yet one can see the interpretation of history merely projecting into the past—or drawing out of it—the meaning of each present major interest. Kant and Hegel fitted into the era of ideologues and nationalist romanticists, and their implications were developed under the reaction following the French Revolution. Buckle drew his inspiration from the trend of science which produced—in the same year—the *Origin of Species*. Marx was the interpreter of the Industrial Revolution.

But this does not mean that interpretations of history are nothing more than the injection into it of successive prejudices. It means progressive clarification. Each new theory that forces itself upon the attention of historians brings up new data for their consideration and so widens the field of investigation. The greater knowledge of our world today reveals the smallness of our knowledge of the past, and from every side scholars are hastening to make the content of history more worthy of comparison with the content of science. From this point of view, therefore, interpretation, instead of assuming the position of a final judge of conduct or an absolute law, becomes only a suggestive stimulus for further research.

We have, therefore, an historical interpretation of interpretations themselves. It accepts two main factors, material and psychical, not concerning itself about the ultimate reality of either. It is not its business to consider ultimate realities, though it may be grateful for any light upon the subject. Less ambitious than theological, philosophical, or even economic theories, it views itself as part of the very process which it attempts to understand. If it has no ecstatic glimpses of finality, it shares at least to the full the exhilaration of the scientific quest. It risks no premature fate in the delusive security of an inner consciousness. When you ask it "Why?" it answers "What?"

CHAPTER VI

⁂

THE OLD TESTAMENT AS HISTORY

WHEN WE TURN from these poor and thin records of the great empires of the East to the history of that little branch of the Semites which clung to the perilous post on the land-bridge between the Euphrates and the Nile, the Hebrews of Palestine, we are struck at once with the comparative wealth of its national annals. In contrast with the product of Egypt or Babylonia, the Bible stands out as an epoch-making achievement. A composite work of many centuries, filled with much that the historian rejects, it yet embodies the first historical work of genuinely national importance which has come down to us.[1] Modern criticism has robbed it of its unique distinction as a special revelation of Jehovah, denied the historicity of its account of the Creation, and destroyed the claim of the legends of the patriarchs to be regarded as authentic; the great name of Moses disappears as the author of the Pentateuch, and that of David from the book of Psalms; the story of Joseph becomes a romance, the Decalogue a statement of late prophetic ideals; the old familiar books dissolve into their component parts, written at different times and by different hands. In short, a national record, of varying value and varying historical reliability, has replaced the Bible of the churches, of stately uniform text and unvarying authority. Never-

---

The History of History by James T. Shotwell (Columbia University Press, 1950) Vol. I, pp. 107-112.

theless, it is possible to claim that, judged as historical material, the Old Testament stands higher today than when its text was protected with the sanctions of religion. For it was not until its exceptional and sacred character was denied that it could be appraised by the standards of history and its value as repository of national, if not of world, story be fairly appreciated. So long as the distinction existed which exalted the Jewish scriptures as sacred inspiration above the rest of the world's literature, the historicity of the Old Testament had to be accepted on a different basis from that of other narratives. Sacred and profane history are by nature incomparable; for the author of the one is God, of the other, man. Now, no higher tribute could be paid to the historical worth of the Old Testament than the statement that, when considered upon the profane basis of human authorship, it still remains one of the greatest products in the history of history, a record of national tradition, outlook, and aspiration, produced by a poor, harassed, semibarbarous people torn by feud and swept by conquest, which yet retains the undying charm of genuine art and the universal appeal of human interest. That is not to say that, viewed from the standpoint of modern history, it is a remarkable performance, for while it embodies some passages of great power and lasting beauty, the narrative is often awkward, self-contradictory, clogged with genealogies, and overloaded with minute and tiresome ceremonial instructions. The historian, however, should not judge it from the modern standpoint. He should not compare Genesis with Ranke, but with the products of Egypt and Assyria. Judged in the light of its own time the literature of the Jews is unique in scope as in power. It is the social expression of a people moving up from barbarism to civilization; and if its pastoral tales reveal here and there the savage Bedouin and its courtly chronicle is touched with the exaggerations of hero myths, if its priestly reforms and prophetic morals are allowed to obscure the currents of more worldly politics, all of these elements but mirror a changing outlook of different ages in the evolution of one of the most highly gifted peoples of the ancient world.

The trouble has been that this mass of literary remains has been taken for something other than what it was. The rabbis came to view its last editorial revision as the authoritative and divine statement of the whole world's story, and the theologians of succeeding centuries accepted their outlook with unquestioning faith. In short, the Bible became more and more unhistorical as it became more and more sacred. Higher criticism, viewing the texts historically, at last reveals their setting in their own time and place, and presents them as a national product instead of a record of creation in the words of the Creator. For the former it is adequate; for the latter no doctrinal apologies could save it from the shafts of ridicule.

The most important service, however, which higher criticism has rendered the Old Testament, is that it has allowed us to distinguish between the validity of different parts, to detect the naive folk tale in which Jahveh and the patriarchs meet at old hill-sanctuaries and the late priestly narrative reconstructing the whole in terms of the temple at Jerusalem. The finer passages are no longer involved in the fate of the rest. It is therefore possible to appreciate (for the first time) the genuine achievements of the chief historians of Israel.[2]

The Bible, as the name implies, is a collection of books.[3] It is not a single, consistent whole, but a miscellany. The first step in understanding it is to realize that it comprises the literary heritage of a nation—all that has survived, or nearly so, of an antiquity of many centuries. It includes legends from the camps of nomads, borrowings from Babylon, Egypt and Persia, annals of royal courts, laws, poems, and prophecies. It preserves these, not in their original form, but in fragments recast or reset to suit the purpose of a later day, for, down to the very close of Jewish history the process of editing and reediting this huge, conglomerate mass went on. Moreover, as the editors were theologians rather than historians, the result was as bad for history as it had been accounted good for theology, and the historian today has to undo most of this work to reach the various layers of sources upon which they built the Bible as we know it—sources which represent the real heritage of the ancient days. One must dig for these beneath the present text, just as one digs the soil of ancient cities for the streets and walls of former times. For the literary and the material monuments of a people share a somewhat similar fate. The Bible of today stands like some modern Athens or Rome upon the fragments of its former elements. The legends and laws of the early time are buried deep beneath the structure of later ages. More than once they have been burned over by conquest and civil feud, and, when restored, built up to suit new plans and different purposes. Today, however, the historian can lay bare the various strata, recover the ancient landmarks, and from their remains reconstruct in imagination each successive stage of the story. So, like the archaeologist, who sees not merely the city of the present or of its classic splendor, but the cities of every era in the long, eventful past, the student of higher criticism can now trace the process of the formation of the Bible from the crude, primitive beginnings—the tenements of barbarian thought—to the period when its contents were laid out in the blocks of books as we have them now, faced with the marble of unchangeable text, and around them all were flung the sacred walls of canonicity. The walls are now breached; and the exploring scientist can wander at will through the historic texts, unhampered by any superstitious fears. We shall follow him—hurriedly.

There was once a historian of our southern states who prepared himself for his life's work in the highly controversial period of the Civil War by taking a doctorate in mediaeval history. In an alien field, where his personal feelings could not warp his judgment, he learned the scientific temper. Something of his discipline is incumbent upon every student of the Bible. Let us imagine, for instance, that instead of the Jewish scriptures we are talking of those of the Greeks. Suppose that the heritage of Hellas had been preserved to us in the form of a Bible. What would be the character of the book? We should begin, perhaps, with a few passages from Hesiod on the birth of the gods and the dawn of civilization mingled with fragments of the *Iliad* and both set into long excerpts from Herodotus. The dialogues of Plato might be given by Homeric heroes and the text of the great dramatists (instead of the prophets) be preserved, interspersed one with another and clogged with the uninspired and uninspiring comments of Alexandrian savants. Then imagine that the sense of their authority was so much obscured as centuries passed, that philosophers—for philosophers were to Greece what theologians were to Israel—came to believe that the large part of this composite work of history and philosophy had been first written down by Solon as the deliverence of the oracle of Zeus at Dodona. Then, finally, imagine that the text became stereotyped and sacred, even the words taboo, and became the heritage of alien peoples who knew nothing more of Greek history than what this compilation contained. Such, with some little exaggeration, would be a Hellenic Bible after the fashion of the Bible of the Jews. If the comparison be a little overdrawn there is no danger but that we shall make sufficient mental reservations to prevent us from carrying it too far. Upon the whole, so far as form and structure go, the analogy holds remarkably well.

The Jews divided their scriptures into three main parts: the Law or Torah, the Prophets, and a miscellany loosely termed the "Writings." The Law is better known to Christians by the name given it by the Jews of Alexandria when they translated it into Greek, the Pentateuch [4]—or five books—or by the more definite title of the "Five Books of Moses," an attribution which rests on late Jewish tradition.[5] It is with these books that we have mainly to deal, for they furnish most of the fundamental historical problems of the Old Testament; but the finest narrative lies rather in the second group, which included as well as the books of prophecies, the four histories, Joshua, Judges, Samuel and Kings.[6] The third division, the "Writings" or "Scriptures," of which the Psalms, Job, and Proverbs are typical, also contained some of the later histories—Chronicles, Ezra and Nehemiah,[7] and the amazing book of Daniel.

NOTES

THE OLD TESTAMENT AS HISTORY

1. The treatment of the historical records of the Jews is here taken up from the standpoint of the completed output, the Bible as we now have it. This is mainly for the sake of clarity. A more historical treatment would be to begin with the elements as they existed in the earliest days and bring the story down, as it really happened, instead of going backwards, analyzing the completed text. The volume by Julius Bewer (in "Records of Civilization"), *The Literature of the Old Testament in Its Historical Development*, should be at hand to develop, and perhaps to correct the points touched upon in these pages.
2. The analysis of the text which is given here was based upon a survey of biblical criticism as it stood at the time these chapters were written. While it is believed that recent discoveries have not shaken the conclusions here stated, it may be said that, in general, they have tended to give support to the more conservative historical outlook as over against conclusions drawn solely from internal evidence.
3. βίβλος was the innerbark of the papyrus, hence applied to the paper made from it. From this it was applied to the book made of the paper. βίβλια (bible) is the plural of βιβλίον, a diminutive of βίβλος.
4. They are also responsible for the names of the separate books, Genesis, Exodus, Deuteronomy, Leviticus. Numbers (*Numeri*) comes from the Latin. It is customary now to group with these five books Joshua, which is closely connected both in form and matter. This makes a Hexateuch instead of a Pentateuch.

5. This attribution to the Pentateuch to Moses is probably found in II Chronicles 23:18, 25:4, 35:12; Ezra 3:2, 6:18; Nehemiah 13:1; Daniel 9:11, 13. It is found in Philo (fl. at the time of Christ), and in Josephus (first century A.D.). It also occurs in the New Testament.
6. The "Prophets" included the three major prophets, Israel, Jeremiah and Ezekiel, and the "Twelve" (i.e. minor prophets), whose prophecies formed one book.
7. The full list of the "Scriptures" is: Ruth, Psalms, Job, Proverbs, Ecclesiastes, Song of Songs, Lamentations, Esther, Daniel, Ezra, Nehemiah, Chronicles.

CHAPTER VII

⚜

CHRISTIANITY AND HISTORY

I. INTRODUCTION

THE GREAT HISTORIANS of antiquity were writers of modern history. Herodotus, Thucydides, Polybius, Tacitus, were interested in what had happened because of what was happening, and great things were happening in their day. Herodotus writing, as he said, "in order that the great and wondrous deeds of both Greeks and barbarians may not be effaced by time," massed his facts around that world-stirring crisis which had just been passed, the Persian wars. Thucydides, persuaded that "former ages were not great either in their wars or in anything else," believed that the war that passed before his eyes was the greatest event in the world's history, and he bent his life's energies to describing it. Polybius, too, carried off to Rome in the track of her victorious armies, saw as a captive the miraculous dawn of that first empire of the Mediterranean world, and he wrote his history to explain it. "Who is so poor-spirited," he says, "or so indolent as not to want to know by what means the Romans in something less than fifty-three years subdued the world." Livy's vision was also always fastened upon the imperial present and the calm, clear-headed patriotism which had brought it about. Tacitus lacked this generous enthusiasm, but his interests were never antiquarian; the great age in which he lived drew his ob-

Reprinted from The Journal of Philosophy, Psychology and Scientific Methods, Vol. XVII, Nos. 4 (February 12, 1920), pp. 85-94; 5 (February 26, 1920), pp. 113-120; and 6 (March 11, 1920), pp. 141-150.

servation and supplied him with his task. From the clash of East and West in the Ionian cities in the sixth century b.c., whereby the critical curiosity of men and societies was first made active, to the tragic close of the drama of the ancient world, almost a thousand years later, history was centered upon the few great epochal events and the characters that dominated the world in which each writer lived.

But there was one event of supreme importance that had no Herodotus to gather up its priceless details, no Polybius to weld it into the world's history with scientific insight and critical acumen— the rise of Christianity. The product of obscure enthusiasts in an obscure and despised oriental people, it did not win more than a disdainful paragraph (in Tacitus) at the hands of pagan historians. Its own writings were but poor attempts at history compared with what other lesser events produced. When the scanty texts of the sayings and doings of Jesus were taking the shape in which we have them now, a Plutarch was writing biographies of all the pagan heroes. But no Christian Plutarch appeared for another three centuries; and then all that the learned Jerome was able to preserve for us was three or four paragraphs on the lives of the leading apostles.[2]

There were several reasons for this. In the first place Christianity began in a most humble way and among the unlettered. It did not burst out in a flame of conquest like Mohammedanism, but crept, half-hidden, along the foundations of society. Its very obscurity left little to chronicle. If it changed the lives of men, they were lives too insignificant to be noticed by history. Only in the present age, after democracy itself has learned to read and begun to think, is the historian awakening to the spiritual forces in the lives of the obscure. But even now we pay little attention to such seemingly extraneous elements as the beliefs of foreign immigrants settled in our city slums—the class that furnished the majority of the early converts to Christianity. In any case the Greco-Roman world troubled itself little about the history of the Jews and less still about that of the Christians.[3]

Even when Christianity had penetrated the society of the learned, moreover, it stimulated little historical investigation. Pagan savants, like Celsus,[4] sometimes challenged the sources of Christian tradition and scripture,[5] but for the most part the great controversy between Christian and pagan writers took place in fields that lay beyond the scope of history. Christianity was a religion, not a thing of politics, and although, as we shall see, the problem of fitting it into the Jewish and then into the gentile setting did involve historical conceptions, yet the main interests awakened by it were theological. This meant that history, as a record of mere human events, was bound to suffer; for the theology, in so for as it concerned itself with those events, sought to transfer them from the realm of human action to that of divine grace, and so to interpret the phenomena of time and change in terms of a timeless and unchanging Deity.[6] The western world has since gratefully built its theology upon the conceptions so brilliantly worked out by the Fathers, and the historian whose business it is to register the judgments of society can not fail to appreciate their great formative influence in the history of thought. But their very success was a loss to history; for it placed the meaning of human effort outside the range of humanity, and so impressed upon the western world a fundamentally unhistorical attitude of mind.

The motive force which accomplished this theological victory was faith. Faith was the chief intellectual demand which Christianity made of its converts.[7] By it the mind was enabled to view events in a perspective which reached beyond the limits of time and space into that imaginary over-world which we know as Eternity. Faith did more than remove mountains, it removed the whole material environment of life. There have been few such triumphs of the spirit as it achieved in those early days of the new religion. But the fact remains that this achievement was largely at the cost of history. Faith, one can see from the criticism of those first really conscious historians, the Ionian Greeks, is an impediment to genuine history, unless the imagination which it quickens is kept within control. The historian needs rather to discipline his imagination with skepticism and to be more upon his guard against believing whenever he feels the will to believe than at any other time—which, in the realm of religious virtues has generally been mistaken for a sin.[8] Moreover, over and above the fact that faith puts a premium upon credulity,[9] it indicates an absence of any real, serious interest in historical data. When one "takes a thing on faith," it is because one is intent upon using it for something else of more importance— so important, indeed, that often while still unrealized it can clothe with reality the very condition upon which it depends. Thus the "will to believe" can master phenomena in a way not permitted to historians. Faith and scientific history do not readily work together.

If this is clear in the dawn of Greek history, when science conquered faith, it stands out even more clearly still in that very antithesis of the creations of Hellas, which we may best term the gospel according to Paul.[10] Nowhere else in the world's literature is there a call to faith like that of Paul, and few, even of the great creators of religious doctrine, have been more indifferent than he to the historical data, upon which, in the order of nature, that faith would seem to rest. The Apostle to the Gentiles cared little for the details of the life of Jesus, and boasted of his indifference.[11] He learned of the divinity of Christ by a flash of revelation which marked him out as one of the prophets. Then the desert, rather than Jerusalem, furnished him that tremendous plan of Christian doctrine upon which Christian orthodoxy still rests, which included the whole drama of humanity from the Creation and the Fall to the Redemption and the vision of its meaning, revealed on the road to Damascus. The plan was based upon the law and the prophets, but only because Paul's thought ran in terms of their teaching. His scheme was one that needed no verification from the sources even of sacred scripture, if once it could carry conviction by inner experience.[12]

Finally the faith of early Christianity was largely involved in a doctrine which centered attention not in this world but in the world to come; and the world to come was about to come at any moment. Immortality for the individual was a doctrine shared by other mystery religions of the pagan world; but only Christianity developed —out of the apocalyptic literature of the Jews—the vaster dream of an imminent cataclysm in which the world to come should come for all at once. While this doctrine appears in full force in Christian circles only from the latter part of the first to the middle of the second century, and was most developed in circles given over to what might be viewed, even by ecclesiastics, as extreme spirituality, it undoubtedly had a large and damaging influence upon Christian historiography. There is nothing which so effectively destroys our interest in the past as to live under the shadow of a great and impending event. It would not have been the same had each individual convert merely been keenly aware of the shortness of his own life and the vision of the coming day of judgment. That is still and has always been a perspective before religious minds; and however strange it may seem, it does not entirely kill the interest in the origin and evolution of these things which are so soon to vanish from before the eyes of death. Such is the vital instinct in us.[13] But it is a different thing for heaven and earth and all mankind to pass away at once as these early Christians expected them to do at any time. A few years ago we were to pass through the tail of a comet and there was some speculation as to whether its deadly gases might not exterminate all life on this globe. Had the probability been more probable, had astronomers and men of science determined the fact by some experimental proof, with what breathless and hypnotic gaze we should have watched the measured coming of that star across the gulfs of space! Our vast, unresting industries would cease; for there would be no to-morrow to supply. Our discoveries in science, our creations in art would be like so many useless monuments in an untenanted world—and science and art would have no incentive to go on. The one interest for us all would be that growing point of light—that doom, swift, inevitable, universal. Here comes a problem in psychology. For as a matter of fact that same doom is coming; we know it with absolute certainty; we know there can be no escape. How many of those who saw that comet pass will be alive fifty years from now? In a century, at most, the earth will be the sepulcher of all—just as much a sepulcher as if the race had perished in one grand catastrophe. And what a little interval is a century! Yet our mills worked on, our discoveries continued, our art went on producing its visions of beauty; and above all, we increased our interest in the distant past, digging for history in the hills of Crete and Asia and working as never before to rescue and reconstruct the past from archives and libraries. Why? Because humanity is more to us than our individual lives; and the future is a reality through it. If humanity were to disappear and no future be possible we should lose our reckoning, along with our sense of values, like Browning's Lazarus, who has had a vision of eternity, but has lost track of time.

So it was in the millennial atmosphere of the early church. However vaguely or definitely the triumph of "the Kingdom" was reckoned,[14] the belief in its approach carried the mind away from earthly affairs and their history. Men who drew their inspiration from it had but little interest in the splendor of a Roman state or in the long procession of centuries in which were painfully evolved the institutions of pagan law and government, institutions which not only safeguarded the heritage of antique culture but made possible the extension of Christianity.

The only history of importance to the Christian was that which justified his faith, and it all lay within the sacred writings of the Jews. So, as the vision of the judgment day became fainter and the Church proceeded to settle itself in time and not in eternity it looked back to a different past from that which lay beyond the pagan world. The sacred scriptures of the Jews had replaced the literature of antiquity. A revolution was taking place in the history of history. Homer and Thucydides, Polybius and Livy, the glory of the old régime, shared a common fate. The scientific output of the most luminous minds the world had known was classed with the legends that had grown up by the campfires of primitive barbarians. All was pagan; which meant that all was delusive and unreliable except where it could be tested in the light of the new religion or where it forced itself by the needs of life into the world of common experience.

There is no more momentous revolution in the history of thought than this, in which the achievements of thinkers and workers, of artists, philosophers, poets and statesmen, were given up for the revelation of prophets and a gospel of worldly renunciation. The very success of the revolution blinds us to its significance; for our own world-view has been molded by it. Imagine, for instance, what the perspectives of history would have been had there been no Christianity, or if it had remained merely a sect of Judaism, to be ignored or scorned! Religion carried history away from the central themes of antiquity to a nation that had little to offer—except its religion.

The story of Israel could not, from the very nature of its situation, be more than an incident in the drama of nations. The great empires of the east lay on either side of it, and the land of promise turned out to be a pathway of conquering armies. From the desert beyond Jordan new migrations of Semite nomads moved in for the plunder of the Jews as the Jews themselves had plundered the land before. On the west Philistine and Phœnician held the harbors and the sea. Too small a nation for a career of its own, exposed and yet secluded, the borderer of civilization, Israel could produce no rich culture like its more fortunately situated neighbors. When unmolested for a time, it too could achieve rapid progress in its fortress towns. But no sooner was its wealth a temptation than the Assyrian was at the gates. It is small wonder, then, if in spite of the excellence of much of the historical literature embedded in the Old Testament, even the best of it, such as the stories woven around the great days of Saul and David, when compared with the narrative of Polybius or even with that of Herodotus, leaves a picture of petty kinglets of an isolated tribe, reaching out for a brief interval to touch the splendors of Tyre and Sidon, and vaguely aware of the might and wealth of Egypt.

The one contribution of the Jews to the world was in a field which offers history few events to chronicle. As we have insisted above, it was a contribution of the first magnitude, to be treasured by succeeding ages above all the arts and sciences of antiquity. But its very superiority lay in its unworldliness, in its indifference to the passing fortunes of man or nations, which make up the theme of history. This at least was the side of Judaism which Christianity seized upon and emphasized. But there could be little for history in any case in a religion born of national disaster and speaking by revelation. The religion which is born of disaster must either falsify realities by a faith which reads victory in defeat—like the inspiration of Mahomet fleeing on his camel from the victorious unbelievers, yet chanting, "Who hath given us the victory!" Or it must take refuge in the realm of the spirit, where the triumphs of the world, its enemy, are met with indifference or scorn. In either case the perspective is distorted. Revelation may save the future by stirring hope and awakening confidence; but it will falsify the past with the same calm authority as it dictates the conduct of the present— falsify, that is, in the eyes of science. In its own eyes it is lord of circumstance and master of phenomena, and the records of the centuries must come to its standards, not it to theirs.

It was, therefore, a calamity, for historiography, that the new standards won the day. The authority of a revealed religion sanctioned but one scheme of history through the vast and intricate evolution of the antique world. A well-nigh insurmountable obstacle was erected to scientific inquiry, one which has at least taken almost nineteen centuries to surmount.

Not only was the perspective perverted, and the perversion made into a creed, but the stern requirements of monotheistic theology placed a veritable barrier against the investigation. The Christian historian was not free to question the data as presented to him, since the source was inspired. He might sometimes evade the difficulty by reading new meanings into the data and so square them with the rest of history, a device employed by every Father of the church whose erudition and insight brought him face to face with the difficulties of literal acceptance of the scriptures. But however one might twist the texts, the essential outlines of the scheme of history remained fixed. From the prophets of Jahve with their high fanaticism and from Paul, the prophet of Jesus, there was but one worldview, that dominated by the idea of a chosen people and a special dispensation. The only difference between Christian and Jewish outlook was that what had been present politics became past history. The apostle to the Gentiles did not give up the Jewish past. Pre-Christian history was in his eyes the same narrow story of exclusive Providence as it was in the eyes of the older prophets. Gentiles had had no share in the dispensations of Jahve; it was only for the present and future that they might hope to enter into the essential processes of historical evolution. The past to Paul was what it was to a Pharisee.

This exclusive attitude of Christianity with reference to the past was in striking contrast with the attitude of contemporaneous paganism, which was growingly liberal with increasing knowledge. To attack the story of Jahve's governance of the world was, for a Christian, sacrilege, since the story itself was sacred. A pagan, with a whole pantheon to turn to, placed no such value upon any one myth and therefore was free to discount them all. His eternal salvation did not rest upon his belief in them; and, moreover, he did not concern himself so much about his salvation in any case. When the belief in an immortality was bound up with the acceptance of a scheme of history, the acceptance was assured. What is the dead past of other people's lives, when compared with the unending future of one's own? History yielded to the demands of eternity.

Moreover in its emphasis upon the Messiahship of Jesus, Christianity fastened upon one of the most exclusive aspects of Jewish thought. Such history as the proof of this claim involved was along the line of a narrow, fanatic, national movement. Christianity, it is true, opened the Messianic Kingdom to the whole world, but it justified its confidence in the future by an appeal to the stricter outlines of a tribal faith in the past. And yet that appeal, in spite of its limitations, was the source of such historical research as Christianity produced. For, when pressed by pagan critics to reconcile their claims with those of Greeks or Egyptians, the Fathers were obliged to work out not merely a theory of history—their theology supplied them with that—but a scheme of chronology. The simple problem, so lightly attacked, as to whether Moses or the Greeks should have the priority as lawgiver forced the apologists to some study of comparative history. While in this particular issue they had a somewhat easy triumph,[15] there was a danger, which is obvious to us now, in too much reliance upon the chronology of the Old Testament, and especially in placing an emphasis upon the literal text. The trenchant criticism of their opponents, therefore, led the Fathers to adopt that allegorical type of interpretation, which they learned from the Greeks themselves, and which is so useful wherever there is a need for holding fast to a text while letting the meaning go. We shall therefore find the chief developments of Christian historiography during the first three centuries following these two lines, of allegory and symbolism on the one hand and of comparative chronology on the other.

II. ALLEGORY AND THE CONTRIBUTION OF ORIGEN

In spite of what has been said about the weakness of Christian historiography, it is possible to take a quite opposite point of view, and to maintain the thesis that, among religions, Christianity is especially notable as resting essentially on a historical basis.

In so far as Christianity was a historical religion, that was due, as has just been said, to the Messianic element in it. Indeed it can be said to have claimed from the beginning that it was a historical religion—a fulfilment of history, one fitting itself into the scheme of social and political evolution in a particular state. The apostles themselves, in their earliest appeal, demanded that one "search the scriptures"—a demand unique in the founding of religions. There is a vast difference, however, between studying history and studying historically. That they did study it, the one fact that the Christians retained the Old Testament is ample evidence. That they failed to deal with it adequately, the New Testament is also ample evidence. But since the Christian Messiah was offered to the whole world as well as to the Jews, Christian historiography had two main tasks before it: it had to place the life of Jesus in the history of the Jews, upon the one hand, and in the general history of antiquity, upon the other. The latter problem was not forced upon the church until the pagan world began to take the new religion seriously, and its answer is found in the works of the great apologists. The relation of Christianity to Judaism, however, the Messianic problem proper, was of vital importance from the beginning, for it involved the supreme question whether or not Jesus was the one in whom the prophecies were fulfilled.[1]

One "searched the scriptures" therefore for the evidences of the signs by which the advent could be recognized. The invitation to search them was, in appearance at least, a challenge to a scientific test, that of verification. If the data of the life of Jesus corresponded with the details of the promises, there was a proof that the promises had been fulfilled. But since the fulfilment was not literal, the interpretation could not be literal either. The spiritual Kingdom of the Messiah had to be constructed out of fragmentary and uncertain references, and the only satisfactory way to apply many of them was by symbolism and allegory. Modern scholarship has now discarded messianic prophecy, having discovered that the texts so confidently cited as foretelling the life of Jesus had no such purpose in the minds of their authors. But orthodoxy has held, through all the history of the church, that the texts were applicable and that the proof was thereby established of the harmony of the old and the new dispensations.

We can now turn, however, to the problems of higher criticism. The significant thing for history-writing was the creation of what might be called a new *genre*—that of the allegorical interpretation of texts. The use of allegory to explain, or explain away, texts was not a creation of Christian historians, for the device was not unknown to pagan literature or philosophy. As far back as the sixth century B.C., Homer was interpreted allegorically by Theagenes of Rhegium, and pagan philosophy had constant recourse to allegory to harmonize myth with reason. The Jews too were past masters in its use; indeed it runs through the prophetic literature alongside that elusive trace of the unattained which gave the prophecies their fascinating charm. One could track it back farther still to the mind of primitive man, where symbol and reality are often confused into a single impression. But in the hands of the Christian theologians, symbolism emerged from the background of thought to dominate the whole situation. The story of realities depended upon the interpretation of the unrealities; and that story of realities was nothing short of a history of the world itself.

Allegorical interpretation of the Old Testament had been developed by the Jewish scholars, especially those of the diaspora, who found themselves thrown into contact with gentile scholars and felt the need of harmonizing Greek thought with their own intellectual heritage. One finds it to the full in the writings of the greatest Jewish philosopher of antiquity, Philo of Alexandria, who lived at the time of Jesus. The extent to which he carried it may be gauged by his description of the Garden of Eden, whose four rivers became the four virtues, prudence, temperance, courage and justice, and the central stream from which they flow, the Divine Wisdom.[2]

The greatest master of Christian allegory was Origen. While not a historian in the stricter sense, he contributed to Christian historiography one of its most remarkable chapters. He not only denied the literal truth of much of Genesis, and explained away the darker happenings in the history of Israel; but, even in the New Testament, he treated as parables or fables such stories as that of the Devil taking Jesus up into a high mountain and showing him the kingdoms of the world. One reads Origen with a startle of surprise. The most learned of the Fathers of the third century was a modern. His commentaries upon the Bible might almost pass for the product of the nineteenth century. The age of Lyell and Darwin has seen the same effort of mystic orthodoxy to save the poem of Creation, by making the six days over into geological eras and the story of Adam and Eve a symbol of human fate. Many a sermon upon the reconciliation of science and religion—that supreme subject of modern sermons—might be taken almost bodily from Origen. For his problem was essentially like that which fronts the modern theologian; he had to win from a rationalism which he respected, the denial of its inherent skepticism. Like Philo, a resident of that cosmopolitan center, Alexandria, that meeting-place of races and religions, Origen was a modern among moderns. He was a Greek of subtlest intellect and vast erudition, one of the finest products of the great Hellenic dispersion.[3]

Interpretation of the scriptures by allegory is not, in Origen's eyes, an unwarranted liberty. The scriptures themselves sanction it

—allegorically! "There is a hidden and secret meaning," he says, "in each individual word. The treasure of divine wisdom is hid in the vulgar and unpolished vessels of words; as the apostle also points out when he says, 'We have this treasure in earthen vessels.' " [4] Quaintly naïve as such reasoning seems when based upon a single text, its weakness becomes its strength when sufficient texts are adduced to convey the impression that the scriptures themselves do really proclaim their own symbolic character. This Origen endeavors to do. "If the texts of Moses had contained nothing which was to be understood as having a secret meaning, the prophet would not have said in his prayer to God: 'Open thou mine eyes and I will behold wondrous things out of thy law (Psalms, 119.18).' " What, he asks, can one make out of the prophecy of Ezekiel except allegorically? [5] Prophetic literature implies allegory in its very structure. But the strongest proof of the legitimacy of allegorical interpretation is its use in the New Testament, and so largely by St. Paul.[6]

The modern critic sees the vicious circle in which such reasoning moves. But he sees it because he denies the hidden meaning, the secret lore, which to the "intellectuals" of the third century was the real heart of phenomena. Symbolism has deeper roots than one suspects. The mysterious efficacy of numbers is as wide as savagery; the secret value of words is a doctrine as universal as speech. They come from untold ages beyond Pythagoras or Heraclitus. The Christian emphasis upon the logos—"the word which became God and the word which was God"—put the stamp of supreme authority upon a phase of thought intelligible to all antiquity. Gnosticism took hold of that phase, and by insisting upon an inner doctrine which was concealed from the uninitiated, attempted to harmonize Christianity with the parallel cults of paganism. Neo-platonism was doing much the same for paganism itself. The cults of Asia and Egypt were drawn together and interpreted in the light of the worship of Demeter or Dionysus. Origen's point of view is not so naïve as it seems. It was in line with that of his age. The world was a growing one, and yet the world itself was a medley of different civilizations. The only way the ancient could think of overcoming this antithesis between an ideal which unified and phenomena which differed was by denying the essential nature of the differences. We should do the same if it were not for our hypothesis of evolution and the historical attitude of mind. Only when one sees the *impasse* into which the thinkers of antiquity were forced, in their attempts to syncretize a complex and varying world, does one realize by contrast what a tremendous implement of synthesis the evolutionary hypothesis supplies. The only alternative method by which to realize the harmony which does not appear is by symbolism.

If we once grant that texts are not what they seem, there is only one way to learn their true meaning. We must find a key, and that key must be some supreme fact, something so large that the content of the text seems but incidental to it. Christianity supplied such a clue to the interpretation of the Old Testament; and the Old Testament, upon its side, supplied Christianity with the authority of a long antiquity. The value of that antiquity for the basis of a story of obscure, recent happenings in Jerusalem was felt by all apologists, and has been a convincing argument until the present. It was left for the nineteenth century to substitute for symbolism the tests of historical criticism, and thus to see the whole scheme of theological interpretation fade away. But we should not forget that, false as it seems to us in both method and results, the symbolic method made the theologian somewhat of a historian in spite of himself; and we should not expect of the savants of the third century the historical and evolutionary attitude of to-day—which was, so far as we can see, his only alternative.

Symbolism may twist the texts; but a mind like Origen's does not miss the essential point that the texts must be there to twist. Nothing is more interesting in the historiography of early Christianity than to see how Origen came to realize, after all, the paucity of his sources and their inadequacy, particularly those dealing with the history of Christianity itself. He shows this with scholarly frankness in a passage in his famous apology *Against Celsus*. Celsus was a pagan Greek who wrote the most notable attack upon Christianity of which we have record from those early times. His treatise was a powerful and learned criticism of the Christian writings and teachings, especially emphasizing their unscientific character and the credulity of those who believed in them. Origen's reply reveals in more places than one how in him a genuine historical critic was lost in the theologian. To illustrate: Celsus had claimed that before writing his attack he had taken the trouble to acquaint himself with all the Christian doctrines and writings. Origen, drawing on his prodigious knowledge of the Bible, shows time and again what a superficial acquaintance it had been—that is, judged according to Origen's method of interpretation. But when Celsus charges the Christians with obscurantism, stating that their teachers generally tell him "Do not investigate," while at the same time exhorting him to believe, Origen takes another tack.[7] He is apparently a little ashamed of the emphasis taken from reason and placed upon faith by his Christian colleagues. He does not actually say as much, but he reminds Celsus that all men have not the leisure to investigate. After this weak admission, however, he turns round, in what is one of the most interesting passages of patristic writing, and demands if Celsus and the pagans do not follow authority as well. Have not Stoics and Platonists a teacher too, whose word they go back to? Celsus believes in an uncreated world and that the flood (Deucalion's) is a fairly modern thing.[8] But what authority has he? The dialogues of Plato? But Moses saw more clearly than Plato. He was in an incomparably better position to be informed. Why not prefer the account of Moses?

The value of a controversy is that each side sees the other's weak points. It seldom results in admitting the inferiority of your own position; but once in a while a fair-minded man will be courageous enough to state that, through no fault of his own, he is unable to be more accurate than his opponent. This is about what Origen does, in taking up the charge of Celsus that the narrative of the baptism in the Jordan is so improbable a story as to require confirmation of first-hand witnesses, before he as a thinking pagan could accept it. In reply Origen frankly admits the paucity of sources for the history of Christianity, but demands to know if Celsus is willing to give up pagan history because it contains improbable incidents. The passage is worth quoting, for it shows how the most learned man of all the Fathers, the most subtle and comprehensive intellect, with one exception, which Christianity enlisted to its cause, recognized the weakness of Christian historiography but failed to see how it could be remedied.

> Before we begin our reply we have to remark that the endeavor to show, with regard to almost any history, however true, that it actually occurred, and to produce an intelligent conception regarding it, is one of the most difficult undertakings that can be attempted, and is in some instances an impossibility. For suppose that some one were to assert that there never had been any Trojan

War, chiefly on account of the impossible narrative interwoven therewith, about a certain Achilles being the son of a sea-goddess Thetis and of a man Peleus, or Sarpedon being the son of Zeus, or Asculapius and Ialmenus the sons of Ares, orÆneas that of Aphrodite, how should we prove that such was the case, especially under the weight of the fiction attached, I know not how, to the universally prevalent opinion that there was really a war in Ilium between Greeks and Trojans? And suppose, also that some one disbelieved the story of Œdipus and Jocasta, and of their two sons Eteocles and Polynices, because the sphinx, a kind of half-virgin, was introduced into the narrative, how should we demonstrate the reality of such a thing? And in like manner also with the history of the Epigoni, although there is no such marvellous event interwoven with it, or with the return of the Heracleidæ, or countless other historical events. But he who deals candidly with histories, and would wish to keep himself also from being imposed upon by them, will exercise his judgment as to what statements he will give his assent to, and what he will accept figuratively, seeking to discover the meaning of the authors of such inventions, and from what statements he will withhold his belief, as having been written for the gratification of certain individuals.

And we have said this by way of anticipation respecting the whole history related in the Gospels concerning Jesus, not as inviting men of acuteness to a simple and unreasoning faith, but wishing to show that there is need of candor in those who are to read, and of much investigation, and, so to speak, of insight into the meaning of the writers, that the object with which each event has been recorded may be discovered.

In so many words Origen admits that since the sources for Christian history can not be checked up by external evidence, there is nothing left but to accept their main outlines on faith—the same faith the Greek has in the existence of Troy or the Roman in the early kings. But being a Greek—and above all a Greek in argument —he qualifies his faith by reason and explains away what seems improbable. In a way, therefore, we have before us a sort of sophisticated Herodotus after all, who eliminates myth to suit his perspective.

Had the Christian world been and remained as sophisticated as Origen, the conception of biblical history for the next fifteen hundred years would have been vastly different. But, although the allegorical method of biblical interpretation was used by nearly all the Fathers—by none more than by the pope whose influence sank deepest into the Middle Ages, Gregory the Great—and still forms the subject of nearly all sermons, the symbolism and allegory came to be applied less to those passages which contained the narrative, than to the moralizing and prophetic sections. The stories of the creation, of the flood, of Joseph, of the plagues in Egypt, of Sodom and Gomorrah, were not explained away. But about them, and the rest of that high theme of the fortunes of Israel, were woven the gorgeous dreams of every poetic imagination, from Origen to Bossuet, which had been steeped in miracle and rested upon authority. One turns to Sulpicius Severus, the biographer of the wonder-working Martin of Tours, for the Bible story as it reached the Middle Ages. The narrative of the Old Testament was taken literally, like that of the New; the story of a primitive people was presented to a primitive audience. Allegory was not allowed to explain away passages which would have shocked the critical intelligence of Hellenic philosophers, for those were the very passages most likely to impress the simple-minded Germans for whose education the church itself was to be responsible.

There was, however, a better reason than mere credulous simplicity, why Jewish and Christian history were not allegorized away. It was because that history had been made credible by an exhaustive treatment of chronology. Christian scholars took up the task of reconciling the events of Jewish history with the annals of other histories, and worked into a convincing and definite scheme of parallel chronology the narrative from Abraham to Christ. Mathematics was applied to history—not simply to the biblical narrative but all that of the ancient world—and out of the chaos of fact and legend, of contradiction and absurdity, of fancy run riot and unfounded speculation, there was slowly hammered into shape that scheme of measured years back to the origins of Israel and then to the creation, which still largely prevails to-day. This is one of the most important things ever done by historians. Henceforth, for the next fifteen centuries and more, there was one sure path back to the origin of the world, a path along the Jewish past, and marked out by the absolute laws of mathematics and revelation. An account of how this came about will carry us back into that complicated problem of the measurement of time, which we have considered before, in its general aspects. (Now, however, we come upon the work of those who gave us our own time-reckoning, and who in doing so molded the conception of world history for the western world more than any other students or masters of history.)

III. CHRONOLOGY AND CHURCH HISTORY

The history of history repeats itself. Tradition and myth, epic and genealogy, priestly lore of world eras and the marking of time, criticism and history follow each other or fuse in the long evolution of that rational self-consciousness which projects itself into the past as it builds up the synthesis of the present. Similar pathways lie behind all developed historiographies. Indeed, the parallel between the histories of the history of different nations is so close as to rob the successive chapters of much of the charm of novelty. When we have reviewed the historiography of Greece, that of Rome strikes us as familiar. The same likeness lies already in the less developed historiographies of oriental cultures. They all emerge from a common base; and, to use a biological expression, ontogeny repeats phylogeny—the individual repeats the species. The law of growth seems to apply to history as though it were an organism with an independent evolution, instead of what it really is, a mere reflection of changing societies.

The explanation apparently lies at hand, in the similar evolution of the societies which produce the history. But, from such promises one would hardly expect the historiography of a religion to exhibit the same general lines of development. Yet in the history of Christian history we have much the same evolution of material as in that of Greece or Rome. Naturally, the priestly element is stronger, and the attempts at rationalizing the narratives more in evidence. But it is the absence rather than the presence of sophistication which strikes one most. The genealogies play their rôle for the kingdom of the Messiah as for the cities of Hellas,[1] Hesiods of Jewish and Christian theology present their schemes of divinely appointed eras, and through the whole heroic period of the church, legends of saints and martyrs furnish the unending epic of the unending war, where the hosts of heaven fought with men, not for a vanished Troy but for an eternal city. Finally, the work of Christian logographi in the apologists—and every theologian was an apologist—reduced the scheme to prose. The parallel would not hold, however, beyond the merest externals if it had not been for the development of Christian chronology; for the thought of writing history was but little in the minds of theologians, and hardly more in those of martyrologists. From the apologists, face to face with the criticism of the unbelieving world, came the demand for more rigid methods of comparative chronology, by which they could prove the real antiquity and direct descent of Christianity. The same kind of practical need had produced similar, if more trivial, documentation by pagan priests and was later to repeat itself in medieval monasteries. So that in the Christian church, as in the antique world generally, history proper was born of the application of research and chronology to meet the exacting demands of skepticism, as well as of the desire to set forth great deeds.

The path to Christian historiography lies, therefore, through a study of Christian chronology. The basis for this was the work of the Jewish scholars of the diaspora. When the Christian apologists of the second and third centuries attempted to synchronize the Old Testament history with that of the gentiles, they could fall back upon the work of a Jewish scribe, Justus of Tiberius, who wrote in the reign of Hadrian. He prepared a chronicle of Jewish kings, working along the same uncertain basis of "generations" as had been used in gentile chronicles, and so claiming for Moses an antiquity greater than that of the oldest figures in Greek legend. The difficulties in the way of any counter proof lent this statement great value in argument, especially since it was merely a mathematical formulation of a belief already established in the church. But, although the argument of priority was familiar from early days the first formally prepared Christian chronology did not appear until the middle of the third century when Julius Africanus wrote his *Chronographia*. It was a work in five books, drawing upon the writings of Josephus, Manetho and pagan scholars, and arranging the eras of the old dispensation in a series symbolical of creation itself. The duration of the world is to reach six thousand years, after which is to come a thousand-year Sabbath. The birth of Christ is put five thousand five hundred years from Adam, which leaves five hundred more before the end. Half-way along this stretch of centuries, three thousand years from the creation we come upon the death of Palek, under whom the world was parcelled out, as is recorded in the twenty-fifth chapter of Genesis.[2]

A scheme like this is a chronology only by courtesy; and yet a glance at the dating along the pages of the authorized edition of the Bible will show how relatively close to it has been the accepted dating of the world's history down to our own time. Critically considered, it was merely a variation of the symbolism of Origen—an allegory of the general scheme of history instead of an allegory of details. It was symbolism on a bolder and larger scale, all the more convincing because while it supplied the frame-work for events it did not have to harmonize or explain them away. Three main influences made for its success. The absence of any continuous Jewish chronology offered it open field; theology demanded that the world's history should center upon the life of Christ and the coming of the kingdom; and the idea of world eras was just in line with the ideas of pagan savants who had attained a rude conception of natural law in the movement of history. A treatment of history which could appeal to the great name of Varro for its pagan counterpart was not lightly to be rejected. The best minds of antiquity saw—though dimly—the outer world as a reflection of the human reason, but what Platonic idea ever mastered recalcitrant phenomena so beautifully as this scheme of Christian history with its symmetry established by a divine mathematics?

One is tempted to turn aside to the absorbing problems of philosophy which these crude solutions of world history open up. But before us stands a great figure, a Herodotus among the logographi of the early church. Eusebius of Cæsarea, the father of Church History, worked out from materials like these the chronology of the world which was to be substantially that of all the subsequent history of Europe to our own time, and preserved the precious fragments of his predecessors in the first history of Christianity.[3]

Eusebius meets the two qualifications which Polybius prescribed as indispensable for the historian. He was a man of affairs, of wide knowledge of the world, and held high office in the state whose fortunes he described. He it was who at the great council of Nicæa (325 A.D.) sat at the right hand of Constantine and delivered the opening oration in honor of the emperor.[4] Few historians of either church or state have ever had more spectacular tribute paid to their learning and judicial temper. For it was apparently these two qualities which especially equipped Eusebius for so distinguished an honor. At least one likes to think so; but perhaps the distinction fell to him because he was as well an accomplished courtier and as much the apologist of Constantine as of the Christian faith.

This incident fixes for us the life of Eusebius. Born about 260 A.D., he was at the fullness of his powers when the church gained its freedom, and he lived on until 339 or 340. He had studied in the learned circle of Pamphilus of Cæsarea, whose great library was to furnish him with many of his materials,[5] and there came under the spell of Origen, whose influence was supreme in the circle of Pamphilus. Nothing is more difficult in criticism than the estimate of one man's influence upon another—and nothing more light-heartedly hazarded. It would be hard to say what Eusebius would have been without the works of Origen to inspire him, but that they did influence him is beyond question. Eusebius was not an original thinker. He lacked the boldness of genius, but to witness that boldness in Origen must have been an inspiration toward freedom from ecclesiasticism and traditionalism.[6] His history is no mere bishop's history, it is the record of a religion as well as of a church. Its scholarship is critical, not credulous. From Origen, too, may have come the general conception which makes the first church history a chapter in the working out of a vast world-scheme, the "economy" of God.[7] But the time had now come for such a conception to be commonplace. It was no longer a speculation; the recognition by the empire was making it a fact.

If one were to search for influences moulding the character of Eusebius's history, this triumph of the church would necessarily come first. No history of Christianity worthy of the name could well appear during the era of persecutions. Not that the persecutions were so fierce or so continuous as has been commonly believed. Eusebius himself, for instance, lived safely through the most severe persecution, and visiting Pamphilus in prison—for Pamphilus suffered martyrdom—carried on his theological works in personal touch with his master. But though the persecutions have been exaggerated, the situation of the church was not one to invite the historian. Constantine was its deliverer; in a few years it passed from oppression to power. And in the hour of its triumph Christian scholarship was to find, in a bishop high at court, a historian worthy not only of the great deeds of the saints and martyrs but of the new imperial position of the church.

Eusebius was a voluminous writer, "historian, apologist, topographer, exegete, critic, preacher, dogmatic writer." [8] But his fame as a historian rests upon two works, the *Church History* and the *Chronicle*. Both were epoch-making. The one has earned for the author the title of Father of Church History; the other set for Christendom its frame-work in the history of the world.

The *Chronicle* was written first.[9] It is composed of two parts: the *Chronographia* and the *Chronological Canons*. The first of these is an epitome of universal history in the form of excerpts from the sources, arranged nation by nation, along with an argument for the priority of Moses and the Bible. It is a source-book on the epochs of history, much like those in use to-day as manuals in our colleges. The second part consists of chronological tables with marginal comments. The various systems of chronology, Chaldæan, Greek, Roman, *etc.*, are set side by side with a biblical chronology which carries one back to the creation, although the detailed and positive annals begin only with the birth of Abraham. The *Canons* therefore present in a single, composite form the annals of all antiquity—at least all that was of interest to Christendom. It presented them in simplest mathematical form. Rows of figures marked the dates down the center of the page; on the right hand side was the column of profane history; on the left hand the column of sacred history.[10]

The fate of this work is of peculiar interest. It is doubtful if any other history has ever exercised an influence comparable to that which it has had upon the western world; yet not a single copy of the original text has survived; the Latin west knew only the second part, and that in the hasty translation of Jerome. Modern research has unearthed a solitary Armenian translation of the work as a whole, and modern scholars have compared this with the fragments preserved by Byzantine chronographers [11] until finally, in the opening of the twentieth century the work is again accessible—if only to the learned. If, however, recovery of the chronicle is a work of archæological philology, like the recovery of an ancient ruin, yet all the time that it had lain buried this little book of dates and comments had been determining the historical outlook of Europe.[12] For the next thousand years most histories were chronicles, and they were built after the model of Jerome's translation of Eusebius's *Canons*. Every medieval monastery that boasted of enough culture to have a scriptorium and a few literate monks, was connecting up its own rather fabulous but fairly recent antiquity with the great antiquity of Rome and Judea through the tables of Eusebius's arithmetic.

This anonymous immortality of the great *Chronicle* is easily accounted for. It was not a work of literature, but of mathematics. Now mathematics is as genuine art as is literature, art of the most perfect type; but its expression, for that very reason, is not in the variable terms of individual appreciations. It is not personal but universal. It does not deal with qualities but with numbers; or at best it deals with qualities merely as the distinguishing elements in numbers. The structure is the thing, not the meaning nor character of the details. And the structure depends upon the materials. Hence there is little that is Eusebian about Eusebius's *Chronicle*, except the chronicle itself. It has no earmarks of authorship like the style of a Herodotus or a Thucydides. But all the same its content was the universal possession of the succeeding centuries.

There is, however, a simpler reason for the fate of Eusebius's *Chronicle*. It has a forbidding exterior. It had even too much mathematics and too much history for the Middle Ages; they were satisfied with the results of the problem. But behind this forbidding exterior the modern scholar finds a synthesis of alluring charm. Parallel columns of all known eras extend up and down the pages; eras of Abraham, David, Persia, Egypt, Greece, Rome, *etc*. It is interesting to see this tangle of columns simplify as the diverse nations come and go; and finally all sink into the great unity of Rome. At last the modern world of Eusebius's own time was left but four columns, the years of Rome (A. U. C.), of Olympiads, of Roman Consuls, and of Christ. The rest was already ancient history. As one follows the sweep of these figures and watches the steady line of those events where the Providence of God bore down the forces of the unbeliever, one realizes that in this convincing statement lay the strongest of all defenses of the faith. Here, compressed into a few pages, lies the evidence of history for the Christian world-view. Origen's great conception that pagan history was as much decreed by Jehovah as sacred history finds in the *Chronicle* its most perfect expression; the facts speak for themselves.[13] No fickle Fortuna could ever have arranged with such deliberate aim the rise and fall of empires. History is the reservoir not of argument but of proof, and the proof is mathematical.[14]

The human element of humor, however, comes into the situation when one turns back to the opening paragraph and learns the attitude of Eusebius himself. "Now at the very beginning, I make this declaration before all the world: let no one ever arrogantly contend that a sure and thorough knowledge of chronology is attainable. This every one will readily believe who ponders on the incontrovertible words of the Master to his disciples: 'It is not for us to know the times or the seasons, which the Father hath put in his own power' (*Acts* 1:7). For it seems to me that he, as Lord God, uttered that decisive word with reference not merely to the day of judgment, but with reference to all times, to the end that he might restrain those who devote themselves too boldly to such vain investigations." [15]

We have left ourselves little space for the work by which Eusebius is chiefly known, the *Ecclesiastical History*. So far as students of theology and church history are concerned, little space is needed, for the work itself is readily accessible and that, too, in an English edition, and magnificently translated.[16] But the general student of history seldom reads church history now, and the achievement of Eusebius shares the common fate. Yet it is a great achievement, and a genuine surprise awaits the reader who turns to it. One might expect that the age of Constantine would produce a history of the obscure, unstoried institution which had suddenly risen to the splendor of an imperial church, but one could hardly expect to find out of that arena of fierce theological conflict the calm and lofty attitude of generous reserve and the sense of dominating scholarly obligation for accuracy which characterize the first church historian. The judgment of Gibbon, that the *Ecclesiastical History* was grossly unfair,[17] is itself a prejudiced verdict. To be sure it lacks the purely scientific aim; it is apologetic. But Eusebius is not to be blamed for that; the wonder is that he preserved so just a poise and so exacting a standard in view of the universal demands of his time. We should not forget that the apologetic tone of Christian historiography was also sanctioned by the pagan classics. Even Polybius had demanded that history be regarded as a thing of use, and Cicero, Sallust, Livy and Tacitus had applied the maxim generously. Christian historiography should not bear the brunt of our dissatisfaction with what was the attitude of nearly all antiquity.[18]

The *Ecclesiastical History* does not live by grace of its style. Eusebius had no refined literary taste; he wrote, as he thought, in rambling and desultory fashion. But he combined with vast erudition a "sterling sense," and a "true historical instinct" in choosing the selections from his store of facts and documents.[19] Conscious of the value of the sources themselves, he weaves into his narrative large blocks of the originals, and in this way has preserved many a precious text which would otherwise be lost. The *Ecclesiastical History* is less a narrative than a collection of documents, for which every student of Christianity is devoutly thankful, and more thankful yet that the author was so keenly conscious of his responsibility. Wherever his references can be verified they prove correct, which gives a presumption of accuracy for those found in his work alone.

This scholarly accuracy was combined with a vast learning. Eusebius had enjoyed the freedom of the great library of Pamphilus at Antioch, in his earlier days. He tells us that he gathered materials as well in the library at Jerusalem founded by Bishop Alexander,[20] and Constantine seems to have opened his archives to him.[21] But he learned not less from the busy world in which he lived. He was no recluse; he lived at the center of things, both politically and ecclesiastically. His genial nature blinded him to men's faults, and his judgment on contemporaries—particularly upon Constantine— is of little value.[22] But even at his worst he seldom recorded any marvelous event without the Herodotean caution of throwing the responsibility back upon the original narrative. There is no better example of this than the account in the *Life of Constantine* of the emperor's vision of the cross. It was an incident all too likely to find ready that credence in Christian circles which it found in subsequent ages. But, however much a courtly panegyrist Eusebius could be, in matters of fact he is on his guard. His account runs soberly enough: "And while he was thus praying with fervent entreaty, a most marvelous sign appeared to him from heaven, the account of which might have been hard to believe had it been related by any other person. But since the victorious Emperor himself long afterwards declared it to the writer of this history, when he was honored with his acquaintance and society, and confirmed his statement by an oath, who could hesitate to accredit the relation, especially since the testimony of after-time has established its truth?" [23]

For two centuries Christian worship had lain hidden behind the "Discipline of the Secret." The uninitiated knew little of what was held or done by the adherents of this intolerant mystery, "after the doors were shut." Constantine brought the new régime, when persecution and secrecy ceased. Eusebius had lived through the dark days of Diocletian, and although he himself had escaped—a fact sometimes held up against him—his dearest friends and above all his great teacher Pamphilus, had been martyred. Free now to speak, therefore, he turns back from the "peace of the church" to the years of persecution with a feeling for martyrs like that of Homer for heroes, of the Middle Ages for wonder-working saints.[24] He depicts their sufferings, however, not simply as the material for heroic biography, but as forming the subject of a glorious page of history, that of the great "peaceful struggle" by which the Kingdom of the Messiah was to take its place among and above the powers of this world. The martyrs of Palestine are fighting the Punic wars for the kingdom of Christ.

It was reserved for a greater intellect—that of Augustine—to carry this conception to its final form. But the outlines of Augustine's *City of God* are already visible in the opening chapters of the *Ecclesiastical History*, as its foundations were placed by Eusebius's master, Origen. The Messiah is not a recent Christ, but comes to us from the beginning of the world, witnessed to by Moses and the prophets. And when "in recent times" Jesus came, the new nation which appeared was not new but old, the Nation of God's own Providence —Christian and universal. The pæan of the victorious Church is sounded at the opening of its first history: "A nation confessedly not small and not dwelling in some remote corner of the earth, but the most numerous and pious of all nations, indestructible and unconquerable, because it always receives assistance from God." [25] This is the historical prologue to the *City of God*.

NOTES

1. Cf. V. Soden, *Das Interesse des Apostolischen Zeitalters in der Evangelischen Geschichte*, in *Theologische Abhandlungen*.
2. Jerome's *De Viris illustribus*, written after the model of Suetonius' *Viri illustres*.

3. The emphasis which subsequent ages has placed upon references to Judaism and Christianity in pagan writers has given those passages an altogether factitious prominence. There are at best only a very few, and those are mostly incidental.
4. See below.
5. As Apion did those of the Jews.
6. It is significant to see how the conception of the essential unhistoricity of God, as a Being beyond the reach of change, has been growingly modified in modern times. The increase in the number of those mystics who have revised their theology in terms of modern science and philosophy (especially Bergsonian), is, from the standpoint of the history of pure thought, the most decisive triumph of the historical spirit. The Deity himself becomes historical; eternity disappears; all is time—and change.
7. Charity was hardly an intellectual virtue, at least as conceived by the Fathers.
8. There are all kinds of faith, to be sure. We are speaking only of religious faith, which transfers phenomena from the natural to the supernatural world and is, therefore, the chief opponent of rationalism.
9. As Celsus, the pagan critic, so cogently suggested.
10. And we must regard Paul as the intellectual creator of Christian theology.
11. Cf. the first, second and third chapters of Galatians.
12. The Pauline doctrine involved a conceptual parallel to history, which apparently furnished a better past to the world, one more reasonable and more probable than that which actually had been the case.
13. The influence of the belief in immortality upon historical perspectives invites our attention here; but the subject is too intricate for hurried consideration. Undoubtedly the emphasis upon a contrast between time and eternity obscured the understanding of the meaning of phenomena in their time-setting.
14. The conception of a millennium, drawn from the later Jewish literature, was that Christ and his saints would rule for a thousand years; but in spite of much calculation the belief was never quite reduced to successful mathematics. It is interesting, in passing, to see how it drew upon that other interest in chronology, the plotting out of a future instead of a past, which astrology best illustrates. In fact the millennium may be said to be a sort of Christian equivalent for astrology. In the earlier prophets the Messianic Kingdom is to last forever (cf. Ezekiel, 37:25, etc.), a conception found also in the apostolic age (John, 12:34). Jeremiah, however, had risked a prophecy of Jewish delivery from captivity at the end of seventy years (25:12), but when his dream of deliverance was not realized the later prophets had to find an explanation, and apocalyptic literature developed a reckoning which should save the validity of the earlier. This was definitely the occasion of Daniel's attempt (chapter 9), which has taxed the mathematics of every apocalyptic dreamer to the present day. The conception of a thousand years came late, and perhaps rests on very extended use of symbolic interpretation. According to Psalms 90:4, a day with God is as a thousand years. Combine this with the six days of Creation in Genesis and by analogy the world's work will go on for six such days, or six thou-

sand years, and then the Messiah will reign for a Sabbath of a thousand years. This idea is found only once in the Talmud. It was developed in detail, for Christians, in Revelations (cf. 20:4, "They lived and reigned with Christ a thousand years"). Through Jewish and Christian apocalypses the doctrine was taken up, sometimes with, sometimes without, the mathematical data. By the middle of the second century it began to subside, and although Montanism in the early third century revived it, it was henceforth regarded as somewhat tinged with heresy and Judaism. In the learned circles, Neoplatonic mysticism, as taught by Origen, superseded the crudities of the millennistic faith. "It was only the chronologists and historians of the church who, following Julius Africanus, made use of apocalyptic numbers in their calculations, while court theologians like Eusebius entertained the imperial table with discussions as to whether the dining-hall of the emperor—the second David and Solomon, the beloved of God—might not be the new Jerusalem of John's Apocalypse." (A. Harnack, article "Millennium" in *Encyclopædia Britannica*. This article furnishes an admirable survey and bibliography. See the treatment of Christian eschatology in the various works of R. H. Charles in the field of apocalyptic literature.)

15. One of the earliest and best short statements of this claim is that made by Tatian in his *Address to the Greeks*, chapter 31 ff. It is strikingly in line with Josephus's protest in *Against Apion*.

II. ALLEGORY AND THE CONTRIBUTION OF ORIGEN

1. The coming of the Messiah was the main continuation of Jewish national history. Messiahship was to the Jews of the time of Christ the embodiment of somewhat the same thought as stirred the Frenchman of the close of the nineteenth century at the recollection of 1870 and the lost provinces, or lent such inspiration in embittered Poland to the prophet-like poetry of Mickiewicz. It was the dream of a deliverer, a belief strengthened rather than crushed by failure and disaster. The whole sad drama of Jewish history may be said to have concentrated its expression in the messianic hope—a hope against hope itself. Christianity in offering itself as the realization of that hope was steppng into a definite place in Jewish history, but it was a place to which the Jewish nation as a whole has never admitted it.

2. Cf. *Allegories of the Sacred Laws*, 1:19.

3. Cf. Eusebius, *Church History*, Bk. 6, for details of Origen's life.

4. *De Principiis*, I., 1:9.

5. *Against Celsus*, 4:50.

6. *Op. cit.*, 4:49.

7. Cf. I., 12 and 10. The order of citations has been reversed here for clarity.

8. Celsus also had the idea of a common evolution of ideas and customs and of the borrowings of one nation from another, e.g., circumcision from Egypt (1:22).

III. CHRONOLOGY AND CHURCH HISTORY

1. Cf. Julius Africanus's pioneer work in this direction, in harmonizing the variant genealogies of Christ in the Gospel, quoted by Eusebius, I., 7.

2. *Cf.* the monumental study of Gelzer, *Julius Africanus* (1898), which has disentangled the fragile threads of his chronology as preserved in various ways.

3. The name Eusebius was a very common one in the records of the early church. There are 40 Eusebiuses, contemporaries of the historian, noted in Smith and Wace's *Dictionary of Christian Biography*, and in all 137 from the first eight centuries. Eusebius of Cæsarea took the surname Pamphili after the death of his master Pamphilus, out of respect for him.

4. *Cf.* Sozomen, H. E., I., 19.

5. *Cf. Eusebius' Martyrs in Palestine, in loco;* Jerome, *De Viris illustribus*, 75, 81.

6. These at least are the two main influences of Origen upon Eusebius according to McGiffert and Heinrici. *Cf.* McGiffert's edition of the Church History, p. 7, and Georg Heinrici, *Das Urchistentum in der Kirchengeschichte des Eusebius*, Leipzig, 1894. Heinrici here presents the case against F. Overbeck's view (*Über die Anfänge der Kirchengeschichteschreibung*, Basel, 1892), that Eusebius follows the hierarchial episcopal thread in a sort of constitutional history of the church.

7. *Cf.* Heinrici, *op. cit.*, p. 13.

8. Lightfoot in Smith & Wace's *Dictionary of Christian Biography*. A brilliant article.

9. He already refers to it in the opening of his *Church History* (I:1), and also in the *Ecloga Prophetica* (I.1) and in the *Præparateo Evangelica*, X:9. which were both written before 313. As the Chronicle when it reached Jerome was carried down to 325, it is conjectured that there may have been a second edition.

10. In the present text some profane history notes are on the left side, but this was due to the fact that the comments on profane history were fuller than those on sacred history, and were crowded over for reasons of space.

Eusebius was largely indebted for his plan to Castor, whom he invokes at the beginning and end of the lists for Sicyon, Argos and Athens. *Cf.* Gelzer, *Julius Africanus*, II., pp. 63 f.

On the relations between Eusebius and Julius Africanus see Gelzer, *op. cit.*, II., 23-107.

11. Especially Georgius Syncellus. These chronographers preserved such large extracts that Joseph Scaliger was able to risk a reconstruction of the text from them alone. Scaliger's first edition was published in 1606, second edition in 1658. The Armenian version was published at Venice in 1818 by J. B. Aucher with a Latin translation. The text in Migne, that by Cardinal Mai (1833) is based upon this; but the classic work on the *Chronicle* is that of Schoene (Vol. I., 1875, Vol. II., 1866), while the Armenian text has recently been published with parallel German translation by Karst in the great edition of Eusebius' works now appearing in the series, *Die Griechischen Christlichen Schriftsteller der ersten drei Jahrhunderte*. It has also the version of Jerome, ed. by Helm.

12. Joseph Scaliger refers thus to the influence of Eusebius. "Qui post Eusebium scripserunt, omne scriptum de temporibus aridum esse censuerunt, quod non hujus fontibus irrigatum esset." (Quoted in Migne, P. G. 19:14.)

13. This view of universal history places Eusebius on a distinctly higher plane than that of a mere apologist. It enabled him to have somewhat of the Herodotean sweep and breadth. Cf. Heinrici, *op. cit.*, pp. 13 ff. Eusebius. H. E., 1:7.

14. The translation of the *Canons* by Jerome, while apparently superior to the Armenian version, bears the marks of careless haste. He tells us himself (*Præf.* L:13) that it is an *opus tumultuarium*, and adds that he dictated it most hurriedly to a scribe. He must have meant, so Schoene thinks (p. 76), that he dictated the marginal comments, not the rows of figures. Likely a *notarius* translated the figures into Roman, and Jerome added the notes.

A great deal of discussion has arisen over the fact that in the *Church History*, Eusebius differs decidedly from the chronology of the *Chronicle*.

15. *Chronicle*, Preface.

16. By Professor A. C. McGiffert, in *Nicene and Post-Nicene Fathers*, Second Series, Vol. I., pp. 1-403. The same volume contains a translation of the *Life of Constantine* by Ernest C. Richardson, and an exhaustive bibliography.

17. *Decline and Fall* (Bury), II:135; "He (Eusebius) indirectly confesses that he has related whatever might redound to the glory, and that he has suppressed all that could tend to the disgrace of religion"; adding in a footnote: "Such is the fair deduction from I:82, and *De Mart, Palast*, c.12."

18. This point is well made by H. O. Taylor in *The Mediæval Mind*, I., 78-81.

19. Cf. the fine characterization by McGiffert, in the Prolegomena to his edition of the *Ecclesiastical History*, pp. 46 ff.

20. Cf. H. E., VI.:20.

21. Cf. H. E., V.:18.

22. The *Life of Constantine* is a panegyric rather than a biography; and it is unreliable even in questions of fact.

23. *Life of Constantine*, I.:28.

24. Cf. Heinrici, *op. cit.*, p. 3.

25. H. E. I, Chap. 3.

CHAPTER VIII

᯽

WHAT IS HISTORY?

HISTORY. The word "history" is used in two senses. It may mean either the record of events, or events themselves. Originally (see below) limited to inquiry and statement, it was only in comparatively modern times that the meaning of the word was extended to include the phenomena which form or might form their subject. It was perhaps by a somewhat careless transference of ideas that this extension was brought about. Now indeed it is the commoner meaning. We speak of the "history of England" without reference to any literary narrative. We term kings and statesmen the "makers of history," and sometimes say that the historian only records the history which they make. History in this connexion is obviously not the record, but the thing to be recorded. It is unfortunate that such a double meaning of the word should have grown up, for it is productive of not a little confusion of thought.

History in the wider sense is all that has happened, not merely all the phenomena of human life, but those of the natural world as well. It includes everything that undergoes change; and as modern science has shown that there is nothing absolutely static, therefore the whole universe, and every part of it, has its history. The discovery of ether brought with it a reconstruction of our ideas of the physical universe, transferring the emphasis from the mathematical expression of static relationships to a dynamic conception of a universe in constant

Reprinted from the Encyclopaedia Britannica, 11th Edition, Vol. XII, pp. 527-533.

transformation; matter in equipoise became energy in gradual readjustment. Solids are solids no longer. The universe is in motion in
every particle of every part; rock and metal merely a transition
stage between crystallization and dissolution. This idea of universal
activity has in a sense made physics itself a branch of history. It is
the same with the other sciences—especially the biological division,
where the doctrine of evolution has induced an attitude of mind
which is distinctly historical.

But the tendency to look at things historically is not merely the
attitude of men of science. Our outlook upon life differs in just this
particular from that of preceding ages. We recognize the unstable
nature of our whole social fabric, and are therefore more and more
capable of transforming it. Our institutions are no longer held to be
inevitable and immutable creations. We do not attempt to fit them
to absolute formulae, but continually adapt them to a changing environment. Even modern architecture, notably in America, reflects
the consciousness of change. The permanent character of ancient or
medieval buildings was fitted only to a society dominated by static
ideals. Now the architect builds, not for all time, but for a set of
conditions which will inevitably cease in the not distant future. Thus
our whole society not only bears the marks of its evolution, but
shows its growing consciousness of the fact in the most evident of
its arts. In literature, philosophy and political science, there is the
same historical trend. Criticism no longer judges by absolute standards; it applies the standards of the author's own environment. We
no longer condemn Shakespeare for having violated the ancient dramatic laws, nor Voltaire for having objected to the violations. Each
age has its own expression, and in judging each we enter the field
of history. In ethics, again, the revolt against absolute standards limits
us to the relative, and morals are investigated in the basis of history,
as largely conditioned by economic environment and the growth of
intellectual freedom. Revelation no longer appeals to scientific minds
as a source of knowledge. Experience on the other hand is history.
As for political science, we do not regard the national state as that
ultimate and final product which men once saw in the Roman Empire. It has hardly come into being before forces are evident which
aim at its destruction. Internationalism has gained ground in Europe
in recent years; and Socialism itself, which is based upon a distinct
interpretation of history, is regarded by its followers as merely a

stage in human progress, like those which have gone before it. It is evident that Freeman's definition of history as "past politics" is miserably inadequate. Political events are mere externals. History enters into every phase of activity, and the economic forces which urge society along are as much its subject as the political result.

In short the historical spirit of the age has invaded every field. The world-picture presented in this encyclopaedia is that of a dynamic universe, of phenomena in process of ceaseless change. Owing to this insistent change all things which happen, or seem to happen, are history in the broader sense of the word. The encyclopaedia itself is a history of them in the stricter sense,—the description and record of this universal process. This narrower meaning is the subject of the rest of this article.

The word "history" comes from the Gr. ἱστορία, which was used by the Ionians in the 6th century B.C. for the search for knowledge in the widest sense. It meant inquiry, investigation, not narrative. It was not until two centuries later that the *historikos*, the reciter of stories, superseded the *historeōn* ἱστορέων), the seeker after knowledge. Thus history began as a branch of scientific research,—much the same as what the Athenians later termed philosophy. Herodotus himself was as much a scientific explorer as a reciter of narrative, and his life-long investigation was *historiē* in his Ionian speech. Yet it was Herodotus himself who first hinted at the new use of the word, applied merely to the details accumulated during a long search for knowledge. It is not until Aristotle, however, that we have it definitely applied to the literary product instead of the inquiry which precedes it. From Aristotle to modern times, history (Lat. *historia*) has been a form of literature. It is only in the scientific environment of to-day that we recognize once more, with those earliest of the forerunners of Herodotus, that history involves two distinct operations, one of which, investigation, is in the field of science, while the other, the literary presentation, is in the field of art.

The history of history itself is therefore two-fold. History as art flourishes with the arts. It calls upon the imagination and the literary gifts of expression. Its history does not run parallel with the scientific side, but rather varies in inverse ratio with scientific activity. Those periods which have been dominated by the great masters of style have been less interested in the criticism of the historian's methods of investigation than in the beauty of his rhetoric. The scientific historian, deeply interested in the search for truth, is generally but a poor artist, and his uncoloured picture of the past will never rank in literature beside the splendid distortions which glow in the pages of a Michelet or Macaulay. History the art, in so far as it is conditioned upon genius, has no single traceable line of development. Here the product of the age of Pericles remains unsurpassed still; the works of Herodotus and Thucydides standing along with those of Pheidias as models for all time. On the other hand, history the science has developed so that it has not only gained recognition among historians as a distinct subject, but it has raised with it a group of auxiliary sciences which serve either as tools for investigation or as a basis for testing the results. The advance in this branch of history in the 19th century was one of its greatest achievements. The vast gulf which lies between the history of Egypt by Herodotus and that by Flinders Petrie is the measure of its achievement. By the mechanism now at his disposal the scientific explorer can read more history from the dust-heaps of Abydos than the greatest traveller of antiquity could gather from the priests of Saïs. In tracing the history of history we must therefore keep in mind the double aspect.

History itself, this double subject, the science and the art combined, begins with the dawn of memory and the invention of speech. It is wrong to term those ages *pre-historic* whose history has not come down to us, including in one category the pre-literary age and the literary whose traces have been lost. Even the pre-literary had its history, first in myth and then in saga. The saga, or epos, was a great advance upon the myth, for in it the deeds of men replace or tend to replace the deeds of the gods. But we are still largely in the realm of imagination. Poetry, as Thucydides complained, is a most imperfect medium for fact. The bard will exaggerate or distort his story. True history, as a record of what really has happened, first reached maturity in prose. Therefore, although much of the past has been handed down to us in epic, in ballad and in the legends of folklore, we must turn from them to what became history in the narrower sense.

The earliest prose origins of history are the inscriptions. Their inadequacy is evident from two standpoints. Their permanence depends not upon their importance, but upon the durability of the substance on which they are inscribed. A note for a wedding ring baked into the clay of Babylon has been preserved, while the history of the greatest events has perished. In the second place they are sealed to all but those who know how to read them, and so they lie forgotten for centuries while oral tradition flourishes,—being within the reach of every man. It is only recently that archaeology, turning from the field of art, has undertaken to interpret for us this first written history. The process by which the modern fits together all the obtainable remains of an antiquity, and reconstructs even that past which left no written record, lies outside the field of this article. But such enlargement of the field of history is a modern scientific product, and is to be distinguished from the imperfect beginnings of history-writing which the archaeologist is able to decipher.

Next to the inscriptions,—sometimes identical with them,—are the early chronicles. These are of various kinds. Family chronicles preserved the memory of heroic ancestors whose deeds in the earliest age would have passed into the keeping of the bards. Such family archives were perhaps the main source for Roman historians. But they are not confined to Rome or Greece. Genealogies also pass from the bald verse, which was the vehicle for oral transmission, to such elaborate tables as those in which Manetho has preserved the dynasties of Egyptian Pharaohs.

In this field the priest succeeds the poet. The temple itself became the chief repository of records. There were simple religious annals, votive tablets recording miracles accomplished at a shrine, lists of priests and priestesses, accounts of benefactions, of prodigies and portents. In some cases, as in Rome, the pontiffs kept a kind of register, not merely of religious history, but of important political events as well. Down to the time of the Gracchi (131 B.C.) the Pontifex Maximus inscribed the year's events upon annual tablets of wood which were preserved in the Regia, the official residence of the pontiff in the Forum. These pontifical "annals" thus came to be a sort of civic history. Chronicles of the Greek cities were commonly ascribed to mythical authors, as for instance that of Miletus, the oldest, to Cadmus the inventor of letters. But they were continued and edited by men in whom the critical spirit was awakening, as when the chroniclers of Ionian towns began the criticism of Homer.

The first historians were the logographi of these Ionian cities; men who carried their inquiry (*historiē*) beyond both written record and oral tradition to a study of the world around them. Their "saying" (*logos*) was gathered mostly from contemporaries; and upon the basis of a widened experience they became critics of their traditions. The opening lines of Hecataeus of Miletus begin the history of the true historic spirit in words which read like a sentence from Voltaire. "Hecataeus of Miletus thus speaks: I write as I deem true, for the traditions of the Greeks seem to me manifold and laughable." Those words mark an epoch in the history of thought. They are the introduction to historical criticism and scientific investigation. Whatever the actual achievement of Hecataeus may have been, from his time onward the scientific movement was set going. Herodotus of Heraclea struggled to rationalize mythology, and established chronology on a solid basis. And finally Herodotus, a professional story-teller, rose to the height of genuine scientific investigation. Herodotus' inquiry was not simply that of an idle tourist. He was a critical observer, who tested his evidence. It is easy for the student now to show the inadequacy of his sources, and his failure here or there to discriminate between fact and fable. But given the imperfect medium for investigation and the absence of an archaeological basis for criticism, the work of Herodotus remains a scientific achievement, as remarkable for its approximation to truth as for the vastness of its scope. Yet it was Herodotus' chief glory to have joined to this scientific spirit an artistic sense which enabled him to cast the material into the truest literary form. He gathered all his knowledge of the ancient world, not simply for itself, but to mass it around the story of the war between the east and west, the Greeks and the Persians. He is first and foremost a story-teller; his theme is like that of the bards, a heroic event. His story is a vast prose epos, in which science is to this extent subordinated to art. "This is the showing forth of the Inquiry of Herodotus of Halicarnassus, to the end that neither the deeds of men may be forgotten by lapse of time, nor the works, great and marvellous, which have been produced, some by Hellenes, some by Barbarians, may lose their renown, and especially that the causes may be remembered for which these waged war with one another" (*i.e.* the Persian war).

In Thucydides a higher art than that of Herodotus was combined with a higher science. He scorned the story-teller "who seeks to please the ear rather than to speak the truth," and yet his rhetoric is the culmination of Greek historical prose. He withdrew from vulgar applause, conscious that his narrative would be considered "disappointing to the ear," yet he recast the materials out of which he constructed it in order to lift that narrative into the realm of pure literature. Speeches, letters and documents are reworded to be in tone with the rest of the story. It was his art, in fact, which really created the Peloponnesian war out of its separate parts. And yet this art was merely the language of a scientist. The "laborious task" of which he speaks is that of consulting all possible evidence, and weighing conflicting accounts. It is this which makes his rhetoric worth while, "an everlasting possession, not a prize competition which is heard and forgotten."

From the sublimity of Thucydides, and Xenophon's straight-forward story, history passed with Theopompus and Ephorus into the field of rhetoric. A revival of the scientific instinct of investigation is discernable in Timaeus the Sicilian, at the end of the 4th century, but his attack upon his predecessors was the text of a more crushing attack upon himself by Polybius, who declares him lacking in critical insight and biased by passion. Polybius' comments upon Timaeus reach the dignity of a treatise upon history. He protests against its use for controversial pamphlets which distort the truth. "Directly a man assumes the moral attitude of an historian he ought to forget all considerations, such as love of one's friends, hatred of one's enemies. . . . He must sometimes praise enemies and blame friends. For as a living creature is rendered useless if deprived of its eyes, so if you take truth from History, what is left but an improfitable tale" (bk. xii. 14). These are the words of a Ranke. Unfortunately Polybius, like most modern scientific historians, was no artist. His style is the very opposite of that of Isocrates and the rhetoricians. It is often only clear in the light of inscriptions, so closely does it keep to the sources. The style found no imitator; history passed from Greece to Rome in the guise of rhetoric. In Dionysius of Halicarnassus the rhetoric was combined with an extensive study of the sources; but the influence of the Greek rhetoricians upon Roman prose was deplorable from the standpoint of science. Cicero, although he said that the duty of the historian is to conceal nothing true, to say nothing false, would in practice have written the kind of history that Polybius denounced. He finds fault with those who are *non exornatores rerum sed tantum narratores*. History for him is the mine from which to draw argument in oratory and example in education. It is not the subject of a scientific curiosity.

It should be noted before we pass to Rome that with the expansion of Hellenism the subject of historians expanded as well. Universal history was begun by Ephorus, the rhetorician, and formed the theme of Polybius and Deodorus. Exiled Greeks were the first to write histories of Rome worthy of the name. The Alexandrian Eratosthenes placed chronology upon the scientific basis of astronomy, and Apollodorus drew up the most important *chronica* of antiquity.

History-writing in Rome,—except for the Greek writers resident there,—was until the first half of the 1st century B.C. in the form of annals. Then came rhetorical ornamentation,—and the Ciceronian era. The first Roman historian who rose to the conception of a science and art combined was Sallust, the student of Thucydides. The Augustan age produced in Livy a great popular historian and natural artist and a trained rhetorician (in the speeches),—but as uncritical and inaccurate as he was brilliant. From Livy to Tacitus the gulf is greater than from Herodotus to Thucydides. Tacitus is at least a consummate artist. His style ranges from the brilliancy of his youth to the sternness and sombre gravity of age, passing almost to poetic expression in its epigrammatic terseness. Yet in spite of his searching study of authorities, his keen judgment of men, and his perception of underlying principles of moral law, his view was warped by the heat of faction, which glows beneath his external objectivity. After him Roman history-writing speedily degenerated. Suetonius' *Lives of the Caesars* is but a superior kind of journalism. But his gossip of the court became the model for historians, whose works, now lost, furnish the main source for the *Historia Augusta*. The importance to us of this uncritical collection of biographies is sufficient comment on the decline of history-writing in the latter empire. Finally, from the 4th century the epitomes of Eutropius and Festus served to satisfy the lessening curiosity in the past and became the handbooks for the middle ages. The single figure of Ammianus Marcellinus stands out of this age like a belated disciple of Tacitus. But the world was changing from antique to Christian ideals just as he was writing, and with him we leave this outline of ancient history.

The 4th and 5th centuries saw a great revolution in the history of history. The story of the pagan past slipped out of mind, and in its place was set, by the genius of Eusebius, the story of the world force which had superseded it, Christianity, and of that small fraction of antiquity from which it sprang,—the Jews. Christianity from the first had forced thinking men to reconstruct their philosophy of history, but it was only after the Church's triumph that its point of view became dominant in historiography. Three centuries more passed before the pagan models were quite lost to sight. But from the 7th century to the 17th—from Isidore of Seville and the English Bede for a thousand years,—mankind was to look back along the line of Jewish priests and kings to the Creation. Egypt was of interest only as it came into Israelite history, Babylon and Nineveh were to illustrate the judgments of Yahweh, Tyre and Sidon to reflect the glory of Solomon. The process by which the "gentiles" have been robbed of their legitimate history was the inevitable result of a religion whose sacred books make them lay figures for the history of the Jews. Rejected by the Yahweh who became the Christian God, they have remained to the present day, in Sunday schools and in common opinion, not nations of living men, with the culture of arts and sciences, but outcasts who do not enter into the divine scheme of the world's history. When a line was drawn between pagan and Christian back to the creation of the world, it left outside the pale of inquiry nearly all antiquity. But it must be remembered that that antiquity was one in which the German nations had no personal interest. Scipio and the Gracchi were essentially unreal to them. The one living organization with which they came into touch was the Church. So Cicero and Pompey paled before Joshua and Paul. Diocletian, the organizing genius, became a bloodthirsty monster, and Constantine, the murderer, a saint.

Christian history begins with the triumph of the Church. With Eusebius of Caesarea the apologetic pamphlets of the age of persecutions gave way to a calm review of three centuries of Christian progress. Eusebius' biography of Constantine shows what distortion of fact the father of Church history permitted himself, but the Ecclesiastical History was fortunately written for those who wanted to know what really happened, and remains to-day an invaluable repository of Christian antiquities. With the continuations of Socrates, Sozomen and Theodoret, and the Latin manual which Cassiodorus had woven from them (the *Historia tripartita*), it formed the body of Church history during all the middle ages. An even greater influence, however, was exercised by Eusebius' *Chronica*. Through Jerome's translation and additions, this scheme of this world's chronology became the basis for all medieval world chronicles. It settled until our own day the succession of years from the Creation to the birth of Christ,—fitting the Old Testament story into that of ancient history. Henceforth the Jewish past,—that one path back to the beginning of the world,—was marked out by the absolute laws of mathematics and revelation. Jerome had marked it out; Sulpicius Severus, the biographer of St Martin, in his *Historia sacra*, adorned it with the attractions of romance. Sulpicius was admirably fitted to interpret the miraculous Bible story to the middle ages. But there were few who could write like him, and Jerome's *Chronicle* itself, or rather portions of it, became, in the age which followed, a sort of universal preface for the monastic chronicler. For a time there were even attempts to continue "imperial chronicles," but they were insignificant compared with the influence of Eusebius and Jerome.

From the first, Christianity had a philosophy of history. Its earliest apologists sought to show how the world had followed a divine plan in its long preparation for the life of Christ. From this central fact of all history, mankind should continue through war and suffering until the divine plan was completed at the judgment day. The fate of nations is in God's hands; history is the revelation of His wisdom and power. Whether He intervenes directly by miracle, or merely sets His laws in operation, He is master of men's fate. This idea, which has underlain all Christian philosophy of history, from the first apologists who prophesied the fall of the Empire and the coming of the millennium, down to our own day, received its classic statement in St Augustine's *City of God*. The terrestrial city, whose eternity had been the theme of pagan history, had just fallen before Alaric's Goths. Augustine's explanation of its fall passes in review not only the calamities of Roman history—combined with a pathetic perception of its greatness,—but carries the survey back to the origin of evil at the creation. Then over against this *civitas terrena* he sets the divine city which is to be realized in Christendom. The Roman Empire,—the last general form of the earthly city,—gives way slowly to the heavenly. This is the main thread of Augustine's philosophy of history. The mathematical demonstration of its truth was left by Augustine for his disciple, Paulus Orosius.

Orosius' *Seven Books of Histories against the Pagans*, written as a supplement to the *City of God*, is the first attempt at a Christian "World History." This manual for the middle ages arranged the rise and fall of empires with convincing exactness. The history of antiquity, according to it, begins with Ninus. His realm was overthrown by the Medes in the same year in which the history of Rome began. From the first year of Ninus' reign until the rebuilding of Babylon by Semiramis there were sixty-four years; the same between the first of Procas and the building of Rome. Eleven hundred and sixty-four years after each city was built, it was taken,—Babylon by Cyrus, Rome by Alaric, and Cyrus' conquest took place just when Rome began the Republic. But before Rome becomes a world empire, Macedon and Carthage intervene, guardians of Rome's youth (*tutor curatorque*). This scheme of the four world-monarchies, which was to prevail through all the middle ages, was developed through seven books filled with the story of war and suffering. As it was Orosius' aim to show that the world had improved since the coming of Christ, he used Trogus Pompeius' war history, written to exalt Roman triumphs, to show the reverse of victory,—disaster and ruin. Livy, Caesar, Tacitus and Suetonius were plundered for the story of horrors; until finally even the Goths in Spain shine by contrast with the pagan heroes; and through the confusion of the German invasions one may look forward to Christendom,—and its peace.

The commonest form of medieval historical writing was the chronicle, which reaches all the way from monastic annals, mere notes on Easter tables, to the dignity of national monuments. Utterly lacking in perspective, and dominated by the idea of the miraculous, they are for the most part a record of the trivial or the marvellous. Individual historians sometimes recount the story of their own times with sober judgment, but seldom know how to test their sources when dealing with the past. Contradictions are often copied down without the writer noticing them; and since the middle ages forged and falsified so many documents,—monasteries, towns and corporations gaining privileges or titles of possession by the bold use of them,—the narrative of medieval writers cannot be relied upon unless we can verify it by collateral evidence. Some historians, like Otto of Freising, Guibert of Nogent or Bernard Gui, would have been scientific if they had had our appliances for comparison. But even men like Roger Bacon, who deplored the inaccuracy of texts, had worked out no general method to apply in their restoration. Toward the close of the middle ages the vernacular literatures were adorned with Villani's and Froissart's chronicles. But the merit of both lies in their journalistic qualities of contemporary narrative. Neither was a history in the truest sense.

The Renaissance marked the first great gain in the historic sense, in the efforts of the humanists to realize the spirit of the antique world. They did not altogether succeed; antiquity to them meant largely Plato and Cicero. Their interests were literary, and the un-Ciceronian centuries were generally ignored. Those in which the foundations of modern Europe were laid, which produced parliaments, cathedrals, cities, Dante and Chaucer, were grouped alike on one dismal level and christened the middle ages. The perspective of the humanists was only one degree better than that of the middle ages. History became the servant to literature, an adjunct to the classics. Thus it passed into the schools, where text-books still in use devote 200 pages to the Peloponnesian war and two to the Athens of Pericles.

But if the literary side of humanism has been a barrier to the progress of scientific history, the discovery and elucidation of texts first made that progress possible. Historical criticism soon awoke. Laurentius Valla's brilliant attack on the "Donation of Constantine" (1440), and Ulrich von Hutten's rehabilitation of Henry IV. from monkish tales mark the rise of the new science. One sees at a glance what an engine of controversy it was to be; yet for a while it remained but a phase of humanism. It was north of the Alps that it parted company with the grammarians. Classical antiquity was an Italian past, the German scholars turned back to the sources of their national history. Aeneas Sylvius Piccolomini (Pius II.) had discovered Otto of Freising and Jordanes. Maximilian I. encouraged the search for manuscripts, and Vienna became a great humanistic centre. Conrad Celtes left his *Germania illustrata* unfinished, but he had found the works of Hroswitha. Conrad Peutinger gathered all sorts of Chronicles in his room in Vienna, and published several,— among them Gregory of Tours. This national movement of the 15th century was not paralleled in France or England, where the classical humanities reigned. The Reformation meanwhile gave another turn to the work of German scholars.

The Reformation, with its heated controversies, seems a strange starting-point for science, yet it, even more than the Renaissance, brought out scientific methods of historical investigation. It not only sobered the humanist tendency to sacrifice truth for aesthetic effect, it called for the documents of the Church and subjected them to the most hostile criticism. Luther himself challenged them. Then in the *Magdeburg Centuries* (1559–1574) Protestantism tried to make good its attack on the medieval Church by a great collection of sources accompanied with much destructive criticism. This gigantic work is the first monument of modern historical research. The reply of Cardinal Baronius (*Annales ecclesiastici*, 1588–1697) was a still greater collection, drawn from archives which till then had not been used for scientific history. Baronius' criticism and texts are faulty, though far surpassing anything before his day, and his collection is the basis for most subsequent ones,—in spite of J. J. Scaliger's refutation, which was to contain an equal number of volumes of the errors in Baronius.

The movement back to the sources in Germany until the Thirty Years' War was a notable one. Collections were made by Simon Schard (1535–1573), Johannes Pistorius (1576–1608), Marquard Freher (1565–1614), Melchior Goldast (1576–1635) and others. After the war Leibnitz began a new epoch, both by his philosophy with its law of continuity in phenomena, and by his systematic attempt to collect sources through an association (1670). His plan to have documents printed as they were, instead of "correcting" them, was a notable advance. But from Leibnitz until the 19th century German national historiography made little progress,—although church historians like Mosheim and Neander stand out among the greatest historians of all time.

France had not paralleled the activity of Maximilian's Renaissance historians. The father of modern French history, or at least of historical research, was André Duchesne (1584–1640), whose splendid collections of sources are still in use. Jean Bodin wrote the first treatise on scientific history (*Methodus ad facilem historiarum cognitionem*, 1566), but he did not apply his own principles of criticism; and it was left for the Benedictine monks of the Congregation of St Maur to establish definitely the new science. The place of this school in the history of history is absolutely without a parallel. Few of those in the audiences of Molière, returning home under the grey walls of St Germain-des-Prés, knew that within that monastery the

men whose midnight they disturbed were laying the basis for all
scientific history; and few of the later historians of that age have
been any wiser. But when Luc d'Achery turned from exegetics to
patristics and the lives of the saints, as a sort of Christian humanist,
he led the way to that vast work of collection and comparison of
texts which developed through Mabillon, Montfaucon, Ruinart,
Martène, Bouquet and their associates, into the indispensable implements of modern historians. Here, as in the Reformation, controversy called out the richest product. Jean Mabillon's treatise, *De re
diplomatica* (1681), was due to the criticisms of that group of Belgian Jesuits whose *Acta Sanctorum quotquot toto orbe coluntur*
(1643, &c., see BOLLANDISTS) was destined to grow into the greatest
repository of legend and biography the world has seen. In reply to
D. Papebroch's criticisms of the chronicle of St Denis, Mabillon
prepared this manual for the testing of medieval documents. Its
canons are the basis, indeed, almost the whole, of the science of
diplomatic (*q.v.*), the touchstone of truth for medieval research.
Henceforth even the mediocre scholar had a body of technical rules
by which to sort out the vast mass of apocrypha in medieval docu-
mentary sources. Scientific history depends upon implements. Without manuals, dictionaries, and easy access to texts, we should go as
far astray as any medieval chronicler. The France of the Maurists
supplied the most essential of these instruments. The great "glossary"
of Ducange is still in enlarged editions the indispensable encyclopaedia of the middle ages. Chronology and paleography were placed
on a new footing by Dom Bernard de Montfaucon's *Palaeographia
graeca* (1708), the monumental *Art de vérifier les dates* (3rd ed.,
1818–1831, in 38 vols.), and the *Nouveau Traité de diplomatique*
(1750–1765) of Dom Tassin and Dom Toustain. The collections of
texts which the Maurists published are too many and too vast to be
enumerated here (see C. Langlois, *Manuel de bibliographie historique*, pp. 293 ff.). Dom Bouquet's *Historiens de la Gaule et de la
France*—the national repertory for French historians—is but one of
a dozen tasks of similar magnitude. During the 18th century this
deep under-work of scientific history continued to advance, though
for the most part unseen by the brilliant writers whose untrust-
worthy generalities passed for history in the salons of the old régime.
Interrupted by the Revolution, it revived in the 19th century, and

the roll of honour of the French École des Chartes has almost rivalled that of St Germain-des-Prés.

The father of critical history in Italy was L. A. Muratori (1672–1750), the Italian counterpart of Leibnitz. His vast collection of sources (*Rerum Italicarum scriptores*), prepared amid every discouragement, remains to-day the national monument of Italian history; and it is but one of his collections. His output is perhaps the greatest of any isolated worker in the whole history of historiography. The same haste, but much less care, marked the work of J. D. Mansi (d. 1769), the compiler of the fullest collection of the Councils. Spain, stifled by the Inquisition, produced no national collection of sources during the 17th and 18th centuries, although Nicolas Antonio (d. 1684) produced a national literary history of the first rank.

England in the 16th century kept pace with Continental historiography. Henry VIII.'s chaplain, John Leland, is the father of English antiquaries. Three of the most precious collections of medieval manuscripts still in existence were then begun by Thomas Bodley (the Bodleian at Oxford), Archbishop Matthew Parker (Corpus Christi at Cambridge), and Robert Cotton (the Cottonian collection of the British Museum). In Elizabeth's reign a serious effort was made to arrange the national records, but until the end of the 18th century they were scattered in not less than fifteen repositories. In the 17th and 18th centuries English scholarship was enriched by such monuments of research as William Dugdale's *Monasticon*, Thomas Madox's *History of the Exchequer*, Wilkins's *Concilia*, and Thomas Rymer's *Foedera*. But these works, important as they were, gave but little idea of the wealth of historical sources which the 19th century was to reveal in England.

In the 19th century the science of history underwent a sort of industrial revolution. The machinery of research, invented by the genius of men like Mabillon, was perfected and set going in all the archives of Europe. Isolated workers or groups of workers grew into national or international associations, producing from archives vast collections of material to be worked up into the artistic form of history. The result of this movement has been to revolutionize the whole subject. These men of the factory—devoting their lives to the cataloguing of archives and libraries, to the publication of material, and then to the gigantic task of indexing what they have produced—

have made it possible for the student in an American or Australian college to master in a few hours in his library sources of history which baffled the long years of research of a Martène or Rymer. The texts themselves have mostly become as correct as they can ever be, and manuals and bibliographies guide one to and through them, so that no one need go astray who takes the trouble to make use of the mechanism which is at his hand. For example, since the papal archives were opened, so many *regesta* have appeared that soon it will be possible to follow the letter-writing of the medieval popes day by day for century after century.

The apparatus for this research is too vast to be described here. Archives have been reformed, their contents catalogued or calendared; government commissions have rescued numberless documents from oblivion or destruction, and learned societies have supplemented and criticized this work and co-ordinated the results. Every state in Europe now has published the main sources for its history. The "Rolls" series, the *Monumenta Germaniae historica*, and the *Documents inédits* are but the more notable of such national products. A series of periodicals keeps watch over this enormous output. The files and indices of the *English Historical Review, Historische Zeitschrift, Revue historique*, or *American Historical Review* will alone reveal the strength and character of historical research in the later 19th century.

Every science which deals with human phenomena is in a way an implement in this great factory system, in which the past is welded together again. Psychology has been drawn upon to interpret the movements of revolutions or religions, anthropology and ethnology furnish a clue to problems to which the key of documents has been lost. Genealogy, heraldry and chronology run parallel with the wider subject. But the real auxiliary sciences to history are those which deal with those traces of the past that still exist, the science of language (philology), of writing (paleography), of documents (diplomatic), of seals (sphragistics), of coins (numismatics), of weights and measures, and archaeology in the widest sense of the word. These sciences underlie the whole development of scientific history. Dictionaries and manuals are the instruments of this industrial revolution. Without them the literary remains of the race would still be as useless as Egyptian inscriptions to the fellaheen. Archaeology itself remained but a minor branch of art until the machinery was perfected which enabled it to classify and interpret the remains of the "pre-historic" age.

This is the most remarkable chapter in the whole history of history—the recovery of that past which had already been lost when our literary history began. The perspective stretches out as far the other side of Homer as we are this. The old "providential" scheme of history disintegrates before a new interest in the "gentile" nations to whose high culture Hebrew sources bore unwilling testimony. Biblical criticism is a part of the historic process. The Jewish texts, once the infallible basis of history, are now tested by the libraries of Babylon, from which they were partly drawn, and Hebrew history sinks into its proper place in the wide horizon of antiquity. The finding of the Rosetta stone left us no longer dependent upon Greek, Latin or Hebrew sources, and now fifty centuries of Egyptian history lie before us. The scientific historian of antiquity works on the hills of Crete, rather than in the quiet of a library with the classics spread out before him. There he can reconstruct the splendour of that Minoan age to which Homeric poems look back, as the Germanic epics looked back to Rome or Verona. His discoveries, co-ordinated and arranged in vast *corpora inscriptionum*, stand now alongside Herodotus or Livy, furnishing a basis for their criticism. Medieval archaeology has, since Quicherat, revealed how men were living while the monks wrote chronicles, and now cathedrals and castles are studied as genuine historic documents.

The immense increase in available sources, archaeological and literary, has remade historical criticism. Ranke's application of the principles of "higher criticism" to works written since the invention of printing (*Kritik neuerer Geschichtsschreiber*) was an epoch-making challenge of narrative sources. Now they are everywhere checked by contemporary evidence, and a clearer sense of what constitutes a primary source has discredited much of what had been currently accepted as true. This is true not only of ancient history, where last year's book may be a thousand years out of date, but of the whole field. Hardly an "old master" remains an authoritative book of reference. Gibbon, Grote, Giesebrecht, Guizot stand today by reason of other virtues than their truth. Old landmarks drop out of sight—*e.g.* the fall of the Western Empire in 476, the coming of the Greeks to Italy in 1450, dates which once enclosed the middle ages. The perspective changes—the Renaissance grows less and the middle ages more; the Protestant Revolution becomes a complex of economics and politics and religion; the French Revolution a vast social reform in which the Terror was an incident, &c., &c. The result has been a complete transformation of history since the middle of the 19th century.

In the 17th century the Augustinian scheme of world history received its last classic statement in Bossuet's *Histoire universelle*. Voltaire's reply to it in the 18th (*Essai sur les mœurs*) attacked its limitations on the basis of deism, and its miraculous procedure on that of science. But while there are foreshadowings of the evolutionary theory in this work, neither the *philosophe* historians nor Hume nor Gibbon arrived at a constructive principle in history which could take the place of the Providence they rejected. Religion, though false, might be a real historic force. History became the tragic spectacle of a game of dupes—the real movers being priests, kings or warriors. The pawns slowly acquired reason, and then would be able to regulate the moves themselves. But all this failed to give a satisfactory explanation of the laws which determine the direction of this evolution. Giovanni Battista Vico (1668–1744) was the first to ask why there is no science of human history. But his lonely life and unrecognized labours leave him apart from the main movement, until his works were discovered again in the 19th century. It was A. L. H. Heeren who, at the opening of the 19th century, first laid that emphasis upon the economic factors in history which is to-day slowly replacing the Augustinian explanation of its evolution. Heeren's own influence, however, was slight. The first half of the century (apart from the scientific activity of Pertz, Guizot, &c.) was largely dominated by the romanticists, with their exaggeration of the individual. Carlyle's "great man theory of history" is logically connected with the age of Scott. It was a philosophy of history which lent itself to magnificent dramatic creations; but it explained nothing. It substituted the work of the genius for the miraculous intervention of Providence, but, apart from certain abstract formulae such as Truth and Right, knew nothing of why or how. It is but dealing in words to say that the meaning of it all is God's revelation of Himself. Granting that, what is the process? Why does it so slowly reveal the Right of the middle ages (as in slavery for instance) to be the Wrong to-day? Carlyle stands to Bossuet as the sage to the myth. Hegel got no closer to realities. His idealistic scheme of history, which makes religion the keynote of progress, and describes the function of each—Judaism to typify duty, Confucianism order, Mahommedanism justice, Buddhism patience, and Christianity love—does not account for the facts of the history enacted by the devotees. It characterizes, not the real process of evolution, but an ideal which history has not realized. Besides, it does not face the question how far religion itself is a product or a cause, or both combined.

In the middle of the century two men sought to incorporate in their philosophy the physical basis which Hegel had ignored in his spiritism—recognizing that life is conditioned by an environment and not an abstraction for metaphysics. H. T. Buckle, in his *History of Civilization in England* (1857), was the first to work out the influences of the material world upon history, developing through a wealth of illustration the importance of food, soil and the general aspect of nature upon the formation of society. Buckle did not, as is generally believed, make these three factors dominate all history. He distinctly stated that "the advance of European civilization is characterized by a diminishing influence of physical laws and an increasing influence of mental laws," and "the measure of civilization is the triumph of mind over external agents." Yet his challenge, not only to the theologian, but also to those "historians whose indolence of thought" or "natural incapacity" prevented them from attempting more than the annalistic record of events, called out a storm of protest from almost every side. Now that the controversy has cleared away, we see that in spite of Buckle's too confident formulation of his laws, his pioneer work in a great field marks him out as the Augustine of the scientific age. Among historians, however, Buckle's theory received but little favour for another generation. Meanwhile the economists had themselves taken up the problem, and it was from them that the historians of to-day have learned it. Ten years before Buckle published his history, Karl Marx had already formulated the "economic theory of history." Accepting with reservation Feuerbach's attack on the Hegelian "absolute idea," based on materialistic grounds (*Der Mensch ist, was er isst*), Marx was led to the conclusion that the causes of that process of growth which constitutes the history of society are to be found in the economic conditions of existence. From this he went on to socialism, which bases its militant philosophy upon this interpretation of history. But the truth or falseness of socialism does not affect the theory of history. In 1845 Marx wrote of the Young-Hegelians that to separate history from natural science and industry was like separating the soul from the body, and "finding the birthplace of history, not in the gross material production on earth, but in the misty cloud formation of heaven" (*Die heilige Familie*, p. 238). In his *Misère de la philosophie* (1847) he lays down the principle that social relationships largely depend upon modes of production, and therefore the principles, ideas and categories which are thus evolved are not more eternal than the relations they express, but are historical and transitory products. In the famous *Manifesto of the Communist Party* (1848) the theory was applied to show how the industrial revolution had replaced feudal with modern conditions. But it had little vogue, except among Socialists, until the third volume of *Das Kapital* was published in 1894, when its importance was borne in upon continental scholars. Since then the controversy has been almost as heated as in the days of the Reformation. It is an exaggeration of the theory which makes it an explanation of all human life, but the whole science of dynamic sociology rests upon the postulate of Marx.

The content of history always reflects the interests of the age in which it is written. It was so in Herodotus and in medieval chronicles. Modern historians began with politics. But as the complex nature of society became more evident in the age of democracy, the economic or sociological history gained ground. Histories of commerce and cities now rank beside those on war and kings, although there are readers still who prefer to follow the pennants of robber barons rather than to watch the slow evolution of modern conditions. The drum-and-trumpet history has its place like that of art, jurisprudence, science or philosophy. Only now we know that no one of these is more than a single glimpse at a vast complex of phenomena, most of which lie for ever beyond our ken.

This expansion of interest has intensified specialization. Historians no longer attempt to write world histories; they form associations of specialists for the purpose. Each historian chooses his own epoch or century and his own subject, and spends his life mastering such traces of it as he can find. His work there enables him to judge of the methods of his fellows, but his own remains restricted by the very wealth of material which has been accumulated on the single subject before him. Thus the great enterprises of to-day are co-operative—

the *Cambridge Modern History*, Lavisse and Rambaud's *Histoire générale*, or Lavisse's *Histoire de France*, like Hunt and Poole's *Political History of England*, and Oncken's *Allgemeine Geschichte in Einzeldarstellungen*. But even these vast sets cover but the merest fraction of their subjects. The Cambridge history passes for the most part along the political crust of society, and seldom glances at the social forces within. This limitation of the professed historian is made up for by the growingly historical treatment of all the sciences and arts—a tendency noted before, to which this edition of the *Encyclopaedia Britannica* is itself a notable witness. Indeed, for a definition of that limitless subject which includes all the phenomena that stand the warp and stress of change, one might adapt a famous epitaph—*si historiam requiris, circumspice*.

CHAPTER IX

⚜

THE GREEK CITY STATES

THE BEGINNINGS OF POLITICS

ALTHOUGH THE CIVILIZATION of the Orient, especially that of China, bears the mark of great antiquity, it seems likely that the earliest origins were not in the Far East but in the lower reaches of the Euphrates Valley, triply favored by the rich soil for farms and gardens, by the caravan routes that crossed it and by the ease with which its defensive earthworks could be thrown up against invaders. This most ancient chapter of history, and that of Egypt which paralleled it, lie outside our survey, however, because the drama of history on a continental scale for both Asia and Europe does not go back beyond the second millennium B.C. It was then that the Chinese were moving down the Yellow River into the Central Plain of China and the Aryans were pushing through the mountain gaps of the northwest frontier into the heart of India.

Almost at the same time similar movements of conquest and migration brought the Greeks and Romans into the drama of Western history. As in Asia, the northern tribesmen found earlier civilizations that reached back beyond history. The Minoan culture of the Aegean Islands and the mainland, and that of the Etruscans in Italy, were linked culturally with Babylon. The history of the pre-conquest peoples does not come within our survey, because it was un-

Excerpted from The Long Way to Freedom, by James T. Shotwell (The Bobbs-Merrill Co., Inc., Indianapolis and New York, 1960), Chapter IV.

known even to the ancients, although now research and archeology have shown how rich were the spoils of war taken over by the northern invaders. The commerce of the Aegean which had centered at Crete never wholly ceased, although the Homeric warriors played no part in it, settling around strongholds that protected the farm lands strung along sheltered valleys. Despite their cultural borrowings from the people they conquered, they held stubbornly to their forms of society and it is from these simple beginnings of government that the political history of the West begins.

The movement of these ancestors of the Greeks was not a single migration but a series of tribal incursions, which, in the course of time, took over the settlements along the broken contour of the northern shores of the eastern Mediterranean, the islands of the Aegean, the coasts of Asia Minor and even trading posts on the Black Sea. As the settlements were mostly shut off from each other by rugged, rocky barriers, progress in the arts of peace was slow. There was always the temptation to go out on forays against neighboring settlements, a temptation to which the Greeks continued to yield to the very end of their history. In addition to raids by land, the character of the Mediterranean favored sea raiding as well. While it can be rough in winter, it is almost tideless, and supplied with innumerable harbors. But the advantages of trade over piracy led, in the course of time, to a mingling with foreign traders, for if they could be induced to come back, there would be more and more chance of mutual profit as the primitive bazaars developed into market places by the gates of the settlements.

This Aegean world was a vastly different home for tribal life than the lush plains of India or the great river valleys of China. It was a small world of separate settlements or groups of neighboring settlements in which the kinship groups of family, clan and tribe furnished a natural basis for society, but where the urgent needs of war and the changes due to commerce and the arts of peace prevented stagnation. Greek life as described in the Homeric poems is cast in much the same mold as that depicted in the legends of the Aryans or even that preserved in the persisting structure of society in both China and Japan. There is nothing extraordinary in this for it was substantially that of early society the world over.

But whereas in the Orient the primitive kinship-taboo elements continued and were never wholly displaced by even the most powerful of monarchs, in Greece and Rome the practical problems of war and peace, especially of war, forced upon the city-states a new device for government, to which in course of time the older basis of society was subordinated. We still give the new device the name the Greeks gave it, "politics," that is to say, management of affairs of the *polis* or city state. It is this, more than anything else, which is the distinctive mark of Western history in contrast with that of the Orient.

The earliest pictures we have of Greek society, those of the Homeric poems, show that, even in its primitive state, it differed from the oriental. It is true that the taboo was dominant in all critical affairs, both of individuals and of the tribes, but the rule was in the hand of "Kings," whose chief function was the practical direction of affairs of peace and war. It is also true that the king was chosen from a royal family, which claimed to trace its descent from the gods. But, unlike the oriental kingship, that of these primitive Westerners was held in check by the fact that the leading warriors, who in council elected him, also claimed divine ancestry, so that the taboo of royalty did not separate the King from his comrades in arms. For the King had to qualify and even to excel as a warrior to face the constant danger of wars with neighboring tribes or lead in incursions on them. He had to be wealthy enough to provide the best of weapons and retainers to use them, and personally maintain his prestige as the bravest of the brave. He had also to be wise in council and keen in debate, for, not being a despot, he had to persuade in order to command.

The kingship, however, was not wholly secular. As both the affairs of state and the fortunes of war depended on the will of the gods, the King had to see to it that the taboos were not broken, and that the proper ceremonies were performed, either by himself or by a qualified priest. But he himself was not a god, however closely he might claim relationship to them. No temples were dedicated to him or identified with his divine descent, as was the case in Egypt or Japan, where the symbol of the sun or of heaven, as the supreme ruler of the universe, was applied to Pharaoh or the Emperor. It was only after the great age of history of the Greek states was over that Alexander, consciously yielding to oriental influences, accepted the utterly unhellenic practice of the Pharaohs and claimed divinity for himself. How completely foreign this was to the native thought of the West is proven by the parallel of Roman history, although the same kind of oriental influences ultimately falsified the ideal of that greatest of all schools of politics, the Roman Republic, by the introduction of the worship of the emperors.

Even in their origins, therefore, as well as throughout their entire histories, there was a striking difference between Western and Asiatic societies. However much the taboo interfered in the affairs of men or nations, it did not determine the structure of their societies, as in the East. The limitation on the power of the early kings because of the need to win the loyal support of their followers was an effective influence for progress toward a rational and secular society. Even in the Homeric age, the sacerdotal functions of patriarchal kingship were making way for the qualifications of good generalship or the possession of weapons that excelled. Agememnon was more of a king than the "kings" who formed his council, but in neither case was it the priestly character or presumed descent from divine ancestors which determined the choice of leadership. The final decisions were made by the council in open debate. In short, the decline of tribal kingships had already set in and we are witnessing the rise of oligarchy, the typical form of government in the Greek city state at the turn of history.

It was not until the sixth century B.C., however, that this secular movement, long in preparation, was finally brought to a head, at the very time when Buddha and Confucius were recasting the old trends in religion and social life. By that time the Greeks were ready for the second great stage in their political development, that which challenged and partly overthrew the oligarchy of chieftains whose rise was already discernible in Homeric times. The next step, which broke down the remaining trammels of taboo in politics, was that which created the first democracy in history, Athens, when the old patriarchal leadership was discarded for an organization based upon the idea of government by all the free citizens of the city. This was a fundamental change, not merely an episode, in the history of government. It was not shared equally or at the same time by other Greek city states, and there were some, like Sparta, in which it never developed the revolutionary quality which made the history of Athens unique in the antique world.

No such development as this ever took place in the Orient. Just why this should have been so, why the Orient remained so firmly planted on its primitive foundations and the West, largely under the tutelage of Greece, moved away to other interests and other ways for satisfying them, raises a question of fundamental importance for this survey. The difference in outlook and in intellectual achievement was not due to a difference in mental endowment, for the Asiatics have shown a capacity equal to the Westerners. It was due chiefly to the fact that the Greeks had the advantage of living in a small but varied world which called for constant ingenuity as the price of safety. Where nature did not provide the means for ready fusion into great empires, which by their very nature would maintain only superficial control, the ancient Mediterranean dwellers had to work out artificial means for their immediate safety and welfare, and the very difficulties which they faced were their stepping stones to progress. Had the problems of government in Greece or Rome been easy to solve by the strengthening of old taboos, as in India, or the submission to a universally accepted authority, as in China, or the fusion of both, as in Japan, Western civilization might never have discovered its ultimate ideal in human freedom.

Life in small communities like those of the early Greeks and Romans had one definite advantage in that everyone could meet in public places, and that quite apart from formal assemblies they could exchange comments and gossip, not only about the day's events, but also about the affairs of the city. One could sharpen one's wits in debate or show what capacity one had for leadership by an appeal to public opinion that was all the more prompt to respond where everyone knew everyone else or at least something about them. In the cities of the Orient there was also discussion of local and public affairs, but they were parts of a much larger whole —a vast impersonal empire—and public opinion had no chance to register its direct effect upon the mass of the population as was the case in the little city states of the Mediterranean. The smaller the public the better the chance for changing not only the policies of the rulers, but the institutions of government itself. In Greece and Rome the conditions were ideal, and it was not long before the primitive society began to change.

The council of the chieftains was at first composed of what we might call the spiritual aristocracy of primitive peoples, that is to say those who were leaders in what has been termed the "organization of safety"; warriors and patriarchs who could best aid the king in defense against the real and imagined dangers confronting the community. In the earliest days one of the council's chief duties was to make sure that the established routines were not violated. But the routine had to be changed when new situations arose, which meant disaster for those who kept to the old technique. For example, when iron supplanted bronze, new methods of defense were used against the new weapons and the strategy of war had to be revised. If one's own settlement remained untouched by change, new developments in neighboring states had to be weighed and the council of the chieftain strengthened to make it more able to deal with the practical problems of security. Changes could not be thorough-going while the old taboos protected the prerogatives of the chieftain, but the qualifications for leadership had henceforth to be, not proficiency in the primitive orthodoxy of sacrifice and ritual, but ingenuity in combat and common sense in council.

In such communities as these the needs of war were direct and compelling for the threat of it was never absent. Even in the intervals of peace there was constant preoccupation with war because one never knew when the peace might be broken. In this regard the Greek city states resembled all other settlements in semi-barbaric, semi-tribal life the world over, and even the organization of life among the nomads like the Arabs. In all such early societies the warriors were privileged members because they might at any time be called upon to protect it from invasion and also because they were the ones who brought home the booty from the invasion of others. The old kinship tie supplies all that is necessary for the organization of the fighting men as long as the fighting is carried on by individual combat, and courage and strength carry the day. But when the army begins to form in solid ranks, as was the case with those innovations which made Sparta a terror to its neighbors, and in which Thebes led for awhile, the old careless reliance upon courage and cunning no longer avails.

The military development in the case of small states is a very different thing from that of the creation of great armies like the semi-feudal, semi-mercenary forces of Asiatic monarchs. Small though they were, the armies of the city states were solid companies of marching men, shield to shield, moving like a bristling fortress, and inspired by a common cause. The contrast between them and the hosts of Xerxes is not unlike that between the archers of England and the cavalry of France on the field of Agincourt. A major change was taking place in the art and science of warfare which, in turn, affected the structure of the city state. For the council of the chieftains had to call in all those who could come in full armour and place them in the ranks of honor on the battlefield even if their ancestry did not qualify them for full participation in the religious ceremonies. The result was that they had a place in the council meetings when the decisions were made on the problems of war or peace.

In this way the structure of politics was largely the creation of military science. There was nothing extraordinary in this, for throughout all history war has played the dominant role in the formation and policies of governments. Strangely enough, however, the analysis of war—as such—is a sadly neglected field in the social sciences. This is perhaps partly due to the fact that when these sciences were developing, during the nineteenth century, (especially during the Victorian Era), war was apparently being narrowed down to a hoped-for vanishing point to make way for the processes of peace.

Now, however, when war strikes not only at the safety of every land but civilization itself, it is well to study the contributions which it has offered to balance the ultimate calamities which it invariably has brought. This can best be seen in the histories of Greece and Rome which here, as in so many other fields, are an intimate part of our history. Between the period of tribal organization and that of mercenary soldiers under professional leadership in the days of imperial Rome, there was a stage of social formation which was the chief political contribution of antiquity to politics, and which retains lessons of the first importance for all time. In Greece this was the period of the supremacy of Athens; in Rome it was that which witnessed the rise of republican institutions, between the decline of the kingship and the rise of the empire.

It was not only the small size of the city states, however, nor the discipline of military organizations, which made the politics of Greece so great a contribution to the history of freedom. For the Greeks had also another advantage in the paradox that their very isolation tempted their citizens to venture abroad, and those who could travel shared their experiences with those who stayed at home, stimulating curiosity and an open mind in them in spite of the narrow confines of their daily life. The intercourse within Greece itself, if sporadic and more or less unfriendly, was still sufficient to maintain a feeling of Greek solidarity against the barbarian world outside the confines of Hellas, a solidarity which found expression in games and religious festivals. But from long before the day of Homer it was the "wine-dark sea" which led them to explore lands as far off as those of the Crimea on the north and Egypt on the south. Ulysses, the wanderer, was typically Greek, both in his daring and his curiosity, finding in the surprises of discovery a substitute for the excitement of battle.

More important than adventure, however, was the movement of colonization. No other people of antiquity spread their settlements around the Mediterranean to the same extent, their only rivals in this regard being the Carthaginians. This movement, whether due to overcrowding or to that mixture of motives which we now call imperialism, scattered Greek outposts as far west as Marseilles and as far east as the Crimea, each settlement cherishing its Hellenic culture but insisting, generally with success, upon independence from the city and the homeland which had founded it. Thus the way was prepared for that extension of Hellas which ultimately, under the aegis of Alexander and his successor was to transform or at least to touch with Hellenic influence the cultural life of western Asia.

In their contact with other people the Greeks remained strongly nationalistic, but their pride in their common heritage of culture never prevented them from adjustments to foreign influences so long as they did not violate the sense of the integrity and the dignity of human life. In this way the experience of other peoples enriched their own, especially when it challenged the accepted ways of thought and conduct.

It would be wholly wrong, however, to think of the ancient Greeks as cosmopolitan in the modern sense. Down to the last period of their history, they continued to regard non-Greeks as barbarians and to treat them with intellectual arrogance justified in their own minds by the fact that they improved upon practically everything they took from the non-Greek world. For the adventurers who thus pioneered on the fringes of the barbarian world, having no powerful monarchs to support them or protect them, had to rely upon themselves, as had been done at home by those whose small groups made up the ancient city states.

Self-reliance, enterprise, and curiosity became the outstanding characteristics of the Greeks throughout the antique world. How much of it there had been in the earliest days of Greece before the Greeks were there is a question to which history has no answer except in the fact that the sailors of Crete, centuries before the founding of Athens, were in touch with Asia and Egypt. This would seem to indicate that the Greek temper was not due to race so much as to circumstances. But in the light of subsequent history of Hellenism this easy generalization seems quite inadequate. The Greeks stood forth as a specially endowed people wherever they were, whether it was in the Athens of Pericles, the cities of Alexander's planning, or as slaves at Rome. They were the leaders of culture in their own right.

The cities which led in what was destined to be a new era of human culture were not those of the European mainland—for their great era came a little later. They were the Ionian seaports which nestled between the headlands of Asia Minor, whose explorers and traders ranged through the Near East before the days of Herodotus and established trading posts which grew into city states along the lines of trade. Sooner or later the citizens of these Hellenic centers were bound to compare their small cities and especially their tribal lore with the great civilizations of Egypt and Mesopotamia, to the south and east, with which Europe had lost touch since the Minoan age of Greece. The vast spectacle of the antiquity of Egypt with its thousands of years of settled life and the enduring creations of its art and culture made the traditions of the Asiatic Greek seaports seem trivial and laid their tribal taboos open to question. An intellectual revolution without parallel until the days of modern science began in the sixth century B.C. when Hecataeus of Miletus, the first of the historians, coming back from his travels to Egypt, challenged traditions and orthodoxy by a declaration as sweeping as that of any of the skeptics: "I write what I deem true, for the beliefs of the Greeks are manifold and ridiculous." This is something very different from the reforms set in motion by the religious leaders and philosophers of Asia. Even the secularly-minded Confucius never cut himself off from the past with such a denial of its validity as was the case with these pioneers of the history of Europe. Instead, he emphasized reverence for the past because in it and not in a divergent civilization of the present, he found the basis for morality.

A new door was opening upon the world, one forced open by the curiosity of inquiring minds. Curiosity is a universal attribute to life, to be found among animals as well as among men. But its peculiar characteristic is that it is highly individual and not a social function of the group. If carried to an extreme, it is frankly antisocial when it questions the truth of what everyone else believes. In the history of Europe it played this double role of stimulating thought by the development of the critical faculty. The pathway to progress which it opened was therefore a dangerous one, because the denial of rooted beliefs weakens a society unless there are substitutes for them that can be relied upon to maintain the common mind in the routine of life and strengthen it in time of crisis. Therefore, such a daring kind of skepticism did not make for political stability. This apparent contradiction between individual freedom of thought and the needs of state was never wholly solved in antiquity—as the death of Socrates and the persecution of the Christians bear witness. It remains the fundamental problem of freedom today.

If Asia Minor was the original home of critical history, it is hardly too much to say that it was also the original home of philosophy. The *histor* was the inquirer or truth seeker as well as the "truth-teller." In Rome, with its trend toward law, he became *questor* or magistrate. But in Greece he was the critic who investigated the evidence of what happened before he ventured to tell his story. Similarly, critics of life and the world around, those whom Plato later called philosophers, began a pioneering movement of the liberation of the mind by questioning and studying the ways of the people with whom they came in contact. Of these, we can mention only one. Almost at the same time as Hecataeus, Xenophanes launched a still more thorough-going critique of the Homeric orthodoxy which, up until then, had been accepted with easy acquiescence by Greeks everywhere.

There are few romances in the history of thought more alluring than the life of Xenophanes. Exiled from his home in Asia Minor, he traveled from city to city, to settle at last in southern Italy at Elea, reciting his poems after the same manner of the ancient bards, not to recall the exploits of the gods, but to deny the stories of those exploits as set forth in the Homeric poems. Thus at the dawn of ancient history in the Mediterranean world, we find a philosopher denouncing the traditional beliefs as superstitions, in which men create the gods in their own image, whether they be the fair-haired, blue-eyed deities of Homer or the black gods of the Ethiopians. "Homer and Hesiod," runs a fragment of his teachings, "attributed to the gods all that is a shame and reproach among men—theft, adultery, deceit and other lawless acts." He held that no one really knows for certain about the gods, for all things are matters of opinion. Nevertheless, this skeptic stated as his own belief that "there is one God, greatest among gods and men, neither in shape nor in thought like unto mortals . . . without an effort he rules all things by thought." It is hard to realize that this ringing challenge to accepted beliefs on the basis of critical reasoning comes to us from a distance as far as those forgotten cities of Magna Graecia, before the Parthenon was built in Athens and while there were still kings in ancient Rome; for it comes to us not as a faint echo of unfamiliar things such as we still hear in the literature of Asia, but as a voice of today challenging that greatest of all servitudes, superstition. We lose the sense of its unique quality because, in the years that followed, it was not unique among the Greeks. In this connection the fact that is next in significance to Xenophanes' teaching is that as far as we know, he was never persecuted for his belief.

The citizens of the Mediterranean city states undoubtedly had no clear idea of the extent of the revolution which they had begun in human affairs, that which was destined in the course of centuries to overthrow the taboo as the directing element in human society and substitute for its politics, that is to say, the secular functioning of organized societies. It would be wholly misleading to interpret ancient history as the conscious embodiment of any such secularizing movement. The emancipation from superstition which marked the trend of intellectual history was by no means taken over by the mass of citizens. There was never any general movement of popular enlightenment through public education—that is a phenomenon reserved for modern times. However much the cultured Greek or Roman freed himself from superstition, and however much the statesmen based their policies upon practical issues of the day, the society of the city states was in its origin and structure deeply religious.

The religion of the family, which looked to the patriarch as priest, was paralleled in each city state by the worship of the special deities whose home in the temple crowning the highest hill or by the market place, was a prouder symbol of sovereignty than that of the secular ruler. The gods themselves might be chosen from a universal pantheon, like Athena on the rock of the Acropolis in Athens or Jupiter on the Capitoline Hill of Rome, but the deities could be counted upon to favor those whose hospitality they could most surely count on. Thus the religion of the city states tended to remain, as in all primitive societies, a science of serving the gods, nicely calculated so as neither to neglect nor overdo the required ceremonies. There is more magic in this than religion, although the word religion itself, in its Latin form *religio*, meant, as Cicero pointed out, the reconsideration (rather than the practice) of all that pertained to the worship of the gods.

The extent to which the ancient city was a repository of magic and religion was not clearly seen until the rise of critical scholarship at the close of the nineteenth century. The pioneer work of Fustel de Coulanges, *The Ancient City*, presented another picture of the city state than that in the school textbooks of the day. The study of social history, analyzing the daily life of the citizens of the ancient world, has now reached the dimensions of encyclopedias, and it reveals a world in which magic and religion interplay with the daily activities as a part of the common scene of the town and countryside. This persistent, deep-rooted mixture of polytheism and magic was, in the eyes of the Christian fathers, the very essence of pagan society. Nowhere else has that gigantic company of uncanny presences been more clearly portrayed than in the pages of St. Augustine's *City of God*. There they are presented as the army of Satan and therefore still alive and active in the affairs of men.

The antique man lived in the presence of these beings. It was therefore but natural that magic and religion continued to play a major role in the affairs of state, with omens and auspices as in ancient Babylon. This situation was not overcome by the rationalization of the philosophers. Battles continued to be won by miracle or lost by the failure to perform the proper ceremonies to appease the gods. Politics itself yielded to their anger in the time of crisis, but in the contest of city with city, those were likely to win who learned the best way to serve both human and divine purposes at the same time. This led to a reorganization of the citizenry, insofar as this could be done without endangering the safety of the state by an undue lack of respect for the gods. The way to do this was therefore to retain the religious structure for the purposes of religion and to set up alongside it a new organization chiefly designed for purposes of war. The patriarchs and those who knew the ancient ceremonies could continue to meet or to exercise their functions in the sphere of taboo, but practical men had more definite things to do. The process of secularization, by which they took over the business of the state, was therefore purposely disguised so that the gods would not notice what was happening.

Incomplete as the process of secularization was, the important point remains that the inhabitants of these Mediterranean cities, in Italy as well as in Greece, never fell under the tyranny of priests, as was the case in Egypt and the empires of Mesopotamia. Those who served the temple did not form a caste which overawed the civil authorities, nor were the beliefs of religion set forth in a sacred text. The Homeric poems were the nearest to a bible that the Greeks produced, yet they were never thought of as inspired writings. Indeed their chief interest was secular rather than religious, mingling myth and legend, the story of gods and men, in what was a substitute for history rather than a theology. The way for freedom of thought and speculation lay, therefore, more open before the ancients of the Western world than was the case in the more ancient civilizations of the Orient, where the authority of the past sanctifying sacerdotalism blocked the path to free inquiry. Viewed from the angle of today, the steps which were taken may seem slight, but they were steps out of that primitive world which had been handicapped by an orthodoxy of superstitious fear for untold centuries.

The drama of ancient history was repeated in different terms in the Middle Ages and Modern Times; for the geographical setting which made Sparta, Athens and Rome at once so like and so utterly unlike each other was continued in the larger theatre of European history, owing to the dissimilarities of one country from another. As in the antique world, war continued its potent role in the relations of state with state and its needs largely determined the form as well as the content of politics down to modern times. But these are the externals of history; neither the institutions of war nor those of peace which it fathered, have any meaning in themselves. Their meaning lies in the uses to which they are put in the poverty or enrichment of human lives. And this in turn is no abstract statement of institutional history. It is the living assertion of the individual's life and place in society. Thus it turns out that in the long run the most important contribution of Greece was not the creation of politics by the remaking of its armies and its policies, in ways which we are about to examine, but its awakening of human reason by the eternal questioning of the great verities of life and the world, including society itself.

Here, then, we have come upon a great new ideal for mankind, that of freedom as the exercise of reason in the conduct of life. This is something wholly different from the escape to nirvana and, in spite of all the work of the church fathers intent upon relating it to theology, its approach to the problems of life is from a different angle from that of the theologians. But human reason is still a feeble and often frustrated guide. The primitive mind lasts on in us all and to an extent that none of us would like to admit. As true freedom lies in the application of reason to human affairs, we have still a long road to follow in its ultimate attainment.

SPARTA, THE POLITICS OF POWER

Unfortunately for the modern student of politics, the scenes of its origins in the Western world were so small that its early history seems trivial in contrast with the vast interests and energies engaged in it today, and its devices for government so varied and confused that they have little interest for any except specialists in Greek history. But in that little laboratory of experience a fundamental advance in the management of human affairs was made which set the model for all the centuries of Western history down to our day.

The best starting point for understanding how politics developed in ancient Greece is the city state which developed it least, Sparta, because it preserved in simplest form the impress of that major force in its creation, war. The origins can only be surmised, for the Spartans did not trouble over history, but it seems quite clear that their Dorian ancestors who overran the central Peloponnesus some time

after the Trojan war, either did not wholly conquer the earlier inhabitants or fought among themselves, as so often happens in barbarian conquests, and that those in the settlement of Sparta saved
themselves not by stone-walled fortresses, but by the strictest military discipline and by a political organization planned for war. Little
advance was made in the arts of peace because the militarism on
which Sparta depended for security could not be safely relaxed, so
long as the Spartans were apprehensive of war—for one of the chief
obstacles to progress, in either politics or the arts, is the sense of
insecurity. The fallacy in the Spartan system was that defense was
built upon a rigid system of discipline. Militarism unqualified proved
to be as much of an obstacle as taboo. Indeed it preserved much of
the primitive taboo, as when the Spartans failed to join in the battle
of Marathon because it was the time of a religious festival during
which warfare was forbidden.

The Spartan was first and foremost a soldier, trained in rigid discipline from a childhood from which every softening influence of
humane custom was removed. This training produced a fighting
caste of youths who were messmates in the barracks, debarred by
law from trade or manufacture, forbidden to possess either gold or
silver, but maintained by the state for the one supreme purpose of
war. The old military virtues of warrior heroes were instilled in the
minds of the warriors by self-inflicted punishments and the admoni-
tion to those leaving for battle to return either with their shields or
upon them. In short, Sparta was a training camp of armed men, settled in the midst of a farming world far enough inland from the sea
to be safe from invasion, and secure there only because of its great
army. Thucydides, coming from the splendor of Athens, described
it in these terms: "The city is not built continuously and has no
splendid temples or other edifices, it rather resembles a group of
villages, like the ancient towns of Hellas."

It is not worth our while pursuing this analysis of Spartan institutions farther except for two reasons. The first is that it left its mark
on the history of the West not only because of the unique discipline
of the Spartan citizen, but also because that very discipline enabled
the soldiers to move in line of battle with solid ranks, shield to
shield, a wholly new device in warfare. Heavy infantry, composed
of well-drilled spearsmen could stand the shock of cavalry and defy
the prowess of the individual fighter. No taunting champion like

Goliath of the Philistines could tempt the Spartans to break rank. The day of the noble chieftain had given way to solidarity and equality of risk and achievement. The Spartan formation of battle might, therefore, be called the introduction of democracy into military organizations. This leaves us with a strange paradox—that the first practice of democracy was in that very field which throughout history had most opposed its development, that of militarism. It would be misleading, however, to make too much of this, because it was not democracy under the regime of freedom, which is the only real democracy. Equality and rigid solidarity under discipline have only a misleading and external resemblance to the voluntary coordination of a citizenry in which the individual preserves his freedom.

The second lesson which Sparta left the world is that where the arts of war are so highly developed those of peace are almost wholly left aside. The soldier must not be distracted by any other interest, and so the Spartans, like other primitive peoples, left the day's work for the non-Spartan inhabitants of town or countryside, the *perioeci* or dwellers around, as they were called, and the slaves or *helots*, the underprivileged and the unprivileged. Never were the defects of militarism more clear. There was no free play of ingenuity, no interest in further change. The present dangers were adequately met, but by the use of familiar weapons in familiar ways. New devices were not to be risked; only better and if possible larger battalions, and these drawn only from the warrior classes.

But war wastes manpower as well as weapons, and the Spartans were few. In the last days of Greek history there were only about a thousand of them left. Whether this decline could have been prevented by paying more attention to Sparta's economic development or to the problems of public health is an open question. Because of its inland location and the backward farming country in which it was set, it could never be a large city. There was no challenge to the mind of the Spartans as there was to that of the Athenians to meet rapidly changing conditions by social and economic, as well as political, adjustment within the state. The fact that the Spartans themselves left the problems of their economic welfare, the tiresome, persistent problems of daily life, to those who had no share in the determination of policy was one of the chief reasons why Sparta made no contribution to Greek civilization to rival its influence, often malign, as a military power. The rigidity of mind which could not adjust itself to changing circumstances failed to appreciate that intelligence is after all the chief asset of a people. That discovery was left for the Athenians.

It is in the light of the contrast with Athens that the un-Hellenic quality of Sparta takes on its full meaning. Sparta lacked not only the tone of modernity of the city of Pericles, but it suppressed the development of freedom by the kind of police suppression which militarism always employs, or longs to employ, over the civilian population. Even the Romans, the supreme militarists of antiquity, early learned the value of extending their citizenship, making non-Romans comrades in arms and in council. But the Spartans remained enslaved by their denial of freedom to others.

There is no better witness to the unique spell which the disciplined life of Sparta cast over Greeks of other cities than that of the soldier-historian, Xenophon, both in his turning from Athens to the service of Sparta after the great retreat from Asia, and in his glorification of Spartan institutions in his *Constitution of the Lacedaemonians*. "I recall the astonishment," he says, "with which I first noted the unique position of Sparta among the states of Hellas, the relatively sparce population and at the same time the extraordinary power and prestige of the community. I was puzzled to account for the fact. It was only when I came to consider the peculiar institutions of the Spartans that my wonderment ceased." Then he describes the education of the Spartan youth, contrasting the softening influences of Athenian instruction in music and literature with the Spartan discipline in which "a body of youths in the prime of young manhood (or young bullies) are provided with whips to inflict punishment when necessary, with this happy result that in Sparta reverence and obedience go hand in hand, nor is there a lack of either."

Xenophon's reactionary militarism might be satisfied with this distortion of Hellenic political ideals, but Aristotle was more critical. While he recognized that "There are many elements of virtue in a soldier's life" he noted that the constitution of Sparta was defective in exhausting its population in wars. The ownership of land was in the hands of a few, government by the ephors was corrupt, and some of them even "did their best to ruin the state." Bribery was practiced by the members of the council of elders; "the revenues of the state are ill-managed; there is no money in the treasury, although they are obliged to carry on great wars and they are unwilling to pay taxes." [1]

Such was the judgment of the greatest authority on Greek politics. Yet the fact that the Lycurgean institutions lasted for centuries, while other states were subject to revolutionary changes, furnished a spurious argument for the iron-bound structure of Spartan society, when in reality its stability was chiefly due to the unchanging nature of an agricultural economy isolated from the impact of commerce or foreign influences. Naturally laws and customs based on taboo and security played a part in this history, but their continuing strength was conditioned on the nature of Spartan economy and environment. Even Plato was not clear on this, and lesser minds than his concentrated their attention upon the merits of the close-knit, communist Dorian mode of life, when compared with the looser, ever-changing, ever-growing response to intelligence of the Ionians. As the execution of Socrates shows, Athens was equally ready to suppress freedom even of philosophic thought, when it felt menaced by a sense of insecurity. From Lycurgus to today, here lies the greatest danger to freedom.

ATHENS AND THE BEGINNING OF DEMOCRACY

Had the development of politics in Greece remained on the level of the constitution of Sparta, it would not be worth more than passing notice; for, in spite of the intensely practical purposes of an organization designed for war, it hardly more than opened the door to escape from the primitive taboo. Superstitious scruples such as those which kept the Spartans from the battlefield of Marathon still dominated policies of state. That is bound to be the case where the process of emancipation stops at the first step which leaves the soldiery supreme; where the servitude of fear still mocks the progress toward freedom. It was in Athens that the Greek genius really came to grips with the fundamental problem and where its solution was worked out in what has aptly been termed the most incredible chapter in all human history.

There have been many attempts to explain this unique achievement which gave a new meaning to life by revealing its capacity to explore both nature and the mind itself and which provided as a home for such high enterprise the first experiment of democracy. But no one explanation will suffice. The Ionian Greeks who built up the Athenian city and empire were highly endowed by nature, as they showed wherever they settled. But was their intelligence a birthright, or did it acquire its sharpened edge by fencing with others in the market places of the Aegean and in the contact with strange customs and strange people? Surely the quality of Athenian history cannot be explained away as the product of trade and colonization. But, granting that the Ionian stock was of the best, the stimulus of contact with the outside world certainly was a dominant factor in bringing out the native capacity.

The contrast with Sparta is enlightening. There the contempt for trade resulted in stagnation. Athenian society, on the contrary, was dynamic, because it was open to the constantly changing influences of a varied world. That intellectual mobility is stimulated by trade is a commonplace in history. Modern times began when the world of medieval life was broken by the rise of capitalism and the opening of the world market. In Athens, as the world of business grew, the institutions of democracy developed to assure not only justice but also freedom for the common man. There was the great exception of slavery, and trade was only partially distinguished from plunder—for the war system dominated economic as well as political life—but compared with other antique societies, the history of Athens was that of a revolution in freedom.

The origins of the revolutionary movement which we are tracing go back in Athens, as in Sparta, to the dawn of history, when the "lawgiver," Draco, of the seventh century B.C., codified and published the laws of Athens, thus preventing them from remaining the secret lore in the possession of the priestly patriarchal government. How much of this story is mythical is not a matter of concern here. Suffice it to say that such a writing down of the law registers the emergence into history of that other dominant interest of mankind, which we have noted in the survey of primitive life, the daily welfare in the common pursuits of life. Whenever a society advances beyond the primitive stage, its first interest, the organization of safety against both the visible and the unseen dangers of life, has always to yield ground to the more persistent demands of food, shelter, and well-being. These have chiefly to do with social and economic justice at home, setting limits to the oppression by the strong, and offering some guarantee for the enjoyment of worldly goods and their increase through the work of the artisan or farmer and with the exchange of goods in trade. While primitive man is just as fond of comfort (as he understands it) and as greedy for property (as he understands it) as the more civilized, his satisfactions are more immediate, in idleness or in delight at the glitter of beads or the flash of color. Such easy satisfaction does not call for any disturbance of taboo or habit. But in the course of settled life, property accumulation and the relationships of the members of the tribe become more complicated and the rules of conduct which were administered by the elders must be made known to all. Only by this means can the society continue to be knit together as it was in the old days of kinship tribalism, for the ownership of property is seen to be a means of power which can rival and, ultimately, displace the prerogatives of primitive chieftainship.

It is in this connection that in the history of almost every country, the figure of a great lawgiver appears, enhanced by the myth-making faculty which tends to attribute to him what may have been a long process or a series of reforms. The laws thus gain in strength by this attribution to a single author because they carry the authority of a great personality which is always an asset in lawmaking. Thus Hammurabi stands out in the annals of early Babylon to establish justice and mete out punishment for wrong doing, and thus the Deuteronomist exalted the figure of Moses in the dim antiquity of the Jews. We have already seen the same process at work in Sparta where Lycurgus was looked back to as the founder of a constitution which probably took a century or two to form. We shall find it again in Rome. There is nothing unique, therefore, in finding the lawgiver Draco at the dawn of Athenian history.

The unique character of Athenian history, however, especially in contrast with that of the Asiatic model, is apparent in the rapidity with which it changed this first code of laws. Later Greek historians are somewhat at odds as to just what happened and how. But it would seem that the writing down of the law had the result of showing up all its faults, and the pressing needs of a rapidly changing economic situation in which trade was beginning to disrupt primitive society, forced an almost complete repeal of Draco's laws only a generation or so later. This was the work of his great successor, Solon, who stands out in the narrative of Greek history as one of the most revolutionary statesmen in the history of the world.

The details of Solon's reforms are matters of controversy among historians, because the Greek source themselves do not agree. But the basic principle was that the most important rights and privileges of citizenship in Athens were no longer to depend upon the old kinship ties of the primitive tribal relationships, but upon the income from landed property. Thus, although the gods were left their place in the religious and social structure of society, the basis of the constitution of the state was shifted from religion to economics. There was to be no more slavery for debt, the mortgages were cancelled on Athenian farms and the amount of land which a citizen might hold was limited. The poorer citizens, thus freed from economic bondage, became members of the Assembly and participants in the law courts. So important indeed had the common people become, that it was they who gave the name by which this form of government by universal participation was to be known in all the subsequent languages in Europe, for the people were the *demos*, and their society democracy.

There was only one factor weighty enough to carry an economic reform over into the field of politics to such an extent as to recast the structure of the states. That was the need of strengthening the army. The demand for social welfare was insistent, but it was a slower force than the demand for safety. For the defense of Athens and for its wars, the rocky citadel that watched over the plain of Attica was not enough, nor the walls which reached around the city itself. The only safety for Athens lay in having an army similar to that of Sparta with its heavily armed foot soldiers, the *hoplites*, wearing cuirass, greaves and helmet, armed with spear and sword and carrying a large shield. Such weapons cost money, and so the main battle line of the new army would have to be composed of those who could afford to buy them. Wealth, rather than birth, determined one's place in the organization of safety. The citizens were therefore divided into four classes, the first of which owned land which produced five hundred measures of corn, oil and wine; the second, those who could provide a war horse; the third, those who tilled their land with oxen; and the fourth, freemen, artisans, fishermen and the like, who could man the fleet.

Viewed from this angle, the reform of Solon was but a more complicated development of the war system of Sparta; but the economic life of Athens, upon which the new structure of the state was based, was not that of a static farming community, protected by a war band. It was a swiftly-changing world, in which, although agriculture remained basic, the artisan and smith, the builder and the trader edged their way into the state alongside the older privileged classes. This process of transformation by economic forces is never a simple one, and in Athens, although the main steps in its progress stand out clearly enough, the details of its history are complex and multiform. The new institutions did not wholly displace the old ones, for the Athenians, like the English, appreciated the fact that it is more important that the machinery of politics should be adjusted to meet practical ends, rather than to comply with the strict requirements of logic.

The reform of Solon remained the fundamental law of Athens for almost a century, although in that interval city bosses, whom the Greeks called tyrants, gave the Athenians an object lesson in the way the demagogues can, with the consent of the citizens, undermine the safeguards of liberty. Then, in the year 509 B.C., the final outlines of the Athenian constitution were drawn by Cleisthenes, who recast the tribal organization to meet the changing citizenship of the growing state. Army service and civil administration were opened more widely to the poorer classes. The Council, composed of Five Hundred, fifty from each of the ten tribal divisions of the citizens, was in course of time provided with boards of ten to deal with military as well as civil matters.

All this looks artificial from the distance but the simplicity of these broad divisions probably made their adoption easier. In both Athens and Rome, however, they seemed to have remained more military than civil, a distinction which could hardly be made with any definiteness so long as war, particularly local war, was so frequent as to be almost the normal state of affairs. In any case the sovereign body in Athens was not this Council but the general Assembly of the citizens (the *ecclesia*) which seemed to have been first definitely organized in Solon's day and which became the central organ of Athenian democracy. Here were discussed not only plans for war but all the interests of the state. It was the school for oratory and intrigue, and a new profession arose, that of the politician, whose arts of persuasion could win not only applause but power. Politics as we know it began in the theatre or market place or wherever the Athenian Assembly was meeting.

As the city grew, however, the broader basis of democracy was lacking because the poorer classes did not have the leisure to attend the meetings at which policies were decided which affected them. From the relatively small state of the days of Cleisthenes, Athens was becoming a metropolitan center and the interest of the citizens in public affairs naturally ceased to be as direct. It was no longer a glorified neighborhood but a great city with varied activities. This was the kind of situation which opened the path to tyranny, which was the Greek term for the seizure of power by illegal means. But the sense of freedom developed in the practical exercise of politics had become so strong that the tyrants of Athens did not establish a monarchy. Instead, democracy was reorganized and stimulated to do its duty by payment for services.

The new deal in Athenian politics was carried out by the greatest of all Athenian statesmen, Pericles. For the time being it made democracy complete (except for the slaves), and Athens a phenomenon unique in world history. But there was danger that the grant of full political rights to the poorer classes, along with pay for exercising them would merely make democracy a proletarian demagoguery, by outvoting the much smaller number of wealthier citizens, who could temper with conservatism any too radical measures involving the stability of the state. This possibility was met by a measure which shows how Pericles kept his statesmanship within the field of practical politics. The number of those in the "third estate" who were permitted to share in the extension of political privilege was limited to those who could claim Athenian parentage on both sides and it was held to 14,000 citizens, which was almost the number of those in the upper classes.

It is impossible to describe this great experiment in self-government in further detail, but we cannot leave it without pointing to its inherent weakness: its provision for pay put a premium on idleness, for it was only by idling in the Assembly that the democracy as a whole could participate. It was not until many centuries had passed that the principle of representative government was worked out in place of government by all of the people meeting and discussing problems together.

It would be an ungenerous judgment of history, however, to demand of Pericles an experience in the art of government for which the city state was inherently ill-qualified. Without exception, history has accepted as essentially true Pericles' own proud tribute to his city as recorded for us by Thucydides in the funeral oration for those who died in its defense in the Peloponnesian War:

Our government is called a democracy because its administration is in the hands, not of the few, but of the many; yet while as regards the law all men are on an equality for the settlement of their private disputes, as regards the value set on them, it is as each man is in any way distinguished that he is preferred to public honors, not because he belongs to a particular class, but because of personal merits; nor, again, on the ground of poverty is a man barred from a public career by obscurity of rank if he but has it in him to do the state a service.

And not only in our public life are we liberal, but also as regards our freedom from suspicion of one another in the pursuits of everyday life; for we do not feel resentment at our neighbor if he does as he likes, nor yet do we put on sour looks which, though harmless, are painful to behold. But while we thus avoid giving offense in our private intercourse, in our public life we are restrained from lawlessness chiefly through reverent fear, for we render obedience to those in authority and to the laws, especially to those laws which are ordained for the succour of the oppressed and those which, though unwritten, bring upon the transgressor a disgrace which all men recognize.

This passage, one of the noblest in the world's literature, is a panegyric not merely of democracy but of freedom. For Pericles (or Thucydides) makes it clear that freedom is not to be found in the institutions of government, essential as they are for its creation and protection, but in the way of life of the people themselves. It is to be found in a sense of tolerance and understanding, of neighborliness and justice. Never was the ideal of freedom better expressed. After over two thousand years of history we can still look back to it not only for inspiration but also for guidance.

It is, therefore, fitting to pause for a moment over the full meaning of these words. In the mind of Pericles—or of Thucydides who is the author of the text before us—freedom is more than the sum of human rights which the state can guarantee. It is to be found in the way in which the citizens use those rights for their own and the common good. It is public spirit, not merely patriotism. This means, however, that the home for freedom is only where the citizen feels that he participates in public affairs and is to that degree the master of his fate.

THE TRAGEDY OF GREECE

The eloquence of this address is deeply moving, both because of the greatness of his theme and of its inherent tragedy. In praising the dead Athenian warriors he was also praising the dying city, for the Peloponnesian War was to bring about the end of Athenian greatness and the note of foreboding is already in the panegyric on democracy. Thucydides had felt this when the war began, but like Pericles himself and all the poets and philosophers who witnessed that supreme drama, he accepted the ultimate reasoning as something beyond the control of politics. It was the use of war as an instrument of politics. Even in Athens, the prevalence of war or the threat of it in the relationship of one Greek city state to another was so constant as to prevent the development of a healthy economic life.

The effect of war on trade and industry can never be stated in a single sweeping generalization, for there are many kinds of war and their effects on the warring peoples vary with time and circumstances. From savage life to civilization the raider and the victor in war have always seemed to have the easiest if the most hazardous of gainful occupations. Taking the goods of others or seizing men as slaves brings not only power but ease and comfort. The ancient world never—to the very end—fully saw the fallacy of this short cut to wealth, how it ultimately exhausts the sources of supply and makes no provision for either its replacement or that of the diminishing body of warriors themselves. These are facts of war which do not reveal themselves at once but only in the long, slow process of decay. If, therefore, the Greeks did not clearly foresee the ultimate disaster to their common economic life which was inherent in the unique prevalence of war, we who have not fully learned that lesson ourselves cannot blame them for shortsightedness. Nevertheless, as we look back over the economic history of Greece, the ultimate effect of war economy is abundantly clear.

Although the Greeks were always traders, yet in the anarchy of the seas in the Homeric age, and even in the great days of Athens, the hazards of war added to the trader's risk as its booty competed with the goods of peaceful barter. Not the least of the achievements of the Greeks was the way in which they met and overcame these obstacles to commerce, and stretched an economic web over land and sea, which became the chief source of wealth for cities with poor agricultural resources. The advantage in the battle of wits in the markets of Greece, as in the oriental bazaars, was on the side of those who could undersell their neighbors, and the one best way to win that advantage in the antique world was by the exploitation of the slaves which war supplied to do the day's work. Industry, therefore, did not have a chance to develop in freedom, but was given over to slave labor. This was the universal situation in the ancient city states, the inevitable step by which peoples living under the economy of war attempted to use it for the betterment of their peacetime conditions.

In one important way, slavery in Greece was limited by the fact that, although prisoners of war were enslaved, it was the practice to allow Greek captives to be ransomed, so that most slaves in Greece were non-Greeks, regarded as barbarians, whose rights were not recognized in any case. In addition to war, piracy furnished an abundant supply of slaves, the slave trade drawing chiefly on Asia Minor and the shores of the Black Sea. At Athens and other cities there were regular slave markets. Freemen, when reduced to extreme poverty, also sold themselves or members of their family into slavery. The total number of slaves was very great; in Attica and a commercial center like Corinth, they apparently sometimes outnumbered the citizens. By the time of Pericles they did most of the farming and had begun to displace free labor in industry and trade. They were not only artisans and builders, but bookkeepers in business concerns, and entertainers. In short, Athens, and all Greece, depended on slave labor.

The slaves in Athens were generally treated almost as part of the family, were not denied access to religious rites, and were permitted to accumulate savings to apply on their emancipation or otherwise. They had redress in law against cruel masters, but the use of the lash was permitted and the slaves were legally held as property, like any other commodity to be bought or sold. Those working in the fields, and especially in the mines, were often in irons, fettered to prevent their escape. Even under the best of conditions, there was always the haunting menace of the use of torture to extract evidence if their owners were involved in criminal, or even civil, proceedings. Torture was a common practice, often over trivial cases.

Yet no Greek philosopher ever thought that the slave system was wrong. The most that Plato provided for his Republic was that no Greeks should be held as slaves by Greeks; slavery was for barbarians only, but that was not a point to quibble over in an ideal state. Aristotle, with customary directness, came straight to the problem with a defense of slavery as a divine institution, due to difference in race—the Greeks being free by the law of nature, the barbarians subject to slavery by the same criterion. Like Plato, he insisted that both master and slave should keep to their places, the master not acting too harshly, the slave rendering loyal service. The lack of any moral denunciation of slavery was shared by the later schools of Greek philosophy. It might have been expected that the Stoics, denying any difference between Greek and barbarian, bond or free, would have applied their cosmopolitanism to a movement for emancipation in the city states. The basic tenets would seem to call for it—that virtue governs the universe, that justice is the natural expression of the law of reason ordained by God, that in the city of God (Zeus) all its members work for one another's good. Yet the Stoics kept their philosophy aloof from the practice of politics in their city states until after Christian influence interworked with it in the vital embodiment of Roman law. Even there, Stoicism, the most highly moral influence in antique life, raised no voice against slavery as an institution.

The extent to which slave labor limited that antique culture which was largely dependent on it cannot be overestimated. It was by slave labor that the materials were furnished for the great monuments, for the art of antiquity, and the comfort of daily life enhanced to resemble externally that of modern times. But when done by slaves, there can be no interest in applying to it the ingenuity of invention. Therefore, science in the antique world remained, for the most part, speculative interest of privileged thinkers and, if applied, devoted to art instead of industry. Here we have the missing clue to the fundamental difference between antique and modern society. Where slavery prevails, the problems of the common man are utterly falsified; and it is from the reservoir of the common life that the intellectual as well as the material advance of society is drawn.

Alongside the exploitation of slavery in the economy of war, was the exaction of tribute in kind and in treasure. In this regard the record of Athens itself rivals that of oriental potentates, especially in the way in which it used the treasure of its associates in the Delian League against the Persians. The need for maintaining the fleet furnished the pretext for seizing the funds exacted for common defense, and it was only a step from that to applying the treasure for the use of Athens itself, to pay for its magnificence. But such a misuse of funds prevented a knowledge of the wholesale use of capital. Although, spurred on by the inflation of war economy, Athens learned to circulate gold and silver coinage, yet instead of making it work as an economic stimulus, it stored it in the temples, hoarding it in the way the oriental rulers did. Aristotle stated the common view of the Greeks, when he stated that money is "barren." Thus, while the political structure of Athens bore the impress not merely of maturity, but of modernity, its economic life remained antique.

More obvious than the effects of war on the economy of Greece were those on the interrelations of the city states. The explanation commonly given for the disunity of the Greek city state system is that the individuality and independence of the Greek spirit were far too strong for any greater bond than that of immediate loyalties. Even if this were true, it is not an explanation, it is a description. The subsequent history of Europe shows that the sense of citizenship is not lost when local unities fuse into the larger unity of the nation. Never has this been shown more clearly than today, not only in the matured democracies of the United States and the British Commonwealth of Nations, but also in the unity of the peoples of China and of Russia. There was a sense of cultural unity in Hellas and the recognition that the Greeks were different from the "barbarians" who made up the rest of the world; but there could be no real development of Greek nationality as long as war was taken for granted as an inherent and inevitable element in their relationships one with the other.

The disunity in Greece itself was accentuated by the planting of colonies. These offshoots from Hellas, which extended from the shore of the Black Sea to the coasts of what are now France and

Spain, broke their political ties with the homeland. The colonies took their language, their religion, their customs, their ideas of art, music and literature with them from the home city, but they set up a new *polis* wherever they established themselves. In Greece itself, the movements for greater unity, when they were something more than merely temporary alliances, either developed imperialistic aims, as in the case of Athen's transformation of the Delian League into its own empire, or were the tragic efforts of a well-meant federalism too weak to stand against the might of a strong neighbor like Macedon.

The early form of intercity league was a confederacy grouped around an outstanding military champion. Of these the most notable was the Peloponnesian League that looked to Sparta as its chief member. But in the closing period of Greek history, especially in the third century, a genuine movement of intercity cooperation produced for a period all too short a new political experiment, that of federalism, which in theory at least, is the culmination of Greek political creations. The Aetolian and the Achaean Leagues were more than military organizations. In them was developed, as nowhere else in Greece, the principle of representation. While the member states were left their internal independence and the League dealt only with foreign politics and war, there was an assembly in which each individual citizen had the right to vote, while a council appointed by the states (at least in the Aetolian League) held the reins of power.

Thus, in the last period of its history, Greece made a contribution to politics which, had it been set to work in the early days or in the period of Athenian greatness, might have done for it what the Roman system did for Italy—developed the city state into a republic extending over the country as a whole. But by the third century it was already too late. The horsemen of Macedon were on the way, and the failure of the experiment in the policy of peace only heightened the tragedy of Greek history.

Looking back over that history, we see that "the glory that was Greece" did not fade because of foreign invasion. It had already begun to decline in the recurring anarchy of intercity strife. The preoccupation with war which prevented the development of a wholesome sense of economic laws, blocked social reforms as well, with the result that the people who prized physical strength and beauty most, died victims of malaria. Because the creators of cities of such marvelous beauty turned over to slaves the fulfillment of their dreams, craftsmanship declined. Finally, the manhood of the country left it to follow the profession of arms as in the mercenaries of the Persian kings or in the track of the armies of Alexander. Greece was left impoverished and depopulated. This failure to escape from even the effects of war in peacetime would have ensured the failure of Greek civilization, even had there been no Macedonian or Roman conquerors.

POLITICS IN THEORY

In this analysis of the history of Greek politics emphasis has been put on the creative, as well as the destructive effects of war. Strangely enough Greek thinkers paid little attention to it, at least in the setting which it takes today in the perspectives of city state organization. Greek philosophy reached its climax in the period after the Peloponnesian War when the data were at hand for a study of its effect in the upbuilding and destruction of the Athenian empire, but neither the greatest historian of antiquity, Thucydides, nor its greatest philosophers, Plato and Aristotle, attempted in their analyses of society to isolate the phenomenon of war and see the part that it had played and was still playing in the evolution of society. As we have just seen, it called forth, in the revolutionary reforms of Solon and Cleisthenes, the framework of the first democracy in the history of the world.

But this change in the internal structure of the state did not bring with it any change in the relation of one state to another. So far as its military purpose was concerned, it was to make Athens more efficient in the age-old relationships with foreigners, those of war and armed truce. Even by the end of its history, Greece had not made any great contribution to international relations. Its treaties, alliances and federations were tentative arrangements compared with the lasting strength which Rome developed out of the same origins. Although Greek philosophy learned to speak in universal terms, the chief interest of all Greeks was in the fortunes of their own city state and their duty as citizens of it. Even Socrates accepted the political anarchy of Hellas as a condition to be bettered by better living, rather than by a far-reaching political reform. He had been a soldier, with a reputation for courage in the army of Athens, and although he questioned almost everything else in the conduct of men and states, we have no record of his questioning the legitimacy of war itself. How could it be otherwise when the fate of the state, and therefore, the existence of the individual depended so often on success in war? Only a purely individualistic philosophy could deny the legitimacy of the war system as long as the whole social order was so closely conditioned by it.

It is this that furnished us with the clue to the failure of Greek philosophy to come squarely to grips with the greatest question that confronts the world today, that of the place of war in the field of politics. For the Greek thinker put all the accent on man as a social, that is to say, a political being. Greek individualism never robbed him of his sense of citizenship. It was but natural that he should concentrate on politics at home because political argument was always within earshot. The voice of the orator reached the passerby and furnished a rival interest to the theater and athletic games. The theme of these discussions was, therefore, chiefly concerned with ward politics and the immediate issues of the day.

And yet the three incomparable leaders of Greek philosophy—Socrates, Plato, and Aristotle—did succeed in drawing from their doctrine of civic duties doctrines of universal application, which in one form or another have challenged the intelligence of all thoughtful men. Socrates lived through the Peloponnesian War and the period of tyranny which followed after Pericles. By the "restoration of the constitution" in 403, democracy was restored to power, and it adds to the tragedy of his death that it was under it, and not under tyranny, that he was put to death on the charge that he was denying the gods and corrupting the young. In reality, he was what we would call today a liberal conservative, opposing the pay for political service, which Pericles had introduced and insisting on rule by the intelligent and limiting the franchise of the irresponsible mob. His influence was that of an educator with a distinctly moral point of view. He defined good as that which is useful: knowledge of it comes from practicing it or observing the effects of good and evil in the daily life of men in the community in which one lives. His sense of duty and of patriotism was based on the idea of a supreme being, a beneficent and intelligent creator of the universe; therefore his patriotism, while centered in Athens, capable of being extended beyond even Hellas to a conception of a universal citizenship under divine guidance. The far reach of this idea was never fully developed by him, however. His aim was the practical education of Athenians and not the exploration of political theory.

It was Socrates' great pupil, Plato, who gave the classic answers to the questions raised by Socrates: "What is a state?" "What is a statesman?" "What is justice?" "What is government?" Like his teacher and his own great pupil and associate, Aristotle, Plato dealt with these fundamental problems in terms of ethics, the difference being that while Socrates kept more to the analysis of individual motives, Plato's imagination carried him over to the ideal against which imperfect reality stands out in such strong contrast. Aristotle welded the ideal and the actual together into a vast system of comprehensive political history. Plato's ideas on politics are chiefly to be found in the *Republic* and the *Politicus*. It is impossible here to do more than touch upon the externals of his great structure of political thought.

The *Republic* begins with Socrates' question: "What is justice?" and finds it in the education of the individual as a citizen, especially with reference to the right division of labor among the classes of the state. There are faculties which correspond to these duties, and the culmination of the whole process is to be found in placing rule in the hands of the highly educated men, the "philosopher kings." In these higher realms of intelligence, justice could be practiced to the point where there would be something approaching communism for the guardians of society.

In the *Politicus* Plato leaves this optimistic world of hope, dreams and aspirations for more practical problems in the field of scientific statesmanship, that kind of control which can maintain a strong grasp upon recalcitrant human nature and which, on that account, needs to be checked within recognized limits. The constitutional monarchy is the best of all forms of government, and then follow, in the order of descending merit, constitutional oligarchy, law abiding democracy and tyranny. At the end of his long life Plato attempted to make this manual of politics still more definite and to leave a code of law sufficiently practical to be adopted by some of the Greek states if not by all. Exiled from Athens, he had studied the Dorian law of Sparta as well as the Ionian law of Athens. But this wider outlook was gained at the loss of the whole of the Socratic method, for Plato now taught that the existing laws were not to be open for free and general criticism, but to be revised only by commissioners appointed for that purpose, who would travel and study the experiences and devices of other states and bring back their suggestions for those who stayed at home. The disciple of Socrates, that arch critic of the common mind, had traveled a long way.

Finally Greek thought reached its encyclopedic culmination in the work of Aristotle, Plato's pupil and the teacher of Alexander the Great. So weighty and so widespread has been his influence upon succeeding centuries that even more than in the case of Plato it seems hardly fitting to summarize his teaching on Politics. Like Socrates and Plato he reached it through ethics, but unlike either of them, he was interested as well in the actual history of the city states and the result was a much more realistic picture of society, that of a historian even more than a philosopher. We know that he made a comparative study of many constitutions, but the only one of such studies which has come down to us is that of the Constitution of Athens, and the text of it had been lost until fifty years ago. Here we have a modern mind at work in a scientific way on problems and practices of politics. His outlook was still limited to that of Greece, even at the very moment when his pupil Alexander was building a greater Hellas throughout the Orient. But Greece was a world so rich in variety of political experience, so keenly felt by all who had been touched by its proud sense of superiority to other peoples, that from its confused pattern he was able to present an outline of a political structure clearly cut, logical and attuned to the moral forces of the world to a degree that made it a real and lasting embodiment of Greek history.

In his treatment of Ethics and the unfinished treatises on Politics, government is characterized in terms suggesting the controversy between responsible and autocratic governments today. The test of good government is that it aims at the general good of those under its rule. It may be monarchy, aristocracy or commonwealth, but in each case, the ruler or ruling class must excel in virtue, that is to say in the attitude toward the common welfare. All of these governments may be denatured, as for instance, when democracy aims only at the good of the majority, oligarchy at the good of the few and tyranny for the benefit of the tyrant. Nevertheless, this denaturing of the categories of government does not justify the denial of the fundamental principle upon which all legitimate authority is based, that of the moral order of the universe.

In Aristotle's mind the world was very different from that of the wayward mythology of Homeric days; it was a world of natural law with which human laws must be in harmony. It was this concept elaborated from a different angle by the Stoics, which had such a notable effect on Roman philosophy and ultimately found a lasting lodgement in Roman law.

It is a perilous undertaking to generalize as to the nature of anything so varied and far-reaching as the intellectual life of Greece. But there is one generalization which can safely be made. It is that with all the genius of great leadership at its disposal Greek thought failed to grapple with the two chief problems which confront the world, the place of war in human society and the adjustment of economic and social justice. The Greeks never reached beyond the threshold of these problems. Even the Stoics, those sternest of moralists, never really learned to turn from their painted corridor (The Stoa) beside the market place of Athens, to study the bearing of that busy scene on the society of their time. The one outstanding lack in Aristotle's great treatise on politics is the failure to deal with economics: the only "art of wealth-getting" which he regards as legitimate is agriculture.

There are two sorts of wealth-getting; one is a part of household management, the other is retail trade: the former necessary and honorable, while that which consists in exchange is justly censured; for it is unnatural and a mode by which men gain from one another. The most hated sort, and with the greatest reason, is usury, which makes a gain out of money itself, and not from the natural object of it. For money is intended to be used in exchange and not to increase at interest.[2]

The contrast between this summing up of economics in the closing period of Greek history and the early picture of farm life in Hesiod's *Works and Days* is hardly more than the difference between simple living and the life of a gentleman farmer. This is a poor showing compared with the splendor of Greek achievements in philosophy; but even this is better than the almost complete absence of intellectual interest in the problem of militarism. We have already indicated the reason for it. This was the new and high note which Greece threw into that ancient symphony of mixed desire which formed the theme of Asian history. Life no longer moved to a minor key but took on the confidence, hope and self-respect of citizens who were pioneers of freedom. It is only when one recalls the splendor of that vision, in contrast with a past shrouded in shadow and haunted by fear, that one realizes the full extent of the tragedy which lay in the failure of the Greeks to grapple with the fundamental weakness in their social and political structure, that which was rooted in the war system.

Nowhere else in Greek history is this sense of tragedy more poignant than in Plato's account of the death of Socrates. It has been called "the earliest justification of liberty of thought," but Socrates did not address it as a protest to the state which had condemned him but rather as a personal defiance to those who would either suppress or turn him aside from what he believed to be the truth:

> In me you have a stimulating critic, persistently urging you with persuasion and reproaches, persistently testing your opinion and trying to show you that you are really ignorant of what you suppose you know. Daily discussion of the matters about which you hear me conversing is the highest good for me. Life that is not tested by such discussion is not worth living.

Thus Socrates met death not in defense of any creed, but of the right to think things through with the full freedom of an unbiased mind. In the history of freedom of thought his life stands out as that of its greatest pioneer, and his death that of one of its greatest martyrs. The accusations brought against him—the denial of the gods recognized by the state, the teaching of heresy, and the corruption of youth—reveal that the same kind of intolerance persisted in Athens as in the primitive taboo, and which lasted on through the Middle Ages to our own days. There is a reminder here, in this most poignant episode of antique history, that freedom of thought may find, any time, anywhere, even in the most enlightened societies, that same fierce, blind reaction against the questioning mind as in the case of the trial of Socrates.

If the Persians Had Won

In this account of the contribution of the Greeks to politics and freedom, nothing has been said about that great chapter of their history which, from that time to this, has been regarded as a supreme crisis in the history of freedom—the war with the Persians. If Persia had won in the invasion of Greece, both the Greeks themselves and most historians since them have held that all the West would have been orientalized. Herodotus, with that deft touch which adds so much charm to his narrative, has Xerxes himself say this in his war speech to the Assembly of the Persian Nobles:

> Once let us subdue his people (the Athenians) and those neighbors of theirs (the Spartans), we shall extend the Persian territory as far as God's heaven reaches. The sun will then shine on no land beyond our borders; for I will pass through Europe from one end to the other, and with your aid make of all lands which it contains one country. For thus, if what I hear be true, affairs stand. The nations whereof I have spoken, once swept away, there is no city, no country left in all the world which will venture so much as to withstand us in arms. By this course then we shall bring all mankind under our yoke, alike those who are guilty and those who are innocent of doing us wrong.

Whatever Xerxes may or may not have said to his officers, here is the issue of the Persian Wars as stated by the Greek historian. And it must be admitted that as we follow the fortunes of Darius and Xerxes in the pages of Herodotus, the chances for world empire seemed good. The conquest of all western Asia had been quickly accomplished, from India to the Mediterranean and the Nile, overthrowing miilitary empires the like of which did not exist in the West, the Assyrian, the Babylonian, including Palestine and Tyre, the Lydian, including the Greek cities of Asia Minor, the Egyptians on the south and the Scythians on the north, beyond the Black Sea.

Conquest was only the beginning of the Persian achievement, however. Darius spent the first ten years of his reign quelling revolts; then he took the next six years "resting" at his capital, Susa, organizing the empire on a new pattern of government. In boldness of conception and magnificence of design, there is nothing in history to equal it. Instead of treating the conquered kingdoms as vassals to be held down by garrisons, he created twenty-three provinces, "satrapies," with governors in control of civil administration, judges to apply the laws impartially to all, and generals in command of the local troops.

The whole vast structure centered in the person of the king, who had a secretary in each satrapy reporting to him. Although royalty as the keystone of the arch was inevitable in Asia, there were checks to despotism such as that recorded in the Book of Daniel, that the king could not do anything against the "laws of the Medes and Persians." If the king reserved to himself the assessment of tributes from the satrapies, the realm profitted in the prevention of corruption and extortion by provincial authorities, which was common in the other vast oriental empire, China. Within the satrapies the subject peoples were allowed a large degree of independence, deciding their law suits among themselves, meeting in their own assemblies and, along the Mediterranean, organizing in city states like those of Greece. Although the king kept close oversight of the administration by his local officials, he used his wars as civilizing missions. "He was no more a conquestador than Augustus." [3] Yet the system was faulty which left the final power in the hands of the king; for however well he might use the machinery of government, it lacked the motive power which lies in the sense of individual responsibility of the citizen for his own welfare and that of the state.

The fault in the Persian system should not be exaggerated, however. We should not confuse freedom with democracy, as the Athenians tended to do. Aristotle's statement that Asiatics are slaves by nature is unworthy of so keen an analyst of politics; for, in grouping Persians in with Babylonians and Assyrians, he shows no appreciation of their fundamental differences which had been fully appreciated by the Persians. It is in line with the racial prejudice of the Greeks, that all but they are barbarians. It was incredible that the tutor of Alexander should not have had in mind the fact that the Persian Empire was the first to use freedom as an instrument of statecraft, delivering peoples who had been enslaved, restoring to them their lands and possessions.[4] The account of the liberation of the Jews from their Babylonian captivity in the Books of Ezra and Nehemiah has no parallel in Greek history. The proclamation of Cyrus was in the first year of his reign. It was part of his plan of empire-building, both to weaken Babylonia and to create a loyal Jewish state which would be a source of strength on the southwestern fringe of his empire. The generosity of Cyrus paid well, as was evidenced by the added support given Nehemiah by Darius when the walls of Jerusalem were rebuilt. The neighboring tribes warned the king that the Jews might use their new military power to rebel, but the Persian confidence in the Jews remained unshaken; and also, it must be supposed, their ultimate confidence in their own strength.

The problem which the Persians faced and solved in the unification of their empire—the use of freedom in the interests of law and order for all—was an issue which Greece never faced until the days of Alexander; and he solved it, for the time being at least, in the Persian way, retaining a structure of government which could take on the trappings of oriental splendor while holding largely to what we may now call "the modern way," of a Hellenized version of Persian statecraft.

Greek citizenship, such as Pericles so eloquently defined it, meant devotion to one's own city. Although there were religious and racial ties that gave all Greeks a sense of kinship, they kept up constant feuds with their neighbors. The Spartans were absent from the battle of Marathon, the Athenians from Thermopylae, and Salamis was an Athenian victory. Such a record leaves much to be explained. If, as everyone agrees, the Greeks were the defenders of freedom and drew their strength from this fact, what kind of freedom was it?

The answer is, of course, that it was the kind of freedom which was suitable for small communities where people know one another—individual liberty. This is what we have found in Pericles and Plato. The unit is man; not every man, but the kind of man one knows or can know intimately, and with whom one can live on an equal footing. It was this sense of freedom which made it almost like a religion to the Greeks, a personal possession about which one could be passionately aware, and in that awareness, discover one's own self. Philosophy thus became a secular study, freed from the religious background of ancient thought, and a precious heritage of the West, when Hellenism was recovered in the Renaissance.

The difference between this and the kind of freedom which the Persians allowed to the peoples whom they liberated lies, not in the nature of the government, but of the governed. For example, it was the Jews themselves who, when liberated from Babylon, reverted to the tribal theocracy of their ancestors instead of trying to explore their more modern world, as the Greeks would have done.

Cyrus, Artaxerxes and Darius wisely did not try to interfere; on the contrary, they helped in the restoration of the temple. Ahuramadzda, the God of all mankind, whom the Persians worshipped, was not forced on the worshippers of Jehovah. Religious tolerance went along with political autonomy. Indeed the use of freedom as an instrument of politics was so successful that in Isaiah 14:1 Cyrus the pagan is the "anointed" one, the Messiah.

All this is utterly un-Greek; but the difference is less between freedom and democracy than between a respect for an established way of life, rooted in religion, and the challenge of it, which makes for science. Would Darius have been as tolerant of the Greek way of thinking about the world and man, as he was of the ancient beliefs? Probably not. He stood for law and order. The troublesome Greeks must have struck the Persian overlords of Asia—if they bothered to try to understand them—almost the way revolutionary Marxian communism strikes the capitalist world today. But Rome began its world conquest by a disregard of Greek liberties and ended by incorporating the finest statement of them in the Roman law and applying them in Roman policy when the Roman Empire was at the summit of its power. Perhaps a Persian West would not have been very different.

NOTES

SPARTA, THE POLITICS OF POWER

1. *Politics*, Book 2, Chapter 9.
2. *Politics*, Book 1, Chapter 10. It would be misleading however to conclude that Aristotle ignored economics in his analysis of the state. Cf. Book 3, Chapter 8. "Tyranny, as I was saying, is monarchy exercising the rule of a master over the political society; oligarchy is when men of property have the government in their hands; democracy, the opposite, when the indigent, and not the men of property, are the rulers. And here arises the first of our difficulties, and it relates to the distinction just drawn. For democracy is said to be the government of the many. But what if the many are men of property and have the power in their hands? In like manner oligarchy is said to be the government of the few; but what if the poor are fewer than the rich, and have the power in their hands because they are stronger? In these cases the distinction which we have drawn between these different forms of government would no longer hold good."

IF THE PERSIANS HAD WON

3. The phrase is that of Eduard Meyer, whose *Geschichte des Altertums* did much to readjust the perspectives of ancient history.

4. An interesting illustration of the benevolent aspects of Persian rule is furnished by an inscription of a letter by Darius to an official of the Ionian province of the empire, quoted in *Hellenic Civilization* (Botsford and Sihler, New York: Columbia University Press, 1915), p. 162: "The king of kings, Darius, the son of Hystaspes, to his slave Gadatas says thus:—I learn that thou dost not obey my commands in all respects. In that thou cultivatest my land by transplanting the fruits (of the country) beyond the Euphrates to the lower parts of Asia, I commend thy purpose, and by reason of this there shall be laid up for thee great favor in the king's house. But, in that thou settest at naught my policy towards the gods, I will give thee, if thou dost not change, a proof of my wronged feelings; for thou didst exact a payment from the sacred gardeners of Apollo and didst command them to dig unhallowed ground, not knowing the mind of my forefathers towards the god, who hath told the Persians the whole truth."

CHAPTER X

⧉

THE ROMAN WORLD

ALTHOUGH THE HISTORY of Greece, and particularly that of Athens, furnished the first great chapter in the history of politics, the lessons of Roman history were of far greater importance in the subsequent development of Europe and Western civilization. Down to our own day the daring achievements of Athenian democracy have remained an inspiration for the thoughtful and studious rather than a model for practical application in world affairs. On the other hand, the Roman experience in government was the largest single influence upon the minds of those who, throughout the long centuries of European history, created the state system of today.

Rome began as a city state, similar to those of Greece. It was a little kingdom centered in the fortress-like enclosure of a group of hills a few miles inland from the mouth of the Tiber. Its government and social life were based on the old clan organization. There were patricians, people who belonged to the clans that composed the ruling class, and plebeians, those who did not. The origin of the latter is obscure. Some of them may have been clans who, as the shifting tides of fortune changed, lost caste with their neighbors; some of them may have been members of the peoples who, whatever their origin, were there before the coming of the tribesmen who conquered and settled in the Tiber valley; some of them were possibly freed-men from these conquests, and some of them the

Excerpted from The Long Way to Freedom, by James T. Shotwell (The Bobbs-Merrill Co., Inc., Indianapolis and New York, 1960), Chapter V.

descendants of foreign settlers. The Greeks, it may be remembered, had colonies in Sicily and other surrounding territories before the "founding of Rome," and the Etruscans had moved in, perhaps from an unknown land beyond the seas. The mixture of peoples is parallel to that in early Greece.

At any rate, the difference between the patricians and plebeians was marked by taboo barriers of the most exclusive sort. Plebeians could not marry patricians nor hold public office over them nor vote in the meetings of the recognized tribesmen, while only patricians could qualify as city fathers, *patres*, from whom was formed a sort of advisory council to the king. The religious secrets and the laws of taboo were in the keeping of this kinship class and its head.

The decisive step in political history is that attributed to the king Servius Tullius by the reorganization of the army and of the constitution, on a property qualification rather than on the old tribal and clan relationship. How long it took to accomplish this revolutionary change and just how it actually happened is of less importance than the fact that some such change did take place, and that this new military organization, arranged in companies or "centuries" was based on land ownership. Therefore it included some plebs as well as the patricians, although it still excluded the foreign merchants whose booths stretched along the Tiber and in the valley between the seven hills.

Under the old kingdom, all power had resided in the king. It was undifferentiated—that is, the power to legislate or make laws was not distinct from the power to administer them, or from the power to lead the army in war, or from the power to settle disputes between citizens, or from the power to preside as high priest of the state religion. Power was not thought of as being divisible. The king was the head of the state, and the head of the state was the source of all authority. In the Orient he remained the source of all authority. But under the Roman Republic, power came to be separated, and to be lodged according to its functions, in different officials and councils, and a series of checks and balances grew up to keep anyone from having too much authority.

First of all, the power that had resided in the king was given to two magistrates, called consuls, who shared the power equally and held office for a year only. They were elected, as were other magistrates, by the assembly of the people, the *Comitia Centuriata*.

According to custom, the consuls had to ask the advice of the Senate on important matters, as had the king before them, but in both cases it was left to executive judgment whether or not the matter was important and whether or not to follow the advice. However, as the Senate was a permanent body, it gradually gained and held the ascendancy over the executive in the government during the period of the Republic. For one thing, it nominated the magistrates to be elected in general assembly.

The Senate was not a legislative body, as is the Senate of the United States. Laws (leges) were supposed to be voted by the people in the *Comitia Centuriata*, but as the awkwardness of that system was apparent in the growing size of the Roman populace and in its general ignorance of public affairs, matters were largely left to the Senate to decide by decree (*Senatus Consultum*). Moreover, it had the authority to approve the laws voted by the people. As a body of about three hundred men, it was generally better fitted for debate and consultation than the *comitia*. The Senate thus became the central and dominant body under the Republic. The standards which the armies bore in the field held the singular device SPQR (*Senatus Populusque Romanus*), "the Senate and the Roman people."

While in office the consuls were the heads of the army, except as the proconsuls cut in upon them, and as such they had *imperium*, a Roman word which has played a large part in the description of the structure of modern states. At first, it meant simply military authority, the kind of authority the old kings had had, personal and general. It could not be divided into the special departments of government like those we have been tracing in Republican Rome. At the front, the command of the general, *imperator*, applied to all.

This situation offered a career to men like Marius, Sulla, Pompey, and finally Julius Caesar, *imperatores*, who went out from Rome not only to protect the state, but to add new conquests in Africa, in the Near East and in Gaul and finally to achieve the empire of the Western World. As proconsuls they became sole masters of the *imperium* of the state on the frontiers, and they had only to exercise this power in Rome itself to undo the long process of the separation of the powers of government on which the safety of the Republic had depended.

Pax Romana

Few conquests were added after the time of Julius Caesar—Britain, Thrace south of the Danube and, for a while, Dacia to the north of it, some territories in Asia Minor and the Holy Land. During the reign of Augustus attention was directed mainly to the establishment of a secure frontier protected by the natural barriers of water or desert. At these frontiers stood the legions of Rome, keeping back the barbarian invader on the north and the Oriental despots on the east, preserving the culture and civilization that had been handed down in turn from Homer to Pericles, to Alexander, to Caesar.

We have to think of the endless wars of the Greeks, of the strife between the generals over the remnants of Alexander's empire, of the perpetual fighting of the tribesmen to the north, of the piracy that was the scourge of the Mediterranean trade, to realize what it meant to the antique world for Augustus to establish and his successors to maintain the Roman peace, the *Pax Romana*. There had never been anything like it in the history of the world. No wonder thoughtful people for the next thousand years were to look back to it as to a paradise lost.

Within the shelter of the outer defenses lay a world more securely at peace than the West had ever known. For centuries men could come and go from the borders of Scotland to the foothills of the Himalayas, from the Gates of Hercules to the Black Sea, without fear of attack because the legions of Rome policed that world and her ships swept the sea free of pirates. This strange interlude of peace between the background of wars did not seem to the people of that time to be something temporary which the world would one day look back to as to something almost unreal. For four hundred years the *Pax Romana* lasted, and while four hundred years may be but a moment in all history, it is a considerable space of time as measured by individual lives. Four hundred years ago today Europe was just emerging from the Middle Ages.

The permanent contribution of Rome to the Western World was not this prodigious structure of empire, however lasting its impression on the minds of statesmen and peoples of succeeding centuries, but the development of a vast and splendid system of law. The history of this great juristic creation runs parallel with that of

Rome itself from the days of kingship of the little city state to that of the Emperor Justinian when the barbarians were already ruling in the West and the last citadel of the ancient world was Constantinople. It began with the process of secularization under the kingship, and the first sign of its independent life was the creation of the office of praetor to take over the administration of justice within the limits allowed it in a society that was still primitive.

The process of secularization was a long one and is still going on; we still have magic in our law; the oath (sacramentum) goes back to the primitive idea of bad luck if the pledge to the god is violated. But with the establishment of a court of law the tendency is to concentrate upon rules of evidence and technical methods to be applied to all alike. The advantage of this is that it offers a greater chance for impartiality and prevents arbitrary decisions. Justice for the Roman, therefore, became a formal proceeding following precedent and thus developed a learned profession, that of the jurist.

This development of the law as a technical scheme of things more or less set apart from the rest of the social and political organization was never paralleled in the Orient, a fact of great importance in dealing with Oriental peoples down to the present time. The administration of justice for the Oriental was personal, depending for the most part on tribal, ancient or local custom or on the moods and whims of a despot. This was also the case, as one might expect, in early Germanic law because it was the perpetuation of the undifferentiated rules of primitive society.

The body of law which was worked out in the practice of the courts received the name *jus gentium,* or the law of the peoples. The more common translation, the law of the nations, is confusing both because the ancient cities were not nations and because the Roman jurists never worked out a system of international law. That could happen only in an international society, a stage of political development never reached in the antique world. Nevertheless, the *jus gentium* became, in course of time, the best expression of the universality of Roman law, because it embodied elements proven, by comparison of the laws of different people, to have the general approval of mankind. Therefore, centuries later it became a vital factor in the formation of that international law which was to spring up in the fifteenth and sixteenth centuries. But the *gentes,* or peoples, to which the *jus gentium* referred, were any people, any single governmental unity, whether of city or tribe; they were not the territorial states which we think of as nations today.

Since the legislative body of the Roman state (the Roman populace acting in assembly) was such an unwieldy body, changes in law were left largely to the Senate, of whose powers in this regard we have already spoken, and to the praetors. The latter, while not legislating, nevertheless changed the law by interpretation and by the promulgation of edicts in which were set forth the way in which certain cases were to be decided for the next year, thereby getting rid of outworn laws that might still be on the statute books. Thus Roman law was to a large extent judge-made. But this creative process became less vigorous in the later empire. While the great code of Justinian in 533 A.D. was of tremendous advantage to later centuries in preserving in concrete form the collected thoughts of Roman jurists, the necessity for putting them into writing shows that during the years the vitality had gone from the Roman courts and Roman judges; they could no longer draw from the basic elements of the profession of the law to fit the case but must have everything in black and white to follow by rote.

Meanwhile, the *jus gentium* was seen, as time went on, to be superior to the formal procedures and complexities of the law. Gradually it tended to take over parts of the sphere of the older law, and in the code of Justinian the two were finally fused.

The result was a body of law without parallel in history, one of the three greatest gifts of the ancient world to Western civilization; the other two being Hellenism and Christianity.

No higher note was ever struck in all history of law than that which opens the manual of Roman law, the *Institutes* of Justinian: "Justice is the fixed and constant purpose that gives to every man his due," thus summarizing the thought in Plato's *Republic*. It was the same thought that Confucius expressed in terms of ethics, and Jesus in terms of religion. The measured concept of fair play in a world of miscellaneous business was phrased by Rome in terms of abstract relationships. In this setting it came at last to embody the spirit of Greek philosophy and Christian teaching. It is a sobering fact that Roman society was on a higher level when it went to pieces than when it conquered the world. The more recent studies of provincial life in the fifth century show a relatively high grade of morals. Earlier historians, however, were misled by taking the word of the Christian critics who were contemporaries of the pagan world, and the Christian critic was naturally not an impartial judge. He has left us a picture of Roman morals which was not fair and no picture at all of the Romans who conquered the world in the first instance. Nevertheless, the formal justice developed by jurists and administered by magistrates did not reach the fundamental evil in the structure of Roman society. The inheritance of war in booty and slaves made impossible that kind of economic justice which is the only basis for permanent health in the social as well as the political organization. The Roman Empire did not fall because of a decline in morals but because the war system by which it was created contained the slow but fatal poison of a false economy.

War was the creator and destroyer of the antique world. It is only now, with the rise of the social sciences as allies of history, that we have begun to see clearly this central fact of the first civilization of the West. The greatest historian of the decline and fall of Rome, Edward Gibbon, did not see clearly the *leitmotiv* of the great drama he described. Writing from toward the end of the eighteenth century with the anti-Christian animus of a *philosophe*, to explain why bare-footed monks should be clambering over the ruins of imperial palaces, he found the reason for the downfall of Rome in the same philosophy that Polybius had advanced for its rise: the character of men and institutions and arbitrary fate. Gibbon's work was a rationalist's reaction against the scheme of history based on the writings of the Church Fathers as summed up for the West by Augustine, according to which disasters were a part of the providence of God, a punishment for sin and a discipline for the spirit.

The nineteenth century enriched our knowledge of both events and institutions by the introduction of scientific method in history, especially in Germany; but from Niebuhr, who recast the story of early Rome, to Mommsen, who described the Empire, they worked for the most part within the traditional limits of political history. The conception of the past was therefore one-sided. Towards the close of the nineteenth century, however, the new analysis of the modern world in terms of economics and the other social sciences began to throw their reflection back across the centuries and a new set of interests developed in the study of the ancient world. The religious basis of the city state, brought into clear light by Fustel de Coulanges, has been taken over by those familiar with similar data in primitive life and early civilizations all over the world. Anthropology, joined with archaeology, is now regarded as a definite part of the training for ancient history.

So long as Rome was a small city of farmers and traders, the slaves were not numerous, as even the patricians worked along with the household slaves they owned. The situation did not change materially with the early conquests of neighboring tribes, for it was the unique characteristic of Rome that until it became militarized in the later years of the Republic, it did not enslave the peoples whom it conquered, but steadily if slowly and reluctantly incorporated them within the expanding state. This extension of the rights and privileges of Roman citizens was forced along by social war and by the heroic championship of reformers like the Gracchi, and ultimately constituted the abiding strength of the Roman State. But it was a process of the extension of political rights which did not reach down to those who had no rights to begin with, the slaves.

At first few in number, the slaves multiplied with the increase of the late Republic and Empire, especially as the conquests reached out beyond Italy. Then the economy of Rome changed from the healthy basis of independent free peasant owners—large and small—to that of slave labor on great estates. The two institutions of war and slavery were interlocked in a joint process which seemed at the time to mark the height of civilized living, but which proved to be the ultimate cause of the decline and fall of Rome, and with it of antique civilization which thus it both preserved and betrayed. With the extension of the conquests, the supply of slaves grew tremendously.

When Epirus, in the mountains of northern Greece, was conquered in 168 B.C., one hundred and fifty thousand of its inhabitants were carried off as slaves to Italy. Another hundred and fifty thousand were taken as captives from German invaders (the Teutons and Cimbri) in 102 B.C. The victories of Pompey over the pirates tapped another great source of supply. Under the Cilician pirates, according to Strabo, as many as ten thousand had been sold in one day. Julius Caesar added many thousands from Gaul, selling sixty-three thousand on a single occasion. They were dragged through Rome on every triumph, either to join the vast army of slaves in city and country or as gladiators to kill each other in the arena for a Roman holiday. At the height of the empire, Trajan brought ten thousand gladiators at one time all the way from distant Dalmatia beyond the Danube. The slave trade with Rome flourished in Spain, Gaul and Africa, but especially in Syria and the adjacent countries of Western Asia. The result was disastrous. Gibbon reckoned that under the Empire half of the population was servile. This may be excessive, but even at the ratio of three free men to one slave, which is a possible estimate, there would have been over twenty million slaves in the Empire at its height under the Antonines.

So far we have been tracing in outline the institution of slavery in antiquity, without regard to the influences of Christianity, although it must be remembered that they were finally traceable in the code of Justinian. The impact of Christianity was meliorating but not revolutionary. Slavery was as much taken for granted by St. Paul as by Aristotle. The slave is to be contented with his lot (if that is what is meant by I Corinthians 7:21), serving his master with "goodwill and singleness of heart as unto Christ" (Ephesians 6:5). Paul admonished the master to give the slave "what is just and equal" (Colossians 4:1) and not to threaten him, "knowing that your Master is in heaven; neither is there any respect of persons with Him" (Ibid.: 9) The first epistle of Peter (2:18, 19) goes further still: "Servants be subject to your masters with all fear, not only to the good and gentle, but also to the forward. For this is thankworthy, if a man for conscience toward God endure grief, suffering wrongfully."

These injunctions were repeated by the early Fathers, urging resignation with one's lot, however hard, because of the perfect freedom in the world to come. Ignatius warned the slave to serve his pagan master with greater zeal because he has no such prospect of future happiness as the Christian. The only voice raised in quiet dissent from this attitude toward slavery was that of Clement of Alexandria, the first of the Fathers to bring a full knowledge of Greek philosophy and culture to bear upon the interpretation of Christianity. There is a note of Stoicism in his insistence the "slaves are men like us" and are to be treated like Christians as they themselves would like to be treated—the Golden Rule in a new setting. Although he nowhere denounced slavery as an institution, he warned against maintaining too many in a household and insisted on their education and the oversight of morals as social obligations almost on a par with those of parents to children.

This high note was not maintained by the later Fathers, some of whom, like Gregory Nazianzen, while admitting equality among all partakers of the Lord's Supper, were slave owners themselves. The accent was upon compassion in human relationship; slavery in itself was to be accepted as any other natural calamity. Chrysostom added a new argument, that the more distinguished the slave the more it is encumbent upon him to continue in servitude, as it offers an excellent chance to influence the whole household in which he is held. It would be hard to find a more perfect example of sophistry twisted to false purpose; but Isidore of Pelusium surpassed it when he argued that slavery might be preferable to freedom if on the day of judgment the slave could argue that his sins were committed at the behest of his master. However, these extreme speculations of theologians were not in the minds of the practical clergy, who, from the fifth century on, even accepted recruits to their numbers from the servile class, although tending to limit this method of enfranchisement to those of outstanding qualities. A general emancipation of slaves was never thought of as a consequence of Christianity in the Roman world.

From this long excursus on slavery in the Roman world, we turn back to the more general effects of war economics. The vitality of the Mediterranean culture had come originally from the free, independent and intensely patriotic city states, whose energy and ingenuity had taken advantage of the natural opportunities of their surroundings for the purposes of trade and their own aggrandizement. Their conquest by Rome brought advantages which at first seemed to outweigh the costs which it imposed, but their gradual absorption into an autocratic empire seemed to rob them of much of their spirit, to which the chaos of the third century was as a death blow. Slowly but steadily the economics of war took its toll of the whole Western world. Tribute was no longer forthcoming and taxes could not be collected. The population declined. The miracle of Roman history was that the Empire could endure so long under these conditions; the explanation lies in the fact that, even in its decline, it maintained a greater degree of peace than any other state of the ancient world.

THE JUDGMENT OF HISTORY

The judgments of history are never final. They change from generation to generation, from age to age, because they are the projection into the past of our outlook and interests in the world in which we live. In proportion as our own horizon is enriched with greater knowledge of ourselves and of the things which influence our action, we are enabled to improve our understanding of what has happened to other people in the past.

It was but natural, therefore, that the growth of the social sciences in our own time should lead to a recasting of the perspectives of ancient history by making us more aware of the economic and social forces of which the purely political historian was only partially aware; but the social sciences themselves have suffered from a limitation which prevented them from dealing with the most important single activity in the formation and in the ultimate destruction of the antique world, the war system. The social sciences have, down to our day, dealt almost exclusively with society at peace. They have continued the tradition of Plato and Aristotle, Cicero and Augustine, concerning themselves with the problems of human association and welfare, of "life, liberty and the pursuit of happiness" at home and wherever there was freedom for their development. The polity of war, which the Greeks neglected, has not yet been brought within the scope of the social sciences. As long as this is the case, history remains fundamentally unadjusted to these sciences because it must deal with war fully as much, and at times even more, than with the data of peace.

Nowhere is this inadequacy more evident than in the history of Rome. It is true that there have been many important studies of the effect of the war system upon the Roman Republic and Empire, and the main results of these studies have been incorporated in the commonest textbooks; but the continuing effects of the war system upon the system of government, as well as upon the economic system, still offer a challenging field for the historian.

We have just seen how the economy of the antique world was falsified by the exploitation of the conquered as they supplied tribute and slaves to the victors. But in the field of government itself we come upon the striking fact that the only creative period in the history of Roman politics was that when the Republic was organizing itself for better government at home, and applying its experience in the extension of its rule over its conquests. The specialization of the functions of government, which produced magistrates of different kinds to deal with justice, money, morals and the like, was a creative process similar to that in the constitution of Athens. Persistent realism marked the treatment of colonies and allies and the grant of citizenship, a progress held in check by prejudice and caution, and yet perhaps all the stronger on that account. In short, so long as the conquests of the Roman Kingdom or Republic were of neighbors living close at hand who could be brought within the orbit of the city state as it expanded to cover all the surrounding territory, there was progress in the interplay of human rights and in the functioning of government itself; but as the Roman state extended to cover distant lands, this process yielded to that of increased military control until at last the whole political evolution was denatured by its very success.

From the time that the Imperator was able to establish the undifferentiated control of sovereignty over the whole state, controlling all the magistracies, down to the close of Roman history—that is throughout the whole imperial period—there was no real progress made in the art and science of government. From Tiberius to Diocletian and Constantine the process is one of increasing regimentation with a continual growth of tyranny, until not only government lost its capacity for adjustment but society itself became almost castelike in its rigidity. There was nothing in all this stretch of Roman history for later generations to copy, because there was a constant process of degeneration instead of growth. It is apparently an iron law of history that despotism produces still greater despotism. When it attempts to relax its control as, for instance, in France in the closing years of the reign of Napoleon III, it runs the danger of increasing its inadequacy in administration through laxness of control.

The tendency is the other way—to increase control—as is so clearly seen in the transformation of the Roman Empire from a state still bearing the outer marks of a republic to one accepting the oriental concept of divine monarchy. Byzantinism has become a synonym for unchanging routine in bureaucratic control. It is, or at least it seems to be, the one safest method of tyrannical government; because under its set forms of organization and administration there is no place for experiment, and experiment is always dangerous for autocratic powers.

In the two great fields of economics and government the history of Rome has lasting lessons for statesmanship, lessons never more pertinent than at the present time. Unfortunately, however, the basic fallacies of the Roman system, which ultimately undermined its strength and caused its downfall, were never clearly seen by the Romans themselves, although there were always thoughtful people who saw some of these consequences. The inability to see how militarized government ultimately leads toward disaster should not be charged up against the Romans as an indication of a lack of intelligence in the theory as well as in the practice of government; for it must be remembered that in the period of the Empire, Roman society bore all the marks of being less militarized than that of any other people in history before then. The *Pax Romana* which reigned inside the far-flung frontiers was a new experience for mankind. The splendor of this achievement was of a character to impose upon the imaginations of peoples who had once been its victims.

Not only was the sovereignty of the Empire universal, that is to say, covering all the Mediterranean world of antique culture, but it bore the marks of seeming permanence. In reality, however, all that was left by the fifth century was a hard shell, one which was easily broken by the battle-axes of its internal weakness, rather than because of any great strength in those who attacked it.

When one turns from this story of politics and government, with its bearing upon economics and social life, to the history of Roman law, it is like turning from a mausoleum to a structure charged with forces still vital in the world today. For Roman law, unlike Roman government, was the embodiment of the sense of justice in simple men and women working out their relations with each other on the basis of their own experience and of that of the jurists who knew the tradition of justice as it has been developed from other cases in the past. The Roman law was in essence like the English common law, an expression of reality in all its varied forms, but unlike the English law, it was generalized from sweeping concepts of high principles, for it was informed within the ethics of stoic philosophy and ultimately of Christian teaching. The real lasting inheritance of Rome was not the great creation of its military chieftains, but the body of Roman law.

CHAPTER XI

⁂

A SURVEY OF THE HISTORY OF THE
MIDDLE AGES

THE FIFTH CENTURY is, in a way, the beginning of the history of Europe. Until the hordes of Goths, Vandals, and Franks came out from the fastnesses beyond the Rhine and Danube and played their part upon the cleared arena of the empire itself, the history of the world was antique. The history of the later empire is still a part of the continuous but shifting history of the Mediterranean peoples. The civilization which the legions of Constantine protected was not the product of Rome; it was the work of an antiquity which even then stretched farther back, three times farther, than all the distance which separates his time from ours. The empire was all antiquity, fused into a gigantic unit, and protected by the legions drawn from every quarter of the world, from Spain to Syria. As it grew old its roots sank deeper into the past. When it had taken all that Greece had to offer in art and literature, the tongue of Greece gave free access to the philosophy of the orient, and as its pantheon filled with all the gods of the world, its thought became the reflex of that of the Hellenised east. If Rome conquered the ancient world, it was made captive in return. The last pagan god to shine upon the standards of the legions was Mithras, the Sun-god of the Persians,

Introduction to Volume VII of The Historians' History of the World (The Outlook Company, New York; The History Association, London, 1904), pp. xiii-xxi.

while Isis shared with Jupiter the temple on the Capitol. This world entrenched behind the bulwarks that stretched from Solway to Nineveh, brooding upon its past, was quickened with but one new thought,—and that was an un-Roman one,—the strange, unworldly, Christian faith. The peoples that had become subjects of Rome were now to own a high allegiance to one whom it had condemned as a Jewish criminal; on the verge of its own destruction the empire became Christian. It is the fashion to decry the evil influences of the environment of early Christianity, but it was the best that human history has ever afforded. How would it have fared with Christian doctrine if it had had to do with German barbarians instead of with Greek philosophers, who could fit the new truths into accordance with the teachings of their own antiquity, and Roman administrators who could forge from the molten enthusiasm of the wandering evangelists, the splendid structure of Catholicism. Before the storm burst which was to test the utility of all the antique civilisation, the church was already stronger than its protectors. And so, at the close, the empire stood for two things, antiquity and Christianity.

In structure, too, the government and society were no longer Roman in anything but name. The administration of the empire had become a Persian absolutism, and its society was verging towards oriental caste. If the art, philosophy, and science of the ancients could be preserved only by such conditions, it was well that they should pass away. The empire in ceasing to be Roman had taken up the worst as well as the best of the past, and as it grew respectable under Stoic or Christian teaching, it grew indifferent to the high impulses of patriotism, cold and formal outwardly, wearying inwardly of its burden.

The northern frontiers of this empire did not prove to be an unbroken barrier to the Germans, however, and for two centuries before the sack of Rome, they had been crossing, individually or in tribes, into the peaceful stretches of the civilised world. Their tribal wars at home made all the more alluring the attractions of the empire. For a long time the Roman armies kept these barbarians from anything resembling conquest, but even the vanquished who survived defeat found a home in Roman villas or among the federated troops. The fifth century merely brought to light what had been long preparing, and it took but few invaders to accomplish the final overthrow. The success of these last invasions has imposed an exaggeration of their extent upon historians. They were not true wanderings of nations, but rather incursions of adventurers. The barbarians we call by the name of Goths were a mixture of many nations, while the army of Clovis was hardly more than a single Roman legion. Yet the important fact is that the invasions of the fifth century were successful, and with them the new age begins.

There were two movements which brought about the overthrow of the Roman Empire; one among the barbarians, the other within the empire itself. The Huns were pressing from the east upon the German peoples, whom long civil wars had weakened to such a degree that they must yield or flee. Just as the strength of the Roman frontier was to be tested whether it could hold back the combined impulsion of Teuton and Hun, the West Goth within the empire struck at its heart. The capture of Rome by Alaric did not end the empire; it does not seem to have created the universal consternation with which we now associate it. Poets and orators still spoke of Rome as the eternal city, and Alaric's successor, Ataulf, sought the service of that state which he felt unable to destroy. But the sack of Rome was not the worst of the injuries inflicted by Alaric; it was one of the slightest. A disaster had been wrought before he reached the walls of Rome for which all the zeal of Ataulf could not atone. For, so the story runs, Stilicho the last heroic defender of the old empire called in the garrisons from along the frontiers to stay the Gothic advance. The incursions of Alaric within the confines of Italy opened the way to the hesitating but still eager barbarians along the Rhine. The storm bursts at once; the Germans are across the Rhine before Alaric can reach Rome. Instead of their German forests, they have the vineyards of the Moselle and the olive orchards of Aquitaine. The proud nobles in Gaul, unaccustomed to war or peril, can but stand by and watch while their villas lend their plunder to the raiders. After all, the storm,—this one at least,—soon passes. The Suabians and the Vandals cross the Pyrenees and the West Goths come up from Italy, with the varnish of culture upon them, to repress their lawless cousins, and drive them into the fastnesses of Leon or across to Africa. Fifteen years after the invasion, the poet Ausonius is again singing of the vine-clad hills of the Moselle, and their rich vintage. Gaul has been only partly changed. The noble Sidonius Apollinaris dines with the king Theodoric and is genially interested in his Burgundian neighbors who have settled in the eastern part. By the middle of the century, unaided by the shadow emperors in Italy, this mixture of peoples, conscious of the value of their present advantages, unite to defeat the invading Huns at the battle of Chalons. But another and more barbarous people is now taking possession of the North. The Franks are almost as different from the Visigoths as the Iroquois from the Norman Crusaders. Continually recruited from the forests of the lower Rhine, they do not cut themselves off from their ancient home and lose themselves in the midst of civilisation; they first break the Roman state north of the Loire and then crowd down the Visigoths towards Spain. By the year 500 Gaul has become Frankland, and the Franks have become Catholic Christians. Add to these facts the Saxon conquest of England, the Ostrogothic kingdom in Italy, and the overthrow of the empire in the West, and we have a survey of part of the transformation which the fifth century wrought in Western Europe. With it we enter upon the Middle Ages.

Such is our introduction to the new page of history. Behind us are now the fading glories of old Rome; the antique society is outwardly supplanted by the Teutonic peoples. But the number of the invaders was comparatively few and the world they conquered large in extent, and it had been Romanizing for four hundred years. The antique element still persisted; in the East it retained its sovereignty for another thousand years, in the West it compromised with the Teutonic element in the creation of a Roman Empire on a German basis, which was to last until the day of Napoleon, and in the recognition of the authority of the Roman hierarchy. The Church and the Empire, these two institutions of which we hear most in the Middle Ages, were both of them Roman, but both owed their political exaltation to the German Carolingian kings. It was Boniface the Saxon, that "proconsul of the Papacy," who bound the Germans to the Roman See; but Pepin lent his strong aid, and Charlemagne doubly sealed the compact.

The coronation of the great king of the Franks as emperor of the Romans forecasts a line of history that was not followed, however, in the way he had in mind. The union of Teuton and Roman, or better, of Teuton and antiquity, was not destined to proceed so simply and so peacefully. Instead of an early revival of the great past, the world went down into the dark age, and was forced to struggle for many centuries slowly upward towards the day when it could again appreciate the antiquity it had forgotten. In other words the Middle Ages intervened to divide the renaissance of Charlemagne from that which culminated in Erasmus. How can we explain the phenomenon? What is its significance? It is essential that we face these questions if we would understand in the slightest the history of Europe. And yet as we examine the phenomenon itself we may find some reconstruction of our own ideas of it will be necessary.

Let us now turn to the Middle Ages. We shall find something of novelty in the act, for in all the world's history there is no other period which ordinarily excites in us so little interest as this. Looking back across the centuries from the heights of Modern Times, we have been taught to train our eyes upon the far but splendid table-lands of Rome, and to ignore the space that intervenes, as though it were nothing but a dreary blank between the two great epochs of our history. Dark Ages and Middle Ages are to most of us almost synonymous terms,—a thousand years filled with a confusion, with no other sign of life than the clash of battle or the chanting of hymns, a gruesome and unnatural world, dominated by either martial or monastic ideals, and void of almost everything we care for or seek after to-day.

Let us look at the details. The break-up of the Roman world which resulted in the first planting of the modern nations, did not cause that vast calamity which we call the Dark Age. The invasion of the Teutons and the infusion of their vigour into the effete society of southern Europe was not a fatal blow to civilization. Rude as they were when first they crossed the frontiers of the empire, the German peoples, and especially their leaders, gave promise that almost in their own day whatever was of permanent value in the Roman world would be re-incorporated into the new society. This series of recoveries had to be repeated with every new people, but it finally seemed about to culminate in the wider renaissance of Charlemagne. By the year 800 it looked as though Europe were already on the clear path to modern times. But just as the young Teutonic civilization reached the light, a second wave of invasion came dashing over it. The Vikings, whom Charlemagne's aged eyes may have watched stealing past the hills of Calais, not only swept the northern seas, but harried Frankland from the Rhine to the Rhone, until progress was at a standstill and the only thought of the ninth century was that of defence. Then the Hungarians came raiding up the Danube valley, and the Slavs pressed in upon the North. Along the coasts of the Mediterranean the Moorish corsairs were stifling the weak commerce of Italian towns, and landing they attacked such ports as Pisa and even sacked a part of Rome. The nascent civilization of the Teutons was forced to meet a danger such as would call for all the legions of Augustus. No wonder the weak Carolingian kings sank under the burden and the war lords of the different tribes grew stronger as the nerveless state fell defenceless before the second great migration, or maintained but partial safety in the natural strongholds of the land.

In such a situation self-defence became a system. The palisade upon some central hill, the hedge and thicket in the plain, or the ditch in the morass, became the shelter and the centre of life for every neighborhood that stood in the track of the new barbarians. The owner of the fastness led his neighbors and his tenants to battle; they gave him their labor for his protection, the palisades grew into stone walls and the "little camps" (castella) became the feudal castles. Those grim, battlemented towers that rise up before us out of the dark age, were the signs of hope for the centuries that followed. Society was saved, but it was transformed. The protection in a time of danger became oppression in a time of safety, and the feudal tyranny fastened upon Europe with a strength that cities and kings could only moderate but not destroy.

From the tenth century to the present, however, the history of Europe is that of one continuous evolution, slow, discouraging at times, with many tragedies to record and many humiliations to be lived down. But all in all, no century from that to this has ended without some signal achievement in one line or another, in England, in France, in Italy, or in Germany. By the middle of the tenth century the first unyielding steps had been taken when the Saxon kings of Germany began to build their walled towns along the upper Elbe, and to plant the German colonists along the eastern frontiers, as Rome had long before shielded the northern frontiers of civilization. By the end of the century the Magyars have settled in the middle Danube, under a king at once Christian and saint, and the greatest king of the Danes is champion of Christendom. In another fifty years the restless Normans are off on their conquest again, but now they carry with them to England and to Italy the invigorating touch of a youthful race who are in the front of their time, and not its enemies.

The age of chivalry was also the age of the universities. Turn from the knight-errant to the wandering scholar if we would find the true key to the age, but still must leave it in the realm of romance. Few have ever guessed that the true Renaissance was not in the Florence of Lorenzo nor the Rome of Nicholas V, but rather in that earlier century when the great jurists of Bologna restored for all future time the code of Justinian. The greatest heritage of Rome was not its literature nor its philosophy, but its law. The best principles that had been evolved in all the ancient world, all progress,—all these invaluable truths were brought to light again through the revival of the Roman law, and incorporated again by mediæval legists into the structure of society two centuries before the literary Renaissance of the Italian cities. The crowds of students who flocked to Bologna to study law, and who formed their guild or university on so strange a basis, mark the dawn of modern times fully as well as the academy at Florence or the foundation of a Vatican library. Already the science of politics was revived and the problems of government given practical and scientific test.

Then came the gigantic tragedy of the Hundred Years' War, retarding for more than a century that growth of industry and commerce upon which even the political structure rests. But while English and French alike are laying waste the fairest provinces of France, the University of Paris is able to dictate the policy of the universal church and for a generation to reduce the greatest absolutism of the age, that of the papacy, to the restrictions of parliamentary government. The Council of Constance was in session in the year of the battle of Agincourt. And, meanwhile, there is another development, far more important than the battles of the Black Prince or the marches of Du Guesclin. Commerce thrives along the shores of Italy, and in spite of their countless feuds and petty wars, the cities of Tuscany and Lombardy grow ready for the great artistic awakening. The story of the Middle Ages, like that of our own times, comes less from the camp fire than from the city square. And even there, how much is omitted! The caravans that line the rude bazaar could never reach it but for the suppression of the robbers by the way, largely the work of royalty. The wealth of the people is the opportunity for culture, but without the security of law and order, neither the one nor the other can be attained. In the last analysis, therefore, the protection of society while it developed is the great political theme of the Middle Ages. And now it is time to confess that we have touched upon but one half of that theme. It was not alone feudalism that saved Europe, nor royalty alone that gave it form. Besides the castle there was another asylum of refuge, the church. However loath men have been in recent years to confess it, the mediæval church was a gigantic factor in the preservation and furthering of our civilization.

The church was the only potent state in Europe for centuries,—an institution vastly different from our idea of it to-day. It was not only the religious monitor and the guardian of the salvation of mankind, it took up the duty of governing when the Roman Empire was gone. It helped to preserve the best things of antiquity; for when the barbarians were led to destroy what was of no use to them, it was the church, as Rashdall says, that widened the sphere of utility. It, more than the sword of Charlemagne, tamed the barbarian Germans, and through its codes of penance with punishments almost as severe as the laws of Draco, it curbed the instincts of savagery, and taught our ancestors the ethics of Moses while promising them the salvation of Christ. It assumed much of the administration of justice in a lawless age, gave an inviolate asylum to the persecuted, and took in hand the education of the people. Its monks were not only the pioneer farmers in the fastnesses of the wilderness, but their entertainment of travellers made commerce possible. Its parish church furnished a nursery for democracy in the gatherings at the church door for counsel and deliberation. It opened to the sons of peasants a career that promised equality with the haughtiest seigneur, or even the dictation over kings. There was hardly a detail of daily life which did not come under the cognizance or control of the church,—questions of marriage and legitimacy, wills, oaths, even warfare, came under its surveillance.

But in depicting this wonderful system which so dominated Europe in the early Middle Ages, when kings were but shadows or military dictators over uncertain realms, we must be careful not to give too much of an air of religiosity to the whole Middle Age. The men of the Middle Ages did not all live in a cowl. Symonds in his brilliant history of the Renaissance in Italy likens the whole mediæval attitude to that of St. Bernard, the greatest of its ascetics. St. Bernard would walk by the blue waters of Lake Geneva intent only upon his rosary and prayer. Across the lake gleam the snows of Mont Blanc,—a sight no traveller forgets when once he has seen it; but a saint, with his cowl drawn over his eyes, sees only his own sin and the vision of the last judgment. So, says Symonds, humanity walked along its way, a careful pilgrim unheeding the beauty or delight of the world around. Now this is very striking, but is it true? First of all, the Middle Ages, as ordinarily reckoned, include a stretch of ten centuries. We have already seen how unlike these centuries were, how they differed from each other as much as any centuries before or since. The nineteenth is hardly more different from the eighteenth than the twelfth was different from the eleventh. So much for the universalization as we go up and down the centuries; it can hardly apply to all. Some gave us the Chansons des Gestes, the Song of Roland, the legends of Charlemagne and his paladins. Others gave us the delicious lyrics of the minnesingers and troubadours, of Walter von der Vogelweide and Bertran de Born. And as for their variety, we must again recall that the same century that gave us St. Francis of Assisi—that jongleur of God— and the Divine Comedy, gave us also Magna Carta and representative government.

But even if we concede that the monks dominated mediæval society as Symonds paints it, we must not imagine that they were all St. Bernards. Few indeed—the sainted few—were alone able to abstract themselves so completely from this life as to be unconscious of their surroundings. The successive reform movements, Cluniac, Carthusian, Cistercian, beginning in poverty and ending in wealth and worldly influence, show what sort of men wore the cowl. The monks were not all alike; some were worldly, some were religious, some were scholars, and some were merely indolent. The monastery was a home for the scholar, a refuge for the disconsolate, and an asylum for the disgraced. And a monk might often be a man whose sensibilities, instead of being dull, were more sharply awake than our own to-day. His faith kindled an imagination that brought the next world down into his daily life, and one who is in communion with eternity is an unconscious poet as well as a devotee. Dante's great poem is just the essence of a thousand years of such visions.

Those phases of the Middle Ages farthest removed from our times and our habits of thought are not necessarily sombre. They are gilded with the most alluring light that ever brightened humanity— the hope and vision of immortality.

It has seemed necessary to say this much at least about the ecclesiasticism of the Middle Ages so that we may get a new or at least a more sympathetic point of view as we study its details. Humanity was not in a comatose condition for a thousand years, to wake up one fine day and discover itself again in a Renaissance. Such an idea gives false conception of both the Middle Ages and that slow change by which men acquired new interests,—the Renaissance.

What then was the Italian Renaissance? What was its significance and its result? First of all no new birth of the human spirit, as we have been commonly taught, could come after the wonderful twelfth and busy thirteenth centuries. It would sound strange to the wandering jongleur or the vagabond student, whose satirical and jovial songs of the twelfth century we still sing in our student societies, to be told that he had no joy in the world, no insight into its varying moods, no temperament capable of the comprehension of beauty. If any man ever "discovered himself," surely that keen-witted, freedom-living scholar, the goliard, was the man, and yet between him and the fall of Constantinople, that commonest date for the Renaissance, there are two hundred years or more. A little study of preceding centuries shows a world brimming with life and great with the promise of modern times. Lawyers were governing in the name of kings; universities were growing in numbers and influence. Not all the men at the universities of Paris or Oxford were busy counting how many angels could dance on the point of a needle, as Lord Bacon implies in his denunciation of the scholastics. If half of them,—and that is a generous estimate,—were busied over theology, not all that half were examining it for their religious edification. Their interests were scientific. In a way they were scientists,—scientists of the world to come,—not of this transient life. They were analyzing theology with about the same attitude of mind as that of the physicist of to-day. When one examines a world which he cannot yet reach, or a providence whose ways are not as the ways of man, he naturally will accept the authority of those whom he believes to be inspired, if he is to make even a little headway into the great unknown. The scholastics stretched the meaning of the word inspired and accepted authority too easily. But they faced their problem with what seems something like a scientific spirit even if they had not yet attained a scientific method. And I may add in passing that to my mind the greatest tragedy of the human intellect is just here,—in this story of the abused scholastics. Starting out confident that all God's ways can be comprehended and reduced to definite data, relying in calm security upon the power of the human intellect to comprehend the ways of Divine governance, they were forced point by point, through irreconcilable conclusions and inexplicable points of controversy, to admit that this doctrine and that, this fact and that one, lay outside the realms of reason and must be accepted on faith. Baffled in its vast endeavour to build up a science of things divine the reason of man turned from the task and grappled with the closer problems of the present world. If the work of the scholastics was futile, as so many claim, it was a grand futility that reaches to tragedy. But out of its very futility grew the science of to-day.

And now with all this intellectual activity of which scholasticism is only a part, where did the so-called Renaissance come in? By the year 1300 the problem of the scholastics was finished. In the works of Thomas Aquinas lay codified and systematized the whole positive product of their work. Not until after that was their work empty and frivolous, but when scholasticism turned back upon itself, even the genius of the great Duns Scotus discovered more and more its futility. Men of culture began to find it distasteful; they did not care to study law,—the other main interest. It was time for a new element in the intellectual realm. The need was no sooner felt than supplied. The study of the antique pagan world afforded scholars and men of leisure the desired change. The discovery of the antique world was not a new process; but the features that had been ignored before, the art and literature of the pagan world, now absorbed all attention. The "humanities" gradually crowded their way into university curricula, especially in Germany and England, and from the sixteenth century to the present day the humanities have been the dominant study at the universities. Looking over the era of the Renaissance, we commonly begin it in the fourteenth century, just where our own previous sketch of the other intellectual conditions stopped. The age of Petrarch was its dawn. France and England, where most progress had been made before, were now to be absorbed in the barbarism of international and civil wars; and so the last stage of that long Renaissance which we call the Middle Ages became the task and the glory of Italy.

It may seem at first as if, in exalting the achievements of the Middle Ages, we have undervalued the work of the humanists. We must give full credit to the influence of that new knowledge, that new criterion, and especially to that new and healthy criticism which came with the Italian Renaissance. Its work in the world was absolutely necessary if modern society was to take up properly its heritage of all those splendid ages which adorned the Parthenon and made the Forum the centre of the world. All the intellectual energy which had gone into antique society must be made over into our own. But after all, the roots of our society are Teutonic and Christian even more than they are Roman or antique. We must learn to date our modern times not merely from the literary revival which witnessed the recovery of a long-lost pagan past; but from the real and splendid youth of Europe when it grappled with the earnest problems of law and order and put between itself and the Viking days the barriers of the national state,—king and people guarding the highways of the world for the protection of the caravans that made the cities. It is as essential for us to watch those boats that ascended the Rhone and the Rhine, and the merchants whose tents were pitched at the fairs of Champagne, as it is to know who discovered the proper derivation of Greek and Latin words.

CHAPTER XII

⤳⤶

THE NEW HISTORY

HISTORY BEGAN in Greece, not the Greece of Athens on the mainland, but on the rocky coast of Asia Minor where the western shore of Asia crumbles and plunges into the Aegean. Here, there was a little group of cities which contributed more to the intellectual history of the world, I imagine, than all the empires of the Orient. They lay by the deep sheltered bays of that rocky coast, where the old-time caravans arrived from the East, down through the river valley of the Meander, to bring their trade for the ships that came and went from the Nile Valley and up the Black Sea. Nursed by such trade, Miletus, for one, grew rich, and about two millennia and a half ago its traders went off in the ships and caravans to see the world. One of these travelers, named Hecataeus, a thinker as well as a traveler, went down into Egypt and talked with the priests in Thebes. A follower of his, Herodotus, tells about him. He says that when this Hecataeus got inside the temple chambers of Thebes, he boasted about the fact that his sixteenth ancestor was a god. The Egyptian priests remarked that that must be strange, as they had something in the next room that hardly fitted his tale. So they took him into it, and there he saw stretched out before him, in a long row on two sides of the hall, figure after figure, statues of great nobles of Egypt; and they told him that these were their ancestors, and that their line stretched back hundreds of years. And

Reprinted from the University of Pittsburgh Bulletin, December, 1916.

they intimated, kindly but clearly, that the Greek ancestors could hardly have been gods in recent times, while theirs were only human.

Then Hecataeus went back to Greece and wrote a book and began it with these words: "I am going to write what I deem true, for the legends of the Greeks seem to me manifold and laughable." With these ringing words, like the phrases of Voltaire in the eighteenth century, he began the critical study of history. Contrasting the ancient world in Egypt with the modern Greece, he corrected the perspective of the centuries. Then as he returned from his travels in Asia, as well as in Egypt, he was also to show the Greeks of his own day and own country in Western Asia that there were new facts outside the narrow range of their little city's life—not simply facts of the past, but facts of the present—which must be taken into account if one were to have an adequate story of the origin of civilization.

In the researches of Hecataeus two things stand out; in the first place, a corrected perspective of the centuries; in the second place, a wider scope of investigation, and a consideration of the arrangement of all the social data which go to make up the complete story of the rise of cities and of civilization.

At the present time we are practically in the position of Hecataeus. We are at the dawn of a new history.[1] In my own time, since I began to teach history, the subject has been remade in almost as thorough-going and effective a manner as it was remade or corrected by these Greek thinkers who first became critics of the past —as thorough-going in spite of all the achievements of history, in spite of all the great historians, the Gibbons, the Macaulays, the Carlyles, the Michelets of our own day. For in our own twentieth century a new historical science has begun to join with the others which are rapidly reforming the content of knowledge. And I might as well take it up as Hecataeus did, both critical of the past on the one hand and its orthodox tradition, and on the other hand aware of a wider horizon than in the old-time narratives. For when Hecataeus talked of "history" in his Ionian Greek, it was the equivalent of the term "philosophy" in Athens, or "science" in the modern world; it meant the inquiry into the accounts of the past and present.

From that double point of view I mean to take up my story now.

In the first place, in reference to the time perspective. I am ready to go as far as to say that until the nineteenth and twentieth centuries the human race had almost no time-sense. It lived in the current world of the day; most people do still. The lives of most people, it seems to me, are about like a trolley ride from one point to another, getting on at the street and getting off at the end, and dealing with immediate facts along the way, with no sense whatever of how far the track of time pushes on to the boundaries of human experience. Until the nineteenth or twentieth centuries we had almost no time-perspective whatever, because, (beyond a few centuries,) the story of the past was lost in the midst of legend and myth. There were only a few years in ancient Roman history—back to 752. In Greek history we could take it only to the story of Homer. Down into the Hebrew past we carried things further, but still less than four thousand years beyond the foundation of Rome, and there we came to a definite stop. This was the limit of the time-perspective, until the latter part of the nineteenth century. Since then fifty to one hundred thousand years of the human past have been added to that old time limit. Even up to the end of the nineteenth century there was almost nothing known of the life which lies beyond written record. Now we have a clear trace of the existence of humanity, I won't say society, but humanity, before the glacial period was over. When the glaciers swept the valleys into the seas, when the Thames emptied into the Rhine, there was humanity, there were men and women wandering over the present battle fields of the Somme, where scholars pick up the remains of their artisanship to this day. Over on the downs of Southern England we have more and more traces of it. And then, as that great ice sheet receded, the caves in which some of them had taken refuge in Southern France were blocked, other soil came down and completely filled them. Thousands and thousands of years passed and they were lost to history. From the end of the ice age to the twentieth century of our era, not a soul knew anything about them. I am speaking now in general. Of course some findings were made back in the middle of the last century, but it was not until the twentieth century that these anthropological data, hidden by the centuries, were brought to light so that we can now tell, not only that man was there, but the work that he was doing. We can find in the caves of Spain and Portugal art which rivals, in painting at

least, that of the futurist of the present time. These things have
been definitely brought to light. They are now in our text books.
No text book written before the beginning of the twentieth century
is worth referring to now with regard to anything which deals
with the origins of history and of civilization.

We have now a definite story to tell, not only of prehistoric
Greece, but also of prehistoric Egypt and Babylon. We can trace,
dimly as yet, throughout the centuries, the stories of the great
Celtic culture north of the Alps, such as that centered near the
shores of Lake Geneva. The history of it is not yet in any text book.
South of the Alps there had been a similar development, but more
rapid, giving us the cultures of antiquity. North of the Alps the
great plains, vast morasses and forests and colder climate retarded
civilization; the rivers ran the wrong way, emptying north. The
half-savage tribes were never secure against the advance of enemies
and could not find safety behind cliffs that stood like city walls
above a fertile valley or a seaport, as in the south. That, in the face
of such obstacles, the northern peoples achieved such culture as
that of La Tène, whose deft artisanship is seen today in the museums
of France, shows what possibilities there were for progress in these
people when the material conditions could be overcome—as Caesar
and the Romans taught them might be done. For the Roman roads
and the Mediterranean *mercatores* laid the basis for a new unity
which gave the promise of political as well as material advance.
The history of northern Europe now goes back to these primitive
origins along the lines of archeology.

But the science of history at the present time has just as definitely
widened its scope as it has lengthened it. In the same way that it has
pushed back across the centuries it had also increased in the number of subjects with which it deals. The old histories, the text books
that I used when I was a boy, had an orthodox definite line of facts
which any person could memorize, and knowing the book meant
knowing history! That orthodox line of facts dealt with politics,
and politics was conceived of as something either romantic, where
you had kings and battles, or something abstract when one read of
constitutions and the problems solved by statesmen. Moreover that
history was shut apart from the rest of the curriculum—not only in
the secondary school, but in the college. One never thought of
co-relation. Economics was a study of the present world; philos-

ophy was a study of the spiritual side of life; science was the study of the material world. History was quite different from any of these. It did not deal with economics, or thought, or science, or art—except when one struck the Renaissance, where some of the Italian art was mentioned, and we heard of Raphael and Michael Angelo. This peculiar, traditional story began with the ancient city states and dealt with medieval Europe, which had just been founding the state system and the national state, and its straight and narrow theme was regarded as the peculiar product of the historian.

In the closing part of the nineteenth century and the opening of the twentieth, it has become obvious that such a story is not only limited in its horizon but is thoroughly misleading. For it fell back —since it was interested only in the development of a certain line of facts—upon the contributory social sciences to offer an explanation for its own particular line of data, and then disowned them as historical. It never stopped to inquire whether it was intelligible in itself. Moreover, it had certain fables which it imposed, thoughtlessly, in its traditional, conservative way, upon the reader. Now we are questioning them, testing its premises, reconstructing its outlines. Just as Hacataeus said: "These old Greek stories are ridiculous with their gods. This is a fabulous history and we will make it common sense," so the new history analyzes the narratives which are imposed on the minds of modern students. And it finds some fables just as unfounded as those he referred to. Among these, to take but one, has been the fable of nationality. For it took for granted in an age which had not applied economics to history, in an age which had not studied anthropology, not only that the nations of history were racially distinguishable, but that each had a peculiar gift and genius as shown in its creations or institutions. Green's History of the English People was a wonderful book, so were Freeman's works, and so was the constitutional history of Bishop Stubbs (although I find that the eminent bishop's name is a myth to my students despite the great reputation he once had). But these historians in the middle of the nineteenth century proceeded to write history upon the presumption that the English race, pure blooded Teutons, isolated from the contaminating influence of the rest of the world, were working out their principles of liberty inherent in the Teuton character or at least revealed in its earliest days. The explanation of the English political system was that this peculiar people, left to itself, fulfilled its mission. Green starts his English history in the marshes of the lower Elbe. Freeman tells us that the Normans came with a little fresher blood from the north to invigorate the Anglo-Saxon—the Danes had been still more Teuton—and this pure-blooded race developed what was inherent in it.

Now, as a matter of fact, this type of nationalist history is largely fallacious. In this case, we know that the old Celtic population was not entirely wiped out by the Saxons. There is sufficient evidence to show that there was intermingling. Even in Serbia, in the First World War, in spite of the German invasion and the Serbian flight into Albania, there were Serbs left behind, especially the women and children. We forget how much history has been written from the standpoint of the men alone. In dealing with race we must remember that historic races are those which have exchanged and mingled blood by way of conquest or settlement, from the earliest times. There is no pure race in Europe and therefore nothing can be said about the varying capacities of the different peoples.

But if the English people are not a race with special aptitudes and tastes, what has caused the triumph of the English institutions? For, of course, I admit that the English institutions, evolved by the English people, have been so excellent as to be copied the world over. There must be some explanation in history. If it is not special racial aptitude, what is it? We have to turn from sweeping generalizations to detailed study.

Look at the evolution of European society in the broadest possible way. In the first place we see that the society of the Middle Ages was agricultural. The nexus between people was land. That, of course, has long been in all our text books, but the implications were not developed. So long as that society was agricultural, advance was impossible beyond very limited horizons. The change came when the use of money loosened up the relations between them. That is what we call the dawn of the capitalistic era. In England you can trace the story from the Norman Conquest down. At the time of the Norman Conquest, Domesday tells us that England was an agricultural country, the land being held by feudal lords and divided up among his vassals in several strips. There was almost no income for the King except from agriculture. When you come on to Henry II's time, you will find that he wants to get money for his army, to police the roads, to pay officers in cash, and to find the money he goes about it in ways important for English constitutional history, but too obscure to discuss here. In the next century, the question of business, private and national, becomes so important that it is necessary to secure somebody representative of those who have the money to vote it. So Parliament came into being. But when they—especially the Commoners—gave the money, they wanted the right to petition the king for the redress of grievances. Then when they petitioned they put their petition into the form of a bill, in the form in which they wanted it answered so that the right of petitioning became the instrument of law-making in the hands of the representatives of the people.

Over in France in the same thirteenth century, feudalism abounded everywhere. But the Crusades and trade with the East were bringing in commerce; industry and the new business were stirring in the towns. This was especially true in the valley of the Seine. Paris was growing rich; its walls were rebuilt to take in the enlarged city; its streets were partly paved—a wonderful and extravagant thing. Notre Dame was rising; the University was begun; and, more than all, the lawyers had come to help carry on the new business of both merchant and king. The king made over part of his palace to them—and they are still there, in the Palais de Justice, though the king has gone. By the middle of the thirteenth century the modern national state was beginning, just as effectively in France as it was beginning at the same time in England. By the end of that century the problem of money was causing the French kings to wage a serious war with the Papacy—between Philip the Fourth and Boniface VIII. Philip seized the money from the church and he got the bourgeois to back him up. He also seized the treasure of the Knights Templar, the wealthiest corporation in France. Capitalistic politics have begun. At the end of the thirteenth century it would seem that the people of France and England were singularly alike in their attitudes.

Now turning to Germany. Bismarck and von Buelow have said that the German has not the same kind of political capacity as that to be found in France and England. When one looks back over German history during the Middle Ages, as presented in our histories, this seems borne out. The weakness of the medieval empire is emphasized throughout its history. But, as a matter of fact, in the purely landed ages of history the king of the Germans was as power-ful as those in France. His weakness lay in the impossible task he attempted. So long as the Emperor had to fall back upon landed estates he could never rule the world. The emperors extended their estates as they did in France and sought to gather in their income from them by sending their counts of the palace (Counts Palatine) to collect their agricultural rents and dues. The counts in time es-tablished themselves on the soil instead. The emperors employed as well the bishops of the Church, misusing their appointing power to try to centralize their government; but this brought them the opposition of the Papacy. In fact all their devices failed because of lack of money. They couldn't hire low-born men whom they could at any time discharge, because they lacked the revenue to do so. So long as a king has to lean on nobles to do his bidding, their very importance as servants of the Crown makes for their independence of it. So, back in the feudal age, Germany failed, not because Ger-mans as such couldn't organize a nation, but because the country lacked the business basis of politics.

Then money came in in the thirteenth century and what was happening to Germany? It was just at the end of the Hohenstaufen period. There was, especially at that time, the anarchy of civil war, and rival cities and princes, rather than the emperor, seized the ad-vantages of business incomes for themselves. The lesser states bene-fitted from the new regime. The emperor did not get a chance to do what was done in England and France, use the power and ad-vantage which had been won by his headship of a land state to monopolize the power or advantage of a business state.

The fate of Germany was decided then, just at the close of the thirteenth century. It became a land of lesser kingdoms with no great emperor. The organization of national business began at the close of the Middle Ages. But it had been going only a while when it became clear that there would be a scarcity of money in Europe generally, partly because Europe is poor in metals, but mainly be-cause of the drain of money towards the Orient. They were im-porting goods from China, India and Arabia, and all the while millions of guldens were passing to the East. Had this gone on for long, Europe would have gotten to the point where it might have been held, for a period at least, to the agricultural stage, which was just beginning to pass.

The discovery of America was of the greatest significance because it supplied Europe with money. Besides, it transformed the center of Europe from around the Mediterranean to the northern and western seashores. If during the fifteenth century one ignores all this and keeps one's eyes fastened on Italian art and Martin Luther, one misses the larger significance of that great age. For modern civilization came not so much by way of the Italian artists, or even the humanists, as by way of the market place and the open sea. Commerce stimulated science and whetted the thirst for knowledge in the great secular world. It was the enlightened middle class which really gave birth to a new intelligence which gave history a new direction. The two economic facts which stand out as determining this movement, were, as has just been intimated, the influx of gold from America and the cheapness of sea freight.

Turn for a moment to this latter question. Just think what a caravan has to face as it brings the goods from the Orient. There is a vast desert barrier, beginning with the Sahara, continuing across the Red Sea into Arabia; then a mountain barrier in Persia, rising into the impassable highlands which Marco Polo found the hardest in his passage to the Orient. Then into the Hindu Kush and the Himalayas, the Roof of the World. On one side lies Europe, on the other Asia. Through their mountains and deserts the caravans must go. Take passage with one bringing its goods from the spice island, up the Ganges to the bazaar say, at Delhi. Then other merchants take the goods and carry them up to the hill country, along that road which Kipling so well describes, perhaps to Kandahar or Samarkand. One must pay ten to twenty per cent profit here, twenty to thirty there; there are heavy expenses for goods and lodging and for armed escorts. Finally the goods arrive at Nineveh of ancient days or medieval Bagdad. After crossing another desert the few goods that can be carried on the back of a few camels are brought to the coast of Asia Minor,—where Hecataeus once could have seen them—Damascus or Beirut. Then the Venetian galleys come and take them to Nuremberg, Munich and the other cities of southern Germany.

Sometimes they avoid the desert by Arab ships from the Indus, through the Persian Gulf and the Red Sea to Alexandria, and since there are fewer bazaars, fewer camels, fewer men, these traders can enable the merchants of Alexandria to outsell the merchants of

Damascus. Then, in a still larger way, Portugal goes all the way by water, and it can outsell Venice. When Vasco da Gama came back from his second voyage to India, in 1502, pepper was sold on the wharves of Lisbon at a price which brought ruin to Venice, and it has never recovered from that day to this. If anyone wants to see the effects of economics on history let him spend a while in Venice, that ancient museum, left untouched by the ravages of time. Along its canals rise the palaces of medieval merchants, but their modern occupants do not control the trade of Europe. There in the Square of St. Mark you can see the trophies of Venetian oriental conquests, but no new trophies have been added; German merchants and bankers go there only as tourists now, where once they bought the products of Asia. It is a silent city, left apart from the great current of world affairs. But go north and see London Bridge, or go to Antwerp and you will find there in the might and wonder of a modern city, the proof that the men of business in the fifteenth century began a greater creation than lay within the power of even the genius of a Michael Angelo. The impersonal forces, the dynamics of business, transformed the history of Europe, cultural and political, as well as economic and so made possible the new era of progressive change we think of as modern.

But the modern world and modern history had still a more significant revolution which has cut our era from all preceding more definitely than the pre-historic world was cut off from the historic. I refer to the revolution due to science.

It is part of the old traditional history that modern science came out of the Italian Renaissance. Now, as a matter of fact, the ancient world had almost nothing to offer as a stimulus towards modern science. Science was the one thing in which antiquity was particularly weak. Had they developed science in ancient Greece and Rome, these civilizations perhaps would not have fallen. But instead of developing science they were more interested in abstract philosophical problems, or more interested in the amassing of booty— which is all very well if it can be safeguarded by sufficient social force; but without the alliance of the forces of nature those of society alone are weak. As Professor Davis put it in his book on the Influence of Wealth in Imperial Rome: "Had Rome been as interested in the mystery of boiling water and the thunder storm, as it was concerned over the theories of philosophy, she might still never have fallen." In any case the Humanists added to the classical heritage of the Middle Ages the study of Plato, and Plato is the last place in the world to go for the study of science. He carried the ideas away from science and its sordid details, and centered attention in the realm of ideals.

Modern science mainly came by itself, I think, from the need of the hour. People became interested in a real world. It was opening out before them, and they were anxious to understand it and get the forces of nature at their disposal; and the only way was to work with the forces of nature. So we have a dawn of experimentation.

This recalls the point I wished to make earlier. No one nation showed a special capacity for science, except as stimulated by special circumstances. Then one nation was as ready as another to contribute. The dawn of modern science was a part of that general movement of enlightenment in which all humanity was to share. Take, as an example, the history of the invention of such a thing as the steam engine. The initial idea came from a Dutchman; his thought became productive in the mind of a Frenchman who lived a while in England and was in touch with English scientists, and who finally became a professor in a German university. His invention was taken up by a Devonshire miner and developed by a Scotch engineer. Denis Papin was the great French inventor and Watt was the Scotchman. The great idea, however, was in a sense a social fact, and an international mind supplied it to the society that had need of it—the Britain of the eighteenth century, already on the verge of the industrial era.

Most of us think of the eighteenth century as beginning with the wars of Louis XIV, and William of Orange, followed by a series of diplomatic moves which one does not carry in one's head; then the reign of Frederick the Great, of Louis XV, of the Georges; thence the French and Indian wars, and the American Revolution; then the Old Regime in France and the French Revolution. This is legitimate enough in history; but it leaves out of the century something of lasting importance, while it concentrates upon details. The application of science to do the world's work was begun while these things were taking place. This great event, known to us as the Industrial Revolution, is the lasting and fundamental fact of that century. When Louis XIV is as dimly remembered as Rameses II, its effects will still be dominant in history.

Our educational system until recently is that which had been determined upon by the successors of the people who had never enjoyed a scientific training or who had never known what a steam engine was, and never cared to know—classicists, the successors of the humanists, as they were of the scholastics. As a matter of fact the steam engine is a part of history itself. It is even part of the human race. Every idea which can be set to work is a part of history and an enlargement and perpetuation of humanity.

Notes

THE NEW HISTORY

1. The pioneer in the New History was Professor James Harvey Robinson, whose book bearing that title appeared in 1912. He had developed the new synthesis in his classes at Columbia University for over a decade earlier.

CHAPTER XIII

⁂

SPENGLER

IN 1918, while Germany was suffering the humiliation of defeat
and before the Nazi movement had hardened into national fanaticism, the one oracle to which intelligent Germans listened was
Oswald Spengler's *Untergang des Abendlandes (The Decline of
the West)*. Its reception by the German people in those post-war
years constitutes an historical event in itself. Under any circumstances the immediate sale of one hundred thousand copies of a
scientific or learned treatise would be notable enough, but the original text of Spengler's work had greater obstacles to overcome than
the natural apathy of the reading public. It was published in a country and at a time when financial and economic chaos forced the
common citizen to the utmost rigorous economies and only the
keenest sense of intellectual need could account for the fact that
practically the entire cultured world of Germany made it a point
to secure in some way or other this ponderous work.

The explanation is surely not to be found in either the style of
the author, on the one hand, nor a quickened interest upon the part
of its readers in world history—which is its ostensible theme. Although there is more than a trace of genius in the presentation of
the material, the author distinctly shunned the field of literature in
the ordinary sense of the word and made no concessions to the populace in tricks of style. The opening sections of the book are, if

*From: Essays in Intellectual History (Harper & Brothers, Publishers, New York,
1929), pp. 57-67.*

anything, more abstruse and difficult to understand than those which follow. Theories of mathematics ordinarily make little appeal to readers of history, and yet, this book plunges at once into discussions of this kind. One wonders what would have been the fate of Mr. H. G. Wells' *Outline of History* if before laying out its historical perspective the author had indulged in a sort of Einsteinian discussion of the relativity not merely of events but of the whole scheme of time and space in which the events occur. Moreover, the text is even more erudite than it is philosophical. It is filled with unexplained allusions to phenomena in almost every field of knowledge, from the history, art and religion of the ancient East to the most recent theories of science in the West, and the reader is supposed to know enough about each of these widely diverse subjects to appreciate a novel synthesis built up out of a new coordination of these varied elements of culture. If the author injects at times the charm of a poet's fancy, yet so massive is the framework of this survey of world history that the explanation of its appeal must be sought in something else than in the form of expression.

A much more natural explanation lies at hand in the German interest in history itself. One might very well imagine that here we have the parallel to what happened in Germany in the opening of the nineteenth century, that in a larger and maturer way the thoughtful public of Germany was recasting its historical perspectives as it did in the days when German historical criticism denied the legends of antiquity, both sacred and profane, and recast the facts of history and all principles of historical writing. But a closer study of both Spengler and of Germany today shows that this analogy is utterly superficial. Not only is there no historical renaissance yet visible in post-war Germany similar to that which a hundred years ago resulted in the disciplines of the historical seminar and the vast output of document and narrative, but there has been, if anything, a definite decline in the taste for history itself. This, at least, is the judgment of one of the most distinguished scholars of Germany, Dr. Carl Becker, Prussian Minister of Education, in a thoughtful study published in 1927, calling attention to the relative decline of the historical seminar and, more especially, to that interest in historical literature which is in Germany an almost equal index of the intellectual output. According to him the thought of the new age is less and less of the purely scholarly type and more and more pragmatic. Although the German seminar still applies the precepts of Ranke, historical research has suffered something like an eclipse in the country which played so large a part in making that research scientific. The detached curiosity concerning the human past is making way for an interest in the present and the future. When we add to Dr. Becker's observation the fact that the controversy over the question of German war guilt has, without the reproof of any outstanding German historian, violated the canons of historical criticism at almost every turn, we find it still more difficult to attribute the German interest in Spengler to any profound stirring of genuine historical interests.

As a matter of fact, the explanation of the appeal which Spengler's work has made to the German mind—and to the minds of many readers of the English text as well—is not the historical appeal in the proper sense of the word. It is a performance that must be judged by different criteria than those of the historical seminar. This is true of content, purpose and method. As to content, it is not a history but a comment upon history; as to purpose, it does not seek to orient us with reference to the past but rather with reference to the present and future, and as to method, it violates boldly and openly at every turn the most elementary precepts of historical scholarship. The fundamental appeal to the public, therefore, must lie in its destructive criticism and in its almost prophetic synthesis; for Spengler speaks with the assurance of a Nietzsche and with equal vigor of assertion and denial. For a society shattered, as his had been, by the tragedy of the war and the chaos which followed it, there was surely an intellectual comfort to be found in a survey of civilization which boldly dared to ignore the passing evils of his day. If the *Untergang des Abendlandes* was a creation of the war, it remained, nevertheless, a monument of intellectual defiance not only to it but to all purely temporary events. In a way it recalls such creations as those of Beethoven in Vienna during the disastrous fall of the Holy Roman Empire, or of Goethe looking calmly at the disturbed world of a revolutionary era. It is perhaps this detachment from the contemporary history of Germany during the World War which furnishes the first clue to its great appeal.

The Decline of the West seems at first sight to be a collection of separate essays or monographs. It deals with the field of social and intellectual evolution, not chronologically but topically. The chapters of Volume I bear such strange titles as "The Meaning of Numbers," "Physiognomic and Systematic," "The Destiny-Idea and the Causality-Principle," "Makrosmos—The Symbolism of the World Picture and the Problem of Space," Faustian and Apollonian Nature Knowledge." Those of Volume II are somewhat more concrete, but are still far removed from the ordinary chapter headings of history. The lower cultures are preceded by a survey of "Origin and Landscape" dealing with plant and animal life, "Being and Waking-Being," and the "Mass Soul." The problem of Arabian culture bears the title "Historic Pseudomorphoses." The volume ends with two great chapters on the "Form-World of Economic Life" in two divisions, "Money" and "The Machine."

When one compares these subject groupings with the arrangement of any general manual of world history, one sees at once that, however suggestive and thought-provoking these monographic chapters may be, they have little to do with the ordinary concepts of history. The purpose of the historian is to reproduce the past as it actually happened, reducing the subjective element to a mere editorial task of deciding whether to devote more or less attention to this or that event; but, upon the whole, intent upon rescuing for knowledge phenomena which have interest in themselves. Spengler's purpose is of an entirely different kind. It is an artistic interest in the formation of a great synthesis, a world philosophy. The incoherent past is to be made articulate and no longer meaningless by stating it in terms of symbols which in themselves have an art-meaning for the author. He is "convinced that it is not merely a question of writing one out of several possible and merely logically justifiable philosophies, but of writing *the* philosophy of our time, one that is to some extent a natural philosophy and is dimly presaged by all."

Now this effort to write "*the* philosophy of our time" is not history in the true sense of that word, but rather the denial of it. It is, as Spengler himself states in the preface to the revised edition, the "intuitive and depictive" arrangement of phenomena for the purpose of illustrating other things, and the whole synthesis is frankly in the subjective world of the thinker. It addresses itself solely to readers "who are capable of living themselves into the world-sounds and pictures as they read"—which means that it is addressed to those who can fit their imaginations into the imaginative creation and attitude of the writer himself. This is myth making; it is poetry. In the hands of Spengler it becomes ultimately massive and splendid poetry because the structure of his thought is architecturally magnificent, powerful in outline and beautiful in detail. Nevertheless, it is a dream structure and should not be mistaken for reality.

The title itself suggests the trend of the narrative. Western civilization is on the threshold of an inevitable and all-embracing decline. In this prediction the author falls back upon a theory of history which arranges events according to a series of cultures which have each their childhood, youth, manhood and old age. There have been eight such ripe cultures, the Chinese, the Babylonian, the Egyptian, the East Indian, the Greco-Roman, the Arabian, the Maya of Yucatan and Mexico, and that of "the West." Each of these cultures lasts for about a thousand years and then decays. The sign of decay is when a culture passes into a civilization, that is, when spontaneous, energetic and creative life exhausts its creative impulses and grows mechanical; when the skeptic denies and the dilettante toys with the things that have been sacred and stimulating to feeling as well as thought. The outward form of this change from culture to civilization is seen in the growth of cities and the socializing process which city life implies. There is no sign of a directing divinity, as in Hegel, no meaning that inspires with confidence or hope, but a recurring cataclysm when the dead nerves no longer respond to impulse and the keen impressions that make the joy of living are burned out, leaving only the ashes of a worn and empty world. It should be said that the emptiness that follows upon disaster receives none of that stressing which it would be given by a moralist.

Spengler is interested in the great and tragic drama which he depicts and wastes little idle sympathy upon the victims of the recurring night. And it is in this depiction of the process that the writer is carried along through a world of suggestion and by ways that open up history in new perspectives. The two huge volumes are packed full with varied data of all kinds of interest, artistic, scientific, political and philosophical. It is a rich and ever stimulating collection of historical detail placed in the strangest juxtaposition, like some vast museum in which things from different eras have apparently been mixed by some irresponsible fancy and yet when studied more deeply one sees a design running through what seems at first mere willful medley.

It is obviously wrong to judge this book as an historical manual or even as history. There is in part the suggestion of a prose Goethe with a range of sensibility that is as capable of lyric outbursts as it is of the enjoyment of abstract formulae. Take the opening paragraphs of Volume II for instance. They are worth quoting, and fortunately the English translator has rendered the full beauty of the original—which, by the way, may be said of the whole translation, and saying this is a high tribute to the translator:

"Regard the flowers at eventide, as, one after the other, they close in the setting sun. Strange is the feeling that then presses in upon you—a feeling of enigmatic fear in the presence of this blind, dream-like, earth-bound existence. The dumb forest, the silent meadows, this bush, that twig, do not stir themselves; it is the wind that plays with them. Only the little gnat is free—he dances still in the evening light, he moves whither he will. A plant is nothing on its own account. It forms a part of the landscape in which a chance made it take root. The twilight, the chill, the closing of every flower—these are not cause and effect, not danger and willed answer to danger.

"They are a single process of nature, which is accomplishing itself near, with, and in the plant. The individual is not free to look out for itself, will for itself, or choose for itself. An animal, on the contrary, can choose. It is emancipated from the servitude of all the rest of the world. This midget swarm that dances on and on, that solitary bird still flying through the evening, the fox approaching furtively the nest—these are *little worlds of their own within another great world.* An animalcule is a drop of water, too tiny to be perceived by the human eye, though it lasts but a second and has but a corner of this drop as its field—nevertheless is *free and independent in the face of the universe.* The giant oak, upon one of whose leaves the droplet hangs, is not."

This is a lyric approach to the problem of the "Cosmic and the Microcosm." It is pure poetry, but leads one from the elements of life and nature to the formation of those "inspired mass units" which become coherent in terms of social or national action. Thus in a few pages we are carried from gnats to the psychology of crowds—"noisy and ecstatic at Eleusis or Lourdes or heroically firm like the Spartans at Thermopylae . . . they form themselves to the music of chorales, marches and dances, and are sensitive like human and animal thoroughbreds to the effects of bright colors, decorations, costume and uniform." Thus Spengler sweeps from "the hours at eventide" to the streets of Paris in 1789, when "the cry, '*A la lanterne!*' fell upon the ear."

The whole book is written with this imaginative freedom, and the marvel of it—for it is a marvel—is that the vigor of the imagination has not been cramped or wearied by the vast scope of the survey. Few books are more learned than this, reaching as it does from Oriental culture through the antique world and medieval thought into the science of today; nevertheless, one feels generally that the author has entered sympathetically into the thinking of these civilizations which in the upbuilding of his scheme of philosophy he moves backward and forward across the ages so as to place Cromwell along with Pythagoras and Mohammed and Buddhism along with Stoicism and Socialism. To be able to move these massive forms and yet to give each age a touch that is almost like a caress is something that makes Spengler's prose the kind of thing that Heine described in the *Nibelungenlied*, which has Gothic proportions that, however, do not distort the realism of detail.

Nevertheless, we must repeat, this poem is not history. The use of historical data should not blind us to the fact that the architectural method employed in building up the synthesis is the very opposite of that which the historian uses. A series of analogies furnishes the pattern according to which this rich pageantry of the imagination is given its design.

Spengler divides world history into four cycles of civilization: the Indian, beginning about 1800 B.C.; the antique, dating from about 900 B.C.; the Arabian, which includes the foundation of Christianity and Islam, and the Western, which began about 900 A.D. Each cycle has its *Spring, Summer, Autumn* and *Winter*. The Western cycle is now depositing its harvest as the Winter of a dark age presses upon us once again. This synthesis is allegorical in character and is akin to that type of thinking which dominated the early Christian Fathers when they had a similar problem to that which Spengler has undertaken, namely, the effort to fit into a single whole the recalcitrant data of life and the world which seemed to be running at cross purposes to the divine plan. They found unity by insisting that not all reality was equally real, but that some phenomena existed for the purpose of foreshadowing others. Thus the primitive Jewish past could be made contributory to the Christian era. Spengler has another synthesis, but his method is substantially the same; the elements of the past are compared with the elements of the present in a vast human allegory, the key to which is a perception of what he calls "the cosmic beat" of life itself.

Now the historical fallacy in this philosophy is that the law of growth is only uniform for civilizations which are uniform in character, and modern civilization, that of today, is not uniform with any that has ever gone before. The drawing of analogies from the Indian and the antique past is a prejudging of contemporary civilization according to standards inappropriate to it. The external resemblances that lie in Cromwellian and Mohammedan world-outlook furnish no criteria as to the contribution made to the world by Cromwell on the one hand and Mohammed on the other. Cromwell may have thought in the accents of Islam, but his work was one that made for human liberty although he himself was impatient of its claims.

But there is a deeper fallacy in Spengler's work than that which consists of the violation of the comparative method. One does not come upon it until the very close of the second volume. While the ultimate aim of the whole work is, as the title points out, to demonstrate the inevitable decline of Western civilization, he, nevertheless, has failed to see that the scientific world of today presents entirely new phenomena which cannot be understood by any analysis of civilizations that have seemed superficially analogous to it. Spengler, it is true, brings in invention and scientific discovery in the closing chapter of his book with a penetrating characterization which seems to promise an understanding of its meaning. But so obsessed is he by the general scheme of his thought that he fails to see that the age of applied science with its conquest of time and space is not merely unlike the civilizations of the past but is undoing the very bases upon which they rested. Winter followed Autumn in the past because life was repetitive and was passed within limited areas of self-contained economy. Intercourse between societies was more predatory than stimulative because mankind had not yet discovered the means to maintain culture without an unjust dependence upon those who had no share in its material blessings. From the savage raid and slavery down to the industrial problems of today, the recurring civilizations have been largely built upon false economic forces backed up by equally false moral and religious casuistry. The civilizations that have come and gone have been inherently lacking in equilibrium because they have built upon the injustice of exploitation. There is no reason to suppose that modern civilization must inevitably repeat this cataclysmatic rhythm. In any case, we can assert with a confidence equal to that of Spengler that the decline—*Untergang*—of Western civilization can be avoided by the application to the social and political organizations of today of that same intelligence which in the physical sciences is enabling us to escape from the routine limitations of time and space.

There is therefore another perspective than that of Spengler, one which sees the present not as the end of the process but as the first beginning of the passing of the barbarian world. The conclusion lies not in disasters, Caesarism and *Machtpolitik*, but in the equilibrium which bears the name of justice and finds its embodiment in the institutions of democracy.

This is not an idealistic conclusion but the simplest statement of historical realism, for in the free play of democratic institutions, there is the widest possible stimulus to the activities of life itself. The achievement of social justice instead of stultifying culture brings into play an ever-increasing reservoir of energy. And so instead of merely repeating the tragic episodes of the past, it seems more likely that we are at the dawn of an era as new in its potentialities as it is different from any that has gone before.

CHAPTER XIV

⊰⊱

BERGSON'S PHILOSOPHY

I T IS FITTING that political science should reckon with all the major
elements in our social consciousness, and Bergson has made philosophy one of the major elements. At least so it was in France, and
to some extent elsewhere in Europe. Forces as far apart as syndical-
ism on the one hand and neo-Catholicism on the other have drawn,
or sought to draw, inspiration from his teaching. It is a work of
genius to have made metaphysics not merely a vogue but the basis
of something like a cult. Neither Schopenhauer nor Nietzsche has
swung so fully into the focal center of a social movement. Bergson's
philosophy touches the heart of that age-long striving from obscurantism to rationalism—touches and partly benumbs—and challenges
the confidence of science. Hence it is acclaimed and condemned

Reprinted from Political Science Quarterly, Vol. XXVIII, No. 1 (March, 1913),
pp. 130-135.
This little study of Bergson's philosophy seems now like an echo from a lost
world. But when it was written Bergson's lectures in the Collège de France had
drawn such crowds to listen to his challenge to the accepted theory of knowledge
as had once thronged the same precincts to listen to Abelard's attack on the scholasticism of the twelfth century. When he came to Columbia University as a
visiting professor in 1913 the largest hall in the university was crowded to over-
flowing. Nor was the interest merely that of personal curiosity. A whole philosophical literature appeared, devoted to the discussion of the major points in
Bergson's philosophy. The bibliography of his writings and the writings on them,
published by the Columbia University Press, had 496 entries. That was only at the
beginning of Bergson's visit to America. No wonder every young professor tried
his hand at criticism.

from all sides, and for all kinds of reasons. It has a negative, critical side, and a positive. On the negative, it boldly asserts that the rational processes of our intellect cannot comprehend reality; on the positive, that life itself can produce a kind of intuitive comprehension of just what intellect misses. We can see the drift of this by a slight analysis of his treatment, stressing two aspects.

The essence of Bergson's theory of the limitation of reason, as presented in his *Creative Evolution*, is that thought cannot comprehend life, and life is the main thing in the universe. The understanding, according to the doctrine of evolution, has been evolved as an adjunct to action. Hence it moves easily among materials and can deal successfully with solids. Bergson grants it in this sphere the possibility of even getting beyond symbols to actuality. The mathematical and physical sciences are sciences in the fullest sense of the word. But life itself falls into categories which the faculty of the understanding cannot supply. Space relations are quantitative, and with them the intellect can deal; but time furnishes qualitative changes which eternally elude the investigator. Life, bound up so thoroughly with time, thus escapes explanation, because it is always becoming something different. It is a creation in time. The inanimate has no history, simply because time makes no difference to it. Its changes can be repeated. Life, on the other hand, is a succession of new phenomena. No present repeats the past, no future the present. That is why it has a past and a future. But, says Bergson, if life is a continuous process of the planting of these new phenomena, by which it is apprehended, in the heart of every fleeting moment, it is itself a disturbing, explosive force, exercising a creative power in the universe. Since change involves the new, the process of change —life—is therefore a sort of creation. Creation, however, is incalculable. The *élan vital*, the life impulse, is the basis of existence; and the nearest one can get to describing it is in terms of itself. So Bergson rejects mechanism, claiming that it neglects the role of time and assumes that incalculable forces may be calculated. The line he draws between the animate and inanimate he regards as impassable from that side. Teleology, on the other hand, the argument that an intelligent purpose underlies the evolution, is treated with incisive and convincing refutation.

Now, continues Bergson, the two most successful applications of the creative life impulse are instinct on the one hand, as developed, say, in ants—and intelligence on the other, as in man. There is nothing more novel and interesting in Bergson's whole scheme than this balancing of these two perfect products of evolution—ants and men. The direction of their achievements, however, Bergson puts in entirely different worlds. Instinct and intelligence are radically different. Instinct, he says, deals with things, intelligence with their relations, though neither one exists quite by itself. This is the more general form of the statement that intellect converts matter into instruments or tools, while instinct operated directly, without their intervention. This distinction, of course, makes pure instinct absolutely incomprehensible, as it eliminates it from the field of consciousness. Man can never quite understand an ant. And since thought is unable to understand instinct, it is cut off from comprehending a large element of life itself.

The same distinction between instinct and thought enables Bergson to limit the scope of intellect even as applied to matter; for intellect deals, not with substance, but with relationships, and therefore never meets more than half of the problem. Moreover, following up the argument, we can see how poorly even the relationships are apprehended. Our knowledge comes to us in cinematographic glimpses, not as a flux, which is the real character of change. We human beings are interested only in positions and juxtapositions, and we have a clear conception only of immobility, whereas solids, as we have been learning, are in constant movement—are, indeed movement itself. Materiality is timeless, and thought works in time. So "as spirit grows more intellectual, matter grows more material."

But now we come to the thing which makes Bergsonism a militant philosophy. For thought, he says, is, after all, relatively successful in dealing with matter compared with its incompetence to deal with life. Here the fixity of his concepts, its cinematographic impressions, are entirely inadequate. "By nature the intellect is characterized by an inability to comprehend life." From the standpoint of life, matter, which is timeless—at least when viewed by rational consciousness on its old mathematical basis—and reason, which cannot comprehend change, are both an arrest of its processes. So we arrive at the paradox that life is interrupted by its own creation, intelligence—the creation in fact which indicates the tendency of the whole creative process!

Where, then, shall we turn? To intuition. Now, what does Bergson mean by intuition? Not the wayward fancies of a dreamer nor the revelations of a mystic, he tells us, but the pure vision that comes from the inner self, such as the genius reveals in art. There is perhaps no clearer statement of what he has in mind than in that famous passage in *Laughter*, in which he discusses the nature of art. From time to time, in a fit of absentmindedness, nature raises up souls that are more detached from life. Not with that intentional, logical, systematical detachment—the result of reflection and philosophy—but rather with a natural detachment, one innate in the structure of sense or consciousness, which at once reveals itself by a virginal manner, so to speak, of seeing, hearing or thinking. This is the way life itself may reveal its secrets. Although Bergson expressly denies that his philosophy connects with art rather than with science, his presentation of the doctrine leaves no doubt as to what are its affiliations.

This scanty survey of a large field cannot do justice to the skill in dialectic, the lucidity in expression and the warmth of sympathetic insight with which the philosophy is conveyed. Nor does it indicate how many illuminating turns the new thought is made to take, how many vital problems it touches. Obviously, then, any critical estimate must be even more unsatisfactory. But since we are rather more interested in Bergsonism than in Bergson, we may point out that it is this last, positive side of the philosophy which gives most comfort to those who are finding comfort in these speculations. For as intuitions are peculiarly irresponsible and respond to all kinds of environment, the neo-orthodox of every faith can accept the illumination of intuition in the way they most prefer, including subliminal senses and sixth senses, along with the more sober illumination that does not shock the common sense. Bergson's own illumination is of this more restricted kind; and this, combined with the rather negative, polemic use he makes of it in the *Creative Evolution*, has apparently blinded some of us to its possibilities when once let loose in a society loaded to the brim with intuitions of another sort—the heritage of untold centuries of sentient adjustment.

It was surely a triumph of dialectic to have forced such matters as intuition to the foreground of philosophic discussion; but it was an even greater triumph to proceed to argue from it and still give the impression that the argument was an induction. If intuitions are valid we have reached the truth of things before the reason has time to get started. It can only manufacture justification for what is already in our possession. The intuitions, moreover, so far as they serve as bases of knowledge, can justify themselves only by other intuitions. For instance, Bergson criticizes our mental inability to conceive of the process of nature as one of flux. But science has already given us much reason to suspect that the flux which his intuition calls for does not really exist. The only radiation which we know is wave motion, the nature of which has been apprehended not by intuition but by reason, as any of us will recall from our earliest experiments in physics. When, therefore, Bergson berates our rational processes for their failure to conceive of flux, he postulates a difficulty which reason has a right to deny at the start. It must not be supposed that Bergson himself has failed to notice the bearing of such facts. He confesses at present that he tends towards a belief in the pluralistic character of change, although from his analysis of rest as the complex, secondary state built out of change itself, it is hard to see how he can do so. But, in any case, it is the caution of that criticism which he tends to disqualify from its office, the criticism of scientific rationalism, which forces the admission of uncertainty. Without that caution, the intuitive process of his philosophical method seems to be much the same thing as we have long been familiar with. "Sharpened perception," left to itself, can develop as with neo-Platonists or Gnostics into an illumination whose fitful glare distorts the phenomena it lightens. It was such intuitionism that furnished to theologians and scholastics, from Alexandria to Monte Cassino, a "truth" which the profane intellect could never attain. Isidore of Seville, the encyclopaedist of the dark ages, registered his ignorance with complacency, falling back upon a sixth-century intuition of the vanity of the intellectual effort to compass reality. Profane was to St. Bernard, as later to Calvin, a "welter of error," because it did not fit the intuitions springing from his monastic vital impulses. It is, in a way, quite unfair to Bergson to classify him with such obscurantists, for his own intuitions are under closest rational control; nor can he fairly be held accountable for the vagaries of his followers. But Bergsonism has already gone pretty far in this direction, and it is time that the trend was pointed out.

In this connection, one of the most interesting developments is the adjustment forced upon pragmatism by Bergson. Nowhere is the practical character of scientific thought more successfully criticized than in *Creative Evolution*, the first treatise on philosophy to catch the full significance of the Industrial Revolution. But if practicality gives a warp to thinking which distorts concepts and falsifies reality, how can *value*, which is practicality incarnate, be the test of truth? It is, surely, rather the test of untruth. The paradox should not be forced; but it suggests itself. It is by clarification of perception, directed upon its problem with virginal aloofness and without preoccupation that one may reach an appreciation of reality, says Bergson. Rational thought deludes us because it is the continuation of biological adjustments. It follows that the values which are apprehended in its grapple with reality are but the shadows of distortions. It is a singular illustration of the mystical character of much recent philosophy to find pragmatism and Bergsonism frequently under the same roof. But that is because both are expressions of the rounded life of action and emotion and not of mere intellectualism. It is significant that the whole Bergsonian scheme is embedded in his little essay on *Laughter*—for laughter, in a word, is the reaction of life when it runs upon mechanistic situations in contrast with it. This is but another reminder of the idea that concepts are static and so envelop obstacles as to conceal that essential changeful character which intuition may reveal. Metaphysics is brought back from abstraction to the realm of science which is the product of unrestricted curiosity in everything affecting life.

CHAPTER XV

❧

THE STATESMANSHIP OF MASARYK

I N THE LIGHT of recent history, the question is sometimes asked, even by those who supported the effort of President Masaryk to introduce Jeffersonian democracy into Central and Eastern Europe, whether it had been justified or worthwhile. There can be no doubt that the history of Europe and of Western civilization has been immensely enriched by the philosophy and statesmanship of Thomas Masaryk. Neither can there be any doubt that the Czechoslovak Republic has left a remarkable record in the annals of history; one which, with all its mistakes—and they must be admitted—proved the competence of this branch of the Slavic peoples in the art and science of government. We must remember that the judgments of history are always relative to the conditions under which events happen; we must also consider the antecedent conditions which determine the outlook and temper of both the people and their leaders. It is with these determining facts in mind that we must come to conclusions whether the great experiment of Czechoslovak independence was justified or not.

It should be stated at the outset that the question is in the main unreal. It would seem to imply that in 1918 the peoples living within the Hapsburg Monarchy had a free choice concerning whether they were to continue on under the old sovereignty or not. The action of the Czechs in setting up an independent government in Prague was

Reprinted from Czechoslovakia, edited by Robert J. Kerner (University of California Press, Berkeley and Los Angeles, 1940),pp. 451-447.

but one of a series of such acts by which the former Hapsburg Monarchy was partitioned. The day before the Czechs took action, national councils had been set up at Lemberg in Galicia, at the far eastern end of the great Austrian crescent, and at Agram, the capital of Croatia, in the extreme southwest. Hungary had already declared herself independent of the Hapsburg Crown, and there was only German Austria left, with revolution in the streets of Vienna. It is true that Emperor Charles delayed his abdication until November 12, one day after the armistic with Germany, but the process of disruption was already fully under way. The Monarchy came to an end as the result of World War I which its foreign minister Berchtold had forced upon the world in 1914 on the theory that the risk of war had to be taken because it was the only way for the monarchy to be preserved. An empire, relying as it did upon the most dangerous of political forces, prestige, was forced to the wall by the fact that the war became a blockade which wore down its civilian as well as its military strength under the strain of continued miiltary and naval pressure. During the war, the military authorities had stepped into control of much of the Austrian bureaucracy, and when the war was over the weakened machinery of government virtually ceased in much of its ordinary functioning. The bureaucracy could not recapture its lost authority; anarchy was rapidly developing, and out of that anarchy came a new States System, which happily for itself could invoke the one principle of Woodrow Wilson's peace terms which most applied to the new order of things, "self-determination."

Neither Wilson nor even Masaryk dominated the situation at this critical junction. It was the change from one regime to another under the force of circumstances at the end of an unsuccessful war. It is, of course, possible to argue that at some time during the war this centrifugal force might have been stopped by a compromise peace, if the question of Germany's terms had not taken precedence over Austria's plight in the eyes of the Allied and Associated Powers in the last phase of the war. The Dual Monarchy was dragged along by Germany to share in a common defeat which, although it brought disaster to the Hohenzollern Empire, meant inevitable extinction for that of the Hapsburgs. These facts should be borne in mind by those who think of the Czech experiment as one which the Czechs were wholly free to try or refuse to try. What other choice was left them in those fateful days of October, 1918? It is true that the Slovaks joined with the Czechs a few days later only to give political reality to the unity proclaimed in America and symbolized by Masaryk himself. But the Hungary out of which the Slovaks came was also facing social as well as political disorders. The strong hand of Prime Minister Count Tisza was no longer there, and that powerful oligarchy of Magyar magnates which had for so long steered the Hungarian ship of state through many perils was not in a position to assert its traditional authority. Under these conditions the oldest of all political forces in that part of Europe, the submerged sense of nationalism, came to the fore, partly through spontaneous movements, partly stimulated by political leaders. Before the Paris Peace Conference met, these elements of the new regime, that of the Succession States, were taking shape, and there was nothing else to replace them.

One hears at times from American commentators on the European scene words of regret and even of blame that President Wilson did not move to prevent the breakup of the Hapsburg Monarchy, so that it might have been kept to serve both as a check upon German ambition, and as a guaranty of economic prosperity for the Danube Valley through maintenance of better conditions for trade and commerce. It does not seem to have occurred to these objectors that this could have been done only by sending American troops into all these different sections of the Hapsburg Monarchy, to police them in the interests of an outworn system. Can anyone imagine what the American people would have said if, after having secured the condition of freedom for these peoples through a costly war, we then had turned upon them and repressed their liberties in the interests of the sovereign whose authority they had renounced?

Even if it had been possible to turn back the clock in this way and secure a reformation of the old Hapsburg Monarchy instead of continuing the war to bring about its dissolution, what guaranty have we that the reform would have been worked out in terms of a genuine federal system? Or that it would have been maintained for any length of time after the immediate pressure of the postwar period had passed away?

A clue to the answer lies in what happened in the Republic of Austria itself. Nowhere else in the Monarchy was there anything like the intellectual leadership and enlightenment which distinguished the capital city, and nowhere else was there such a body of administrators who, while loyal to the dynasty, were also the conscious exponents of the interests of the middle class. Yet it was in Austria, and not in Germany, in which the liberties of the citizens were first repressed in savage domestic conflicts. If it be objected that the real cause of this lay in the economic disasters of Austria and that Czechoslovakia escaped internal disorders because of its greater prosperity, we are at once led to examine the causes of the alleged prosperity, and, although we find them partly in the better balanced economy of the country, we must give much of the credit to the heroic fiscal policy with which the young Republic began its career. Dr. Rasin, the Czech statesman and Minister of Finance, paid with his life for the maintenance of a sound financial policy, but even the assassin's bullet did not check his reforms, and the currency of Czechoslovakia kept its place among the sound moneys of Europe, whereas Austria went bankrupt.

This fact should be borne in mind in judging the capacity of the Czechoslovak state to take its place among the nations of the world. It is true that the structure of Austrian finance had been gutted by the war and that the disruption of the Monarchy called for a reorientation of whatever business was left for Austrian bankers, merchants and industrialists. But, as time was to show, there were hidden resources in the old Austrian economy which in the course of time tended to redress the balance of its losses. The contrast between Austria and Czechoslovakia in the early postwar years is therefore one which, although it cannot be pressed too far, is at least a sufficient answer to those Austrians who in the prewar years had denied the capacity of the Slav for self-government.

If it is perhaps unfair to judge, on the basis of what postwar Austria really was, what a reformed Hapsburg Monarchy would have been, we may perhaps get a less controversial clue by examining the political theories of Austrian liberal thinkers and comparing them with those of Masaryk. It must be remembered that in the prewar period Austria was an outstanding center for the study of the political sciences and that the leaders in this movement of enlightenment were also responsible for the training of those high in government positions. Their ideas were therefore something more than pure academic theory; they represented authoritative trends of thinking. Whereas Masaryk built his hopes upon a system of friendly neighbors under a regime of freedom. His effort to teach the philosophy of Thomas Jefferson not only to his own people but to the others of east-central Europe did not wholly succeed, for the task was well-nigh impossible. The Austrian system of government under which the Czechs had lived, and still more Hungary's rule of the Slovaks within its frontiers, were both far removed from the American democratic federalism, which was the basis of Masaryk's political philosophy. Although the Hapsburgs had been forced to recognize the different national stocks which composed their varied empire, the bureaucracy and the army held these peoples together in a way which failed utterly to satisfy their aspirations for political self-expression. True federalism flourishes only under a regime of liberty, and that was something foreign to the Hapsburg tradition.

No discussion of this subject would be complete, however, which left out of account the extreme nationalism which characterized so much of the history of this part of Europe after the World War— the movement which ultimately found its most extravagant expression in Nazi Germany. The people of the Danube Valley were divided by old antagonisms and resentments which were now given free expression under the divided sovereignties. This situation was accentuated by the fact that the idea of the State which they had been taught in the schools was that of the Germanic concept of absolute sovereignty. Each people, therefore, that achieved its independence was intent upon realizing it in the full sense of the word, even to its own economic detriment. But there were increasing signs that this condition of affairs was being improved as the first decade after the war wore away. But whether or not this betterment in international relations would ultimately have gone on to fulfill Masaryk's conception of the free interplay of free peoples is a question that can never be answered, for two things blocked such progress: the economic difficulties of the thirties, and the intransigence of the new and menacing power of German Nazism. Against these powerful forces of economic and political reaction, the young liberalism of Central Europe had small chance of holding its own. This became fully evident when Great Britain and France betrayed Czechoslovakia at the Munich Conference. But the tragic history which followed that betrayal came after Masaryk's death.

CHAPTER XVI

❧❧

JUSTICE, EAST AND WEST

WORDS ARE like houses; most of them we know only from the outside. Using them without thinking is like finding one's way along a street by the numbers on the doorplates, without even stopping to look at the timeworn facades. It is only on rare occasions that we really become aware of them, and rarer still we push past their outer hallways into the inner recesses, into quiet, pleasant rooms where thoughts can dwell without disturbance from outside. But there are some words that rise like temples from a busy street, and it is one of these which we are now about to explore, one of the noblest words that were ever built into the congeries of human speech. It is known everywhere and is as old as civilization, though with varying facades; but though it has been surveyed by thinkers of every age, it is so vast in scope, so puzzling in design, that only its outer precincts are familiar to most people.

"Justice" is a universal concept, and is defined everywhere in practically the same terms. The dictionaries give it in the very phrase with which Plato began his discussion of it in *The Republic*, over twenty-two centuries ago. It is "rendering to every man his due." Long before this, the prophets of Israel, and still longer before them the moralists of Egypt, weighed its implications in other speech and other setting. Confucius, closer to Plato's time, built his philosophy upon it. Later, the Roman Law took over unchanged

Reprinted from Pacific Affairs, Vol. V, No. 5 (May, 1932), pp. 393-403.

the precept of the Greeks, and the opening words of the *Institutes* of Justinian, that summary of the great principles of the Roman Code, read as follows: "Justice is the fixed and constant purpose to give to every man his due." The religion, philosophy, and law of the ancient world were at one in this definition.

But defining justice is only locating it, enabling one to find it on the vast, labyrinthine streets of experience. It tells but little of what lies within. It is, as Plato showed, only the beginning of the exploration. Both *The Republic* and Justinian's *Institutes* pass quickly from the statement of the general principle to its application to the affairs of daily life. For, after all, this is the real problem, and unless it is solved the definition remains an empty form of words—a signboard on the deserted rooms behind. "To render to every man his due" may mean as many different things as there are men to render or receive what they think to be their due. So the content of justice is by no means determined by its definition, and, in spite of the study of general principles in the field of morals—the field of Plato's exploration—and the study of law in courts and universities, we are still but little farther on than the ancients in our knowledge of the subject.

This is why the student of history looks with such interest to those schools of law which are today experimenting and exploring in the field of human conduct in the same spirit as the physical scientist has analyzed the world of nature. Here is one of those constructive movements which break with the routine of the past to lay the foundations of future advance. The rights and wrongs of the citizen are not to be determined for him by the set rules of ancestors living under conditions unlike his own, nor even by the ignorant action of contemporaries, however necessary may be a temporary compliance. Both custom and law are to be subject to analysis. Law is to be based upon a sound knowledge of human needs, aptitudes and desires, conditioned by local circumstances of time, place and association. It is to be a fitting expression of historic processes, not the rigid embodiment of preconceived ideas. It is not simply a set of rules to be administered but an intelligent expression of the vital interests of a society. Therefore the clue lies in the study of society, and law must fit the conclusions of scientific analysis.

If this experiment should succeed in making jurisprudence a synthesis of the social sciences, it will mark an epoch in history. The challenge which it presents to intelligence touches the whole range of human interests. If the challenge can be taken up, if intelligence is adequate to so great a task, then this experiment is the initial chapter or phase of the development of morals without parallel in the past. For it marks a turning point in the attitude toward conduct, as revolutionary a change as the Jewish prophets or Greek philosophy brought to the West and Buddha, Confucius or Mencius to the Orient. I am fully aware how incongruous this sounds, especially with the mention of the founders of religions. It will be necessary to justify it by a glance back over the past.

There is little to record of the history of justice in the beginnings of civilization. Justice is a secular concept; it has to do with the relations of man to man and not with those of men to supernatural powers. In all early societies it is this latter relationship which is of supreme importance and, therefore, from the fact that religion dominates, justice develops only incidentally. We surely do not have to go back to Plato to show that the relations of mankind with the gods do not rest upon the same principles as those which determine secular society. If the definition of justice holds and it means rendering to everyone his due, then the measurement of what is due cannot be the same with reference to a divinity as under the mutual conditions of human conduct. Hence theology moves in a different sphere from that of ethics. Theology calls for resignation where ethics demands protest; it makes a virtue of compliance with the blows of angered gods; and sacrifice, which is the epitome of suffering, is exalted as a center of religious ritual.

Even more important than the theologies of religion, however, in the effect upon conduct, is the still more primitive tabu, that subconscious overtone which lasts on down into the heart of even modern civilization from the rude wizardry of savage life. The rule of the tabu, still with us in so many of our social sanctions, once dominated all of conduct that was not already set in the pattern of habit. The new, the strange, the unexplained, the un-understood, all the realm of mystery into which every unaccustomed act carried the anxious nerves of our savage ancestors, called for some equally mysterious rite to avert the lurking evils of the unexplored. Anniversary ceremonies were mostly not to mark the happy ending, but to avert the disasters of the new beginning at a turning point in human affairs.

When the laws of tabu govern the world of change, it is but common sense to have as little change as possible. So habit with its dull unconscious repetition takes over the rules of magic and superstition, and reduces them to commonplace in the everyday routine of life. Now, it goes without saying, that neither tabu nor the habit that grows out of it is based upon any conscious striving for an ideal of justice. Yet because the things the gods prescribe are often but the echo of a demand for human rights and the expression of tribal experience, the tabu embodies along with its magical incantations and its supernatural apparatus most of these rules of conduct which bring order and organization out of the chaos of mere savagery. The priest is the earliest lawgiver, and the fact that the gods ordain what he decrees gives his precepts the power to dominate where force and violence would otherwise be unchecked. Religion, therefore, although its task is to link mankind to the gods, not only supplies the rudimentary beginnings of the idea of justice, but protects it by those very supernatural forces which, as we have seen, tend at the same time to destroy it.

These are strange and contradictory facts, but their contradiction is as nothing compared with that which the historian finds when he turns from these prehistoric beginnings to the origins of the great religions of today. Both in the West and in the East these have been the work of revolutionary leaders in revolt against the religious heritage of that prehistoric past. They either made over the existing religious beliefs on an ethical basis, that is to say, on the basis of a frank interest in human welfare, or, leaving the creeds untouched, built a secular philosophy alongside them, which in turn a credulous world made over into a religious faith as its founder became divine. Thus Buddha taught his ethical concepts in a revolt against the overladen tabu world of India, which, however, proved stronger than his moralizing and made his benign figure the center of the vastest system of organized tabu in the world today. Still more secular was the thought of Confucius, as secular as the Greeks' and as un-Asiatic. He taught philosophy, not theology; a philosophy in which the gods play almost no role. Mankind stands out at last with problems of its own, not those that the gods have given it, problems of human welfare to be solved by rules that have no sanction of tabu behind them but embody experience and are projected as an ideal. His precepts, therefore, are of universal application and the chief of them are as strongly held by the leaders of revolutionary China today as by the scholars of so many centuries who learned by heart the five books of the Confucian classics. But alongside this secular teaching, Confucius preserved a reverence for tradition and so helped to strengthen and perpetuate the world of magic and superstition which, as in the case of Buddha, though in far less degree, tended to distort into a sacred and unalterable canon the homely lessons of experience of the sage.

When we turn back from the religions of the Orient, we find the same historic laws at work. If Confucius recalls the Greeks, the affinity between Buddha and the reforming prophets of Israel is too familiar to call for more than passing comment. The prophetic message was, of course, cast in the fullest terms of religion. A universal deity began to replace the tribal Jewish god, but worship of the old tribal sort was to make way for righteousness—a human virtue even when copied upon the divine. Burnt offerings and all the paraphernalia of sacrifice were henceforth to be reckoned less than upright conduct and the cherishing of social ideals. The pure in heart are to be granted the ecstatic glimpse of the divinity, not because of prayers or ritual but by reason of their attitude towards other men. But again the religious background of this teaching grew stronger than the simple precepts of the prophets, stronger even than those of Christ himself. The chief concern was drawn away from the human element to the divine. Jewish teaching held to the half mystical, half magical lore of the Talmud and as for Christianity, as its faith strengthened in the expectation of the world to come, the evils of the present world seemed insignificant and transitory. Christian morals had injected the most revolutionary concept that had been yet offered to the world in the demand for charity not only to one's friend but to one's enemy; but no one, certainly not the church, thought of building society upon its model. It was too revolutionary for adaptation to the secular world. Those who sought to realize it, therefore, retired from the world into a purely religious organization.

From this analysis we see that although the concept of justice was at the heart of the doctrines of the founders of the great world religions, nevertheless religion itself was not the proper field for its development. This fact alone supplies a clue to that great cleavage in the history of civilization which marks off the Orient from the

West. The ethical teaching of Asiatic religions is almost identical with that which Europe borrowed from Old and New Testaments. Confucius' teaching that men should not do to others what they do not want others to do to them states the same principle as the Golden Rule, not in such daring and ideal terms, it is true, but perhaps in more practical form. But although the ethics of Oriental religions struck these high keys, they were so submerged in the great tide of religious belief and ritual as to fail to secure for themselves adequate instruments for their own application in the world of everyday, especially when the everyday world begins to move from its ancient mooring and takes on the quality of the unchanged West until our own time. Oriental politics never developed that process of secularization which the kings of European nations maintained against the claims of pope or bishop and, consequently, its history has little to record that is parallel with the development of justice in the Western world. This does not mean that there has been an absence or even any weakness of the sense of justice as between individuals and groups in nations such as China; but their ethical teaching remained attached to its religious root because religion was an all-pervading element. The result is that ethical teaching dealt with the individual, personal morals or the morals of the family or community expressed in terms of personal relationships. In the business world the guild carried these principles over into a social setting. But it was still a limited community based upon functional relationships and not an expression of the whole life of the nation. The absence of political institutions charged with the duty of applying and developing the ethical doctrines of the sages was the outstanding fact which has differentiated China from the West. The magistrates, it is true, were schooled in the aphorisms of the classics which the sages wrote, but as these teachings were handed down with religious reverence, the magistrates' task was not to modify or adapt the ancient prescript, but to find the existing appropriate one. For it was a part of the accepted belief that in the perfect body of classical teaching some appropriate precept could be found for any and all the exigencies of life. Thus even in a society so naturally unreligious as the Chinese, the development of justice was hampered by a sense of its perfection and by its continued association with the sanctions of religion.

It is only against this background that one begins to appreciate the development of justice in the Western world. Starting from almost the same beginnings, it has had a totally different history and one which was largely responsible for the chief differences between Oriental and Occidental society today. The struggle between the church and state throughout the Middle Ages was one of the fundamental liberations of European society. It was a process extending over almost the whole stretch of Christian history and cleared the path for the great experiment of law as a social expedient instead of a semi-divine ordinance. Justice, in this secular setting, shook off its religious antecedents. In doing so it created its own institutions, and they, in turn, jealous of their liberty and independence, fought back against the religious guardianship which had safeguarded morals before courts were founded. These two facts are chiefly responsible for the development of justice in the West, the secularization of law in the first place, and the erection of courts devoted solely to its application and maintenance. These two things the Orient never fully achieved.

Now what clue does history offer as to the reason for this divergence in the civilizations of East and West? The question cannot be answered by any of those ready generalizations so commonly in use, that the Oriental peoples were by nature more religious than those of the West, or by an equally sweeping generalization as to the practical character and interests of the Western world. These generalities are merely descriptions, not explanations. Even as descriptions they are open to challenge. No other people has been more strongly attracted into the current of modern secular business than the Japanese, who, up to fifty years ago, would have been characterized as outstanding examples of the Asiatic trend. They are still a highly religious people, but the administration of justice has been taken over into the framework of the secular life, and the code of law which the courts of Japan today apply is the borrowed experience of the Western world, varied only by its application to local needs. The history of Japan is a proof that the Oriental peoples do not differ in any inherent tendencies from the nations of the West. For, apart from what we call the modernization of its politics and its business, Japan remains distinctly more religious than China; its temples are still thronged with worshippers as in the past, pilgrims visit its shrines in undiminished numbers, and the religious tie is still dominant in personal and private life. Nevertheless, in little more than a single generation, Japan took over and made its own that process of the secularization of justice which the West had evolved.

This page of Japanese history shows the capacity of Asiatic peoples to enter into the full current of Western development. Why then, did they not do so at an earlier age? Why did this great divergence actually occur? How is it that it was left to the West to develop the principles and the institutions of law while the East held back in the ancient setting of belief and custom? The explanation surely lies not in inherent capacities but in differing situations.

Around the northern shores of the Eastern Mediterranean there were little valleys shut in by protecting mountains and enclosing rocky hills on which the inhabitants could take refuge when the raiders swept over their open fields below, and little bays at hand where the traders could draw up their open boats for a market on the beach. The settlements were large enough to have an independent life but too small and too close together to keep wholly apart. Traders settled on the flat land by the shore, and the communities, as they grew, not only warred upon each other in the old tribal way but formed their alliances and stretched out in war and commerce over an ever-increasing circle of land and sea. The limit of subsistence on the hot, dry soil was always sufficiently low to make adventure profitable, whether it were by the sack of some city on the Asiatic coast, or the bartering of goods with the primitive tribes of Italy, or the sending of the grain fleet to the prairies of southern Russia. The result was that there grew up in these Greek settlements a mixture of peoples chiefly given over to business of one sort or another, which was already, when history dawns, working out new principles of association unlike any that the Orient had ever tried. The old blood-tie of family, clan, and tribe, which has remained the basis of society in the Asiatic world, was broken down for the practical purposes of organization and intercourse. The city-state which resulted was still conceived of in religious terms, with its special deities and temples, and the tabu still survived in the rites which the magistrates performed and in the scruples which might even determine peace and war. This religious atmosphere of the city-state seems at first glance to throw it back almost wholly into the Asiatic mold. The classic pages of Fustel de Coulanges emphasize this religious aspect of the beginnings of European poli-

tics. But within itself the community was working out new principles of law and government, due to the fact that people of different
origins were living together and dealing in goods and property
without regard to ancestors and without a common feeling for the
ancient tabus.

The process of adjustment by which these matters were arranged
covers over a thousand years of Mediterranean history from the
revolutionary reforms of Solon and Cleisthenes to the codified
embodiment of antique business ethics in the *corpus juris civilis*,
which was the supreme achievement of the genius of Rome. Few
chapters in the history of civilization are more alluring than this
which led from sacrament to contract. Beginning with the fumbling
application of tabu and consecrated custom, it had already become
emancipated in principle in the circles that listened to the question
of Socrates and Plato as to the place of justice in private life and the
organization of the State. But even these free speculations revealed
the narrow framework of admitted rights in the political concepts
of the Greeks; and the philosophers seem never to have guessed—
any more than did Confucius—that it was not so much in the arguments of the Academy as in the laboratory of business intercourse
that the rich ore of justice was mined from experience and minted
for actual use. While they recognized that justice is a social fact
rather than the personal attribute of good or wise men, their chief
interest remained centered in the individual. It was a scientifically
sound starting point for secular thinking at a time when society was
still so largely a reservoir of tabu; but the life of the individual is
so short, his contacts so limited, that to concentrate upon it is to
lose sight of the long-continuing forces of history which play upon
it, and of which it is an unconscious element. The Greek thinkers
lived too much in the present to have a proper sense of time, and
too little among busy people to have a sense of business. They were
too close to the origins of politics to see its institutions as the embodiment of impersonal forces, when the personalities who introduced them were still almost contemporary. So the contribution of
Greece remained more in the field of ethics than of jurisprudence;
justice was an ideal rather than a practical concept.

Fortunately for Western civilization, Rome was the complement
of Greece and put the emphasis upon those things which were the
weakest in the Hellenic world; the individual gave way before the

needs of the community. The Greeks had been the frontiersmen of civilization, and like all people of the frontier they had placed confidence in private initiative and keenness of mind. Rome took their heritage and built upon it, not by repeating the process of bold exploration, but by embodying it in institutions upon which they could rely because they knew and could calculate their routine. This tendency of Rome to fall back upon the institutions broke down in the political sphere before the arbitrary power that was concentrated in the hands of the imperator, for it is the nature of war to destroy the slow upbuilding of the institutions of peace. It was only in the realm of law that the old republican process of institution-making continued and developed throughout the whole imperial period, culminating, when the empire was already falling to pieces, in the final structure of the Roman Code. This is not the place to attempt to trace the intricate history of the development of Roman law, but the point that must be borne in mind if we are to read the lesson of history is that in Rome justice survived because it had become impersonal and was given an institutional expression. To the Greeks a man was a man; to the Romans he was a citizen; but citizenship could not be achieved until the individual had become conscious of his rights in the community.

This double heritage of Greeks and Romans, the secularization of justice and its development into the ethics of business, meant nothing to the barbarians of the north. Again history had to begin at the beginning, but, so far as this page of it is concerned, the conditions, although outwardly so different from those of the early Mediterranean world, were in reality very similar to those which had produced the city-state. Migrations of peoples moving from a prehistoric past cut in upon the settled life of tribes and families and broke the kinship ties almost in the same way as had happened south of the Alps. Village communities arose with minute foreshadowings of political institutions in their elected headmen and other local officials. The old tabus gave way to practical expedients, as well as to the teaching of the church, and out of these backgrounds came such institutions as trial by jury and representative government. Once launched on this career, the nations of the north reached out again for the lesson of Rome, and, doing so, founded the first university as their scholars wandered down to listen to the jurists of Italy who had found a home at the foot of the northern slope of the Apennines just over from the fields of Tuscany in the old walled city of Bologna. Thus, partly borrowing from the past and partly building from their own experience, the national states repeated in only slightly variant form, the later phase of antique history. It was by no mere chance that when the French Revolution had finally proclaimed the full emancipation of the national state from its medieval tutelage, France then went back to the jurists of Justinian for the mold in which to cast the Code of Napoleon. The long cycle of some thirteen hundred years had brought the development of justice once more to where it had been when the first great cycle had been completed.

Viewed in this perspective, one sees the beginnings of our era— for contemporary history began in the period of the French Revolution—as a belated chapter of antique civilization. We moderns are ancients as well. On another and wider stage the drama of Western civilization had been played over again to almost an identical conclusion. And then again just as this was happening, new and unsuspected forces were let loose in the Western world, forces as capable of savagery as any of the hosts of Tamerlane, but equally potent in the rapid upbuilding of new forms of life and new human relationships. We have not yet begun to realize the meaning of the introduction of modern science, how it has ended for all time to come the quiet isolation of the past, the repetition through untold millennia of those simple ways of living which man is forced to lead when he draws his sustenance directly from the struggle with nature. From the first invention onward there has come an ever-increasing change in all the things that most affect human society. Time and space, the two elemental conditions of our living, no longer remain the static and unchanging determinants of conduct, but are growingly within control. While, therefore, the ideal of justice remains what it was in the past before Plato, its application, which is what Plato sought, lies now in the extension to human relationships of that same scientific spirit which has so transformed the material world. This is a task upon which the students of justice have only now begun to work, studying jurisprudence in the light of history, economics and other social sciences, and no one knows what will come of it.

CHAPTER XVII

☙❦

THE HERITAGE OF AMERICA

The mind that has ranged the universe must now itself control,
For the force of the mighty atom is less than the human soul;
And simpler than any equation are the words forever true:
Do ye unto others as ye would they do by you.
This is the missing fulcrum for Archimedes' pry
To lift the weight of ancient hate, so the peoples that pass by
May reach together the shining goal that none can reach alone,
Helping each other along the way that each may make his own,
By joint consent surrendering the ancient right of war,
Alert to thwart betrayal, aware where dangers are
That lie in differing loyalties, where bickering conflicts run,
But offering charity to all, with malice toward none.
Then undismayed by the powers we wield, steady we stand and
    strong,
As the harp of the world keeps measure to life's triumphant song.

                                                                J.T.S.

In the world crisis of today the question which haunts thoughtful
minds is: what is the meaning of it all? This is a very different question from that which confronts the governments engaged in a conflict of power, in which the issue is one of victory or defeat. It
reaches beyond the tactics of action to the understanding of the
fundamental issues involved. This at once carries it into the realm

_"The Way," in Poems by James T. Shotwell, Simon and Schuster, 1953. The
text which follows is but slightly changed from that of an article in Think,
September 1953._

of history, for the forces engaged are as much those of the past as of the present and future. Nothing in human affairs can escape history, not even the revolution which attempts to defy it; for the despotism of the Kremlin is more Asiatic than communistic, and the final issue is the oldest and most constant one, that of freedom.

It goes without saying that this is not the way the Communists view the conflict, for those who have never lived under the regime of freedom cannot understand it. Some of the peoples of eastern Europe and Asia have never known what self-government meant, never having shared in that great experiment which from the days of ancient Greece challenged despotism in the West. We therefore cannot expect them to know what we mean when we present as an ideal of government the principles of the Declaration of Independence or the Gettysburg Address or even the Atlantic Charter.

But, more serious still, we ourselves are not wholly clear about this heritage of ours, won for us by the sacrifice and faith, the creative energy and tireless devotion of our forefathers. What is the harvest of their sowing, garnered into the rich storehouse of the Republic?

This is the supreme question of our time as we confront a future which represents new challenges to the intelligence and courage of men no longer finding either safety or welfare in the static world of habit and repetition. Still, although the scenes of the conditions of life are changing, even too rapidly for thought to follow, the human actors remain the same, limited by the same needs, responsive to the same desires as in the past. The mind that controls the atom is never wholly in control of itself. It responds to the instincts of primitive life as well as to the disciplines of reason.

Therefore, as we stand on the horizon of the future, we need to keep our bearings by tracing the pathway of civilization to our country and our own lives. For the crisis of today is part of that vast and tragic drama which kept throughout the ages—and still keeps—the undertone of primitive savagery, but which also rises to the highest themes of human thought, justice and mercy. As this short survey of an age-old theme makes clear, we are the inheritors of every gain made in the history of justice from the days of Hammurabi to those of the welding of Roman and English law, of the ideals of freedom from ancient Greece to Puritan England and revolutionary France, and of all the creative thought nourished by the arts of peace in every land. But this is only half the story, for the gifts of the Old World were fully matched by those of the New World, as the continent opened new paths of freedom and challenged mankind to rise above the past by making its own the greatest of these achievements, the quiet, long-delayed conquest of peace itself.

To no other land and to no other people has this supreme issue of the welding of the past and the future come with such compelling force. The heritage of other peoples, which becomes ours by right of their choice in coming here, is reinforced by the kind of life they have had to live, concentrating with steadfast purpose upon the conquest not of man but nature in the winning of a continent, intractable but kindly, spacious, and magnificent. Then, just when the New World was won from sea to sea, another new world was opened by the discoveries of science, remaking time and space and recasting human relationships. Once again we are pioneers; but this time the pioneering will never stop; it will go on for ever. For it is a test, not merely of steadfastness and endurance, but of that final attribute of man: intelligence.

It is this new, new world which holds the promise of the future. The promise is by no means clear in the dawn's early light, nor in the red glare which gleams so menacingly on the ramparts of freedom. But one thing is clear: the cause of freedom, justice, and peace will ultimately prevail, for otherwise there is no future for mankind. Science has already seen to that by forging weapons of destruction that leave no hope either for victim or victor, making war—the supreme instrument of politics in the upbuilding of nations—an international crime that brings annihilation.

The drama of history is still enacted on the ill-lighted stage where the animal in man has so long stalked its prey. But even while brute force acquires the most deadly power of mass destruction, the theme of the conflict is changing to the realm of the spirit. The principles of secular society, which each nation accepted for itself but denied in its relations with others, are now being forged in the white heat of controversy into universal concepts of right and wrong, applying everywhere, to everyone. The ultimate ideal with which communism beguiles its devotees is that of a classless world of increased welfare for all; its crime against society is not in its insistence on this goal, but in its ruthless methods of persecution at home and conquest abroad, which substitute for the ideal of a cooperative commonwealth the oppressive might of imperialist despotism. The Communists justify this reliance on force and violence as part of the unfinished revolution by which their regime will be established and, therefore, as only a temporary phase of their policy. But this reasoning is based on the assumption that there can be only one outcome, the triumph of communism everywhere and the submission of everyone to the despotism of those who would wield universal, unquestioned authority in the application of their doctrine. Until that day of triumph, communism accepts war as the instrument of its policy. Its propaganda for peace must be understood in the light of these conditions, which not only deny the validity of the peace movements among noncommunist nations, but distort the ultimate ideal of a world of economic justice by making that justice the synonym for rigid, bureaucratic despotism.

What, then, is the way to meet this challenge to the free world? Both history and the events of these last years of crisis point in a single direction: peace based upon freedom and justice. At last these great ideals must be made real. For too many centuries they have been professed in morals and religion but denied in the practical affairs of daily life and the politics of nations. As long as that hypocrisy mocks our ideals, the enemy has a case. We have, of course, a ready rejoinder in the fact that the Communists themselves have excelled as hypocrites in their dealings with other nations, but that is too easy and cheap an argument for a debate so serious as this should be. The real contrast lies in the fact that the Bolsheviki undertook to change society by a single movement, and that the noncommunist nations held to the slow, evolutionary processes of history. They have been slow to realize or at least to apply the Golden Rule, which is the Einstein equation for the free world, turning the inert mass of self-centered nationalism into the dynamics of mutual aid and welfare; and they have been equally slow to deny the age-long legitimacy of war. Now, however, with the advance of science, the only lasting prosperity comes from a working membership in the world community, and the only lasting peace from a recognition that war has become an anachronism between civilized nations, because its mass destruction escapes all limits of control or direction.

The meaning of history is thus becoming clear in the crisis of today, which seems at first sight to darken and obscure it. The clue to it is to be found, not in the records of great eras in either war or peace, but in measuring the rate of the advance of intelligence in the direction of human affairs, from the Ice Age to today. By far the longest period lies the other side of Egypt and Babylonia, where, through untold millennia, mankind made infinitely slow progress in applying the mind to meet the dangers and problems of life. Then, about five thousand years ago, the process began to speed up in favored sections of the earth, as civilization began to come to grips with its ancient enemies, superstition and war. The great ethical religions, especially in the West, attempted with varying success to get rid of the fears and evil practices of superstition, a process which, by its accent on belief, tended to block criticism, that basic element of reason, but by its controversies prepared the way for future inquiry. Then came science, and in the incredibly short period of two or three centuries, it created a new world for the mind and remade the terms of the problems of war and peace. War must now go the way of superstition. In neither case will the great reform be complete or universal in our time; but there can be no doubt of the ultimate goal. Peace is not merely a vacuum left by the ending of wars. It is, as we have seen throughout this survey, the embodiment of the two eternal principles of justice and freedom —justice as defined in the Golden Rule and freedom as set forth in the declaration of the rights of man, by England and France, by the United States and the United Nations. Some day these rights may be embodied in world law, but that day is still distant, for unless law is the expression of the common will it is worse than meaningless; it is an impediment to progress. But with a rapidity without parallel in history, the varied purposes of nations are being brought into line, the contrary methods of the Communists notwithstanding. For, underlying all conflicting ideologies, the final fact remains that the moral order of the world is at last a living issue in practical politics.

The world has just begun to be civilized. Within a single lifetime we are turning the corner on the long stretch of centuries that reaches from beyond the Ice Age.

There is no parallel to this in all the history of mankind. No wonder, therefore, that the pathway of progress is blocked by ignorance and the ideals of justice and liberty are at times dimmed.

Humanity is on the march, but the goal before it is one that can never be reached; for, as we "follow knowledge like a sinking star beyond the utmost bound of human thought," we shall forever find across our pathway the shadows of heights still to be scaled—of ideals still to be realized.

CHAPTER XVIII

⁂

THE CONSTITUTION AND THE
GUARANTEE OF FREEDOM

IN THIS, the greatest crisis in the history of civilization, it is a sound instinct which carries our minds back across the century and a half of history to that day when the work of the Founding Fathers of the Republic was completed and the great experiment was definitely launched of creating a Constitution that would both ensure effective government and safeguard the citizen against excess of power. Every new phase of the crisis draws us nearer in spirit to those pioneering thinkers who first set forth the fundamental principles upon which the institutions of our political life are based. It is not merely instinct, however, which causes us to refresh our minds by a rereading of history; for the stubborn logic of events forces us into a situation which is fundamentally similar to that confronting the country at its birth. The long enumeration of acts of tyranny in the indictment of George III is more than paralleled by our indictment of our enemies today. At a time when liberty is trampled upon by the oppressor in more than half the world, the reminder of our heritage of freedom is especially valid and important. The fundamental issue of the last war was not the maintenance of the independence of the peoples of Continental Europe, nor of the British Empire, nor even the vast significance of the mastery of

James Goold Cutler Lecture—Delivered at the College of William and Mary, February 9, 1942.

Asia; it was whether freedom itself can survive in nations which have cherished it more than life itself, or whether those who have never lived securely under its benign régime will impose the contagion of their regime upon the rest of the world. This is the issue of 1776 once more in a world-wide setting. The scene has shifted from the quiet precincts of historic Williamsburg to a world-wide debate on the nature of government in which some of us think we can faintly discern the outlines of an international community of free nations looking forward with the same confidence in the triumph of the fundamental principle of justice among nations, which is the basis of civil government at home.

It was in fulfillment of this purpose of domestic clarification that there was recently a nation-wide celebration of the 150th Anniversary of the adoption of the Bill of Rights in the Constitution. The exact terms of that celebration, however, left much to be desired from the standpoint of the historian, however appealing it may have seemed to those who conceived of it as an emotional rededication to a great and national ideal. Listening to the voices that came over the air from Hollywood, one might think that the guarantee of freedom was an invention of our own, that we succeeded where other peoples suffered and failed, that however much the ideals had been illumined by prophets and teachers in the past, it had never been focussed into reality until set forth in the immortal phrasing of the Founding Fathers. It should be our first thought today to protest against this falsification of history; for no one would have protested more than Mason or Jefferson against the idea that the fundamental principles upon which the New Republic rested its case before the public opinion of the world were new and solely and purely American. The principles of government, designed to protect freedom, were not a sudden birth, like a full-armed Minerva from the head of Jove. The antecedents of the American experiment in government go back across the whole history of the Western world to those pioneers in political thinking, Plato and Aristotle, and to the stoic and Christian thinkers who built upon their work. Roman law and the scholastic philosophers of the Middle Ages contributed to this heritage as well, and finally it was once more brought out of the academic cloister by the writers of the period of the Renaissance and those following them to furnish the basis of the new State system of Europe in the seventeenth and eighteenth centuries.

So far, however, we have been speaking of only one stream of influence upon the thought of Colonial America. But before we turn to analyze the nature of that contribution of Continental Europe to political theory, we must place over against it another and different pattern of politics, that which was drawn from the history of England. However much the English of the Middle Ages profited from Greece and Rome, the evolution of their political institutions was a thing apart from that of the Continent. In place of the generalizations of philosophy, they tended always to think in the homely terms of real life, and to build up the safeguards of freedom through the obscure but august process which was registered in the common law.

The Founders of the American Republic were influenced by both these historic trends, the Continental and the English, as is clearly shown by an analysis of the Declaration of Independence itself. The title deeds of the new nation are those granted to it by "the Laws of Nature and of Nature's God," a phrase in the opening paragraph of the Declaration, the full import of which most readers fail to note. For, in contrast with these eternal and immutable laws, the main principles of which are summarized in the sentences which follow, there is traced a detailed picture of civil law which constitutes the picture of actual government under King George III. This series of political acts is clearly of a different character drawn from a different world of experience than the basic principles with which the misgovernment is contrasted. In short, the Declaration of Independence judges the government of England on principles drawn from a Continental source.

This is just the opposite of the procedure by which the English themselves set about redressing their own grievances against the Stuarts. James I, a Scottish king, brought up under French influences, was trained in the Roman law and justified his theory of government upon it. His great legal opponent, Sir Edward Coke, was, on the contrary, the protagonist of the common law, and drew his arsenal of argument from English experience. There was an advantage in the argument with the sovereign in his not being held down to a single set of principles like those which the king was fond of reciting from the Roman law in support of his claims of absolute kingship. In building thus upon the English past, Coke went so far as to strain historic truth in the support of freedom. Maitland's remark that Coke "invented Magna Carta" is but another way of saying that he used it to the full and for perhaps a little more than it was worth. For it was a mighty buttress for the glorification of the common law. Yet, while refusing to follow the lead of the Roman jurists, he fell back upon much the same method in his insistence upon a fundamental law superior to parliamentary statutes, an argument not without influence upon American revolutionary opinion.

Now it is a striking fact that the opposition to George III in the Declaration of Independence was not based upon any such reasoning as that of Coke, for Jefferson fell back upon the method of King James and challenged the existing government of England on the basis of its violation of certain abstract rights with which, according to the Declaration, all men are endowed by their Creator. This contrast of the initial statement of the American Revolution, with that which laid the groundwork for the Civil War and the Revolution of 1689 in England, seems to have escaped attention, so far as I know, and it is certainly an interesting conjecture as to why this should have been the case. I think the answer may perhaps lie in the fact that when the experience of the English Revolution came to be summed up after it was all over, the fundamental principles of the law of nature which were then adduced, were very different from the principles which King James drew from the Roman law. James could fall back upon the precepts of the late Imperial period of Roman history, which emphasized the power and sovereignty of a Divine ruler. By the time John Locke wrote his "Two Treatises on Civil Government," it was not to the late Roman period that the political philosophers were looking but to the period of the Republic and the Early Empire, in which the rights of man were the chief concern of both philosophers and jurists, and there was a place for Freedom in the scheme of eternal things.

It is almost impossible for us today to realize how heavy was the weight of antique learning upon the thought of the sixteenth, seventeenth and eighteenth centuries. The formative period of modern history was dominated to a large extent by antique models. In its first phase this played into the hands of absolutism and the age of despots was the result. The theory of the Divine right of kings drew support, not merely from the precepts of the late Roman Empire, but even more from the Old Testament and that ceremony which amounted to almost an eighth sacrament, the anointing and the coronation of the King. Royalty was thus exalted until it claimed to be the whole body politic, "L'état, c'est moi." This conception, destroyed in England in the seventeenth century, and in France in the Revolution which followed our own, was acted upon by rulers as enlightened as Frederick the Great. How was it that the revolutionary theory which ultimately supplanted it, of the sovereignty of the people, won its way to victory? The answer to this question is that the opponents of absolute monarchy found an even richer arsenal in the classical authors than in the protagonists of kingship.

At the risk of repetition, let us trace this prehistory of the Bill of Rights a little more definitely. We begin with Richard Hooker, "the judicious Hooker," as Locke repeatedly refers to him. Hooker's "Ecclesiastical Polity," published in 1593, was designed as an argument against the Puritans and for the Church as established by Elizabeth, and the application of that argument to civil polity was only incidental. Nevertheless, falling back upon the concept of the law of nature as the embodiment of reason, he reached the conclusion that laws must harmonize with this fundamental test and be upheld so long as they are fitted to that end. In the effort to show the Puritans that they were wrong in their objection to what the majority desired, he argued that reason is subject to change with circumstances, and calls for adjustment to realities. The Puritans had fallen back upon Revelation, but that, said Hooker, is a matter of faith, whereas Reason is the guide for mankind in its secular activities. Society itself is a product of the law of nature because, in the pursuit of happiness (the phrase had not yet acquired currency) the interplay of interests leads men to agree upon some form of government to harmonize their varying desires. There is nothing new in all of this, for it is the old debate familiar to Cicero, and to the scholastics. But it leads also to the fundamental thought which was crystallized by Rousseau, that of a social compact as the basis of society. The wording, however, is very unlike Rousseau. Let me quote one sentence:

> . . . By the natural law whereunto God hath made all subject, the lawful power of making laws to command whole politic societies of men belongeth so properly unto the same entire societies, that

for any prince or potentate of what kind soever upon earth, to exercise the same of himself, and not either by express commission immediately and personally received from God, or else by authority derived at the first from their consent upon whose persons they impose the laws, it is no better than mere tyranny.

Thus Hooker's contribution to English political thought leads to the conclusion that a test of the validity of laws is the consent of the governed. It is a paradox which was bound to be noticed, that in this way, while arguing for the support of the Tudor Queen in her ecclesiastical policy, Hooker enunciated a theory quite at variance with the earlier trend of Tudor despotism. His influence, however, was limited by the fact that he was writing a treatise against the Puritans, and they, in their struggle for power, found support in the more practical mind of Coke. The real battle against the Stuarts was to be fought out on more definitely English terms.

When the battle was over, John Locke summed up the consequences in his "Two Treatises of Government," published in August, 1689, some six months after the Declaration of Rights forced upon William and Mary on their accession to the throne. That document began by reciting Hooker's theory of a contractual basis for the Constitution of England. At this point, we may pause to remark that it is perhaps a fortunate thing for the English that they never codified their Constitution into a single written document, for they might have found it difficult to include in it the contractual basis of the sovereignty of William and Mary along with the declaration of a King by the Grace of God. The advantage of not having codified their texts is that there can be a shifting emphasis upon those particular elements in the body of precedent and statute through which the British government works. In short, seventeenth century England actually worked out in its political history that harmony between the law of nature and civil law which Hooker had made the basis of his argument a century before.

This may seem an unduly long historical introduction to the guarantee of freedom in our Constitution, but we have only now reached the real bridge between English and American thought, for it was John Locke who was the mentor and George Mason the author of the Bill of Rights in the Constitution of Virginia, and we have not even touched as yet upon the contribution of Montesquieu, whose scheme of government would make government itself a check upon the undue extension of its powers. There would, of course, be a certain justification in analyzing Locke's political philosophy in some detail at this point because he was the man who most influenced American political thinking in the period of the Revolution. As this has often been done, however, we shall content ourselves with an attempt to answer the question why it was that the Whig philosophy of social contract which he elucidated triumphed so completely in the England of 1689 and in the thought of the Founding Fathers.

The answer to this is, I believe, to be chiefly found in the economic history of the sixteenth and seventeenth centuries which was the period of the Commercial Revolution. The treasure that was captured by the freebooters who plundered the galleons of Spain was not left in the hands of rulers to accumulate in hoards for the payment of soldiery or the extravagance of courts. The seamen of the northern nations were backed by businessmen who speedily learned how to use capital in productive enterprise. Merchant adventurers, they introduced into the economic life of northern Europe a different sense of property from that which concentrated upon territorial holdings. Fluid property to the extent of these new millions in gold and silver coins had never been known in history before. It followed, therefore, that any social contract in the political framework of government which would be valid for England or the Netherlands, would have to provide safeguards for capitalistic property if the new merchant and moneyed class was to maintain its place within the state.

On the other hand, the King had a greater need for money than ever before because of the increased cost of administration due to the inflationary effect of the influx of gold and silver, which produced the first revolution in prices in the history of Europe. The issue between the Stuart Kings and the Commoners of England was thus largely conditioned by the Commercial Revolution; it was not only personal liberty but money. The control of the purse had become very definitely the test of political power. The argument, however, by which Royalty was met was based upon English precedent. James I, trained in Roman law, met the claims of the English jurists by reiterating the precepts of late Roman law in which the will of the monarch was recognized as supreme. Over against this basic citation in support of Divine Right, Coke, as McKechnie puts it, "read into Magna Carta the entire body of the common law of the seventeenth century, of which he was admittedly a master," and did it so effectively that it assumed substantially the character of a statement of natural law. Thus he and Hooker were approaching from opposite angles that theory of human rights which had played so large a part in the theory of the stoics. The law of nature could evidently be reached by the experimental processes of English justice as well as by the philosophic deductions of Aristotle.

Of these two streams of history, the English and the Continental, the latter runs with limpid current between banks that have been opened and made straight by the logic of legal engineering; while the former meanders obscurely and at times is almost lost to view as it sinks into the soil of English life. But the green meadows of the common law, which it refreshes, spreading out by village and countryside, are a more vital symbol of freedom than the prouder creations of the Roman jurists at the courts of rulers. Let us take two examples of this vitality. Our Bill of Rights of 1791 thunders "nor shall any person be deprived of life, liberty or property without due process of law." These very words, clad in the quaint Norman French of 1354, were enacted by the Parliament of Westminster in the twenty-eighth year of Edward III, six years after the battle of Crecy.[1] The gap between the two texts is four hundred and thirty-seven years, but even an old equity draughtsman might well agree that this is the only gap there is. Another example is our constitutional right of the freedom of speech. This made no change whatever in the rights of free speech which Englishmen were then enjoying. It is the rights of free speech, as defined by the common law, which cannot be abridged.[2]

Let us turn now from legal to political history. Alongside the common law principle of *habeas corpus*, stood the demand that there should not be taxation without representation. The two were combined in that most signal exercise of the right of petition ever made, the Petition of Right of 1628, which by the King's signature became law. England was saved from becoming a land where the King could imprison on *lettres de cachet* such as filled the Bastille, and from the levy of arbitrary taxes. In the subsequent Civil War the free rights of Englishmen to dispose of both person and property were sealed in blood; but, as the forces engaged in the conflict were ranged under banners of political faith, it was the protection of property which took precedence over personal liberty, as the very names of the opposing forces indicate. It was a war of Parliament against the King; not of law courts against despotism, although the two principles were united in their fundamental opposition to rule by Divine Right. The contrast with what happened in France is interesting at this point; for there it was the law courts which led in the civil disturbances of the Fronde. In England in the seventeenth century, the propertied class went beyond juristic to political liberty as the fundamental principle of their Constitution.

When we come to think about it, there is nothing strange in the fact that the Revolution which brought the middle class to power should put the protection of property to the forefront. But it was a *tour de force* for the English philosophers of that period to read this fundamental interest of theirs into the law of nature so completely as to make the identification seem axiomatic. It is true that there was a hint of the possibilities in Greek and Roman literature, but those possibilities were not developed and applied to the conditions of the modern world until Locke wrote his famous Treatises on Civil Government. Perhaps the essence of his philosophy is best summed up in the following sentences: "The great and chief need of men uniting into commonwealths and putting themselves under government is the preservation of their property, to which in the state of nature there are many things wanting," and that the commonwealth must be so organized that "the supreme power cannot take from any man any part of his property without his own consent." This quotation, however, should not be left standing by itself, for by property Locke said that he meant "that property which men have in their persons as well as goods."

So far we have been dealing with the essential English situation with which Locke's Treatises were fundamentally concerned. Nevertheless, his Treatises on Civil Government were not argued on the basis of English precedent but were cast in the mold of natural law. It was perhaps chiefly owing to this fortunate circumstance that they became universal in application and influenced deeply not only the thought of Americans but the philosophers of France, thus furnishing inspiration for two great currents of revolution.

Before we leave the old world for the new, however, there is an interesting parallel to be drawn between the achievement of freedom in the political and economic spheres. The year 1776 was the date of the publication of Adam Smith's *Wealth of Nations*, also a document of freedom. In it, the new capitalism of the Commercial Revolution registered its protest against the rigidity of government control. Although the movement of economic forces is often slower and less evident than that of politics, it is also a fundamental expression of human society. It was not until the middle of the nineteenth century that the doctrine of freer trade broke down the barriers of mercantilism throughout Europe. Had that liberating movement happened a century earlier, it would have produced an entirely different history of the modern world.

This hurried sketch of the European background of Colonial thinking on political matters, slight and imperfect as it is, should be kept in mind as we turn to the ways in which English experience and antique precept were fused into the permanent instruments of government of the New Republic. The first of these to be drawn up was that which took shape here in Williamsburg in June, 1776, the Constitution of the State of Virginia. As everyone knows, it preceded the Declaration of Independence, although by only a short space of time. As we read the text of the Bill of Rights drafted by George Mason, and inserted in this pioneer document of the liberties of America, we see at once how natural such a statement would be from so close a student of Locke. "All men are created equally free and independent and have certain inherent natural rights of which they cannot by any Compact deprive or divest their posterity; among which are the enjoyment of Life and Liberty, with the Means of acquiring and possessing property, and pursuing and obtaining happiness and safety." The second article continues the same theme in the same universal terms, "that all Power is by God and Nature,* vested, and consequently derived from the people; that magistrates are their Trustees and Servants and at all times amenable to them."

Bills of Rights, such as that to which these ringing sentences furnish the prelude, were incorporated in the constitutions of seven of the revolting colonies. This undoubtedly was not due to any tendency to copy the formulations of Virginia, but to a widespread

---

* *The phrase "by God and Nature" of Mason's draft was stricken out of the Virginia Declaration of Rights, which, it should be said, was not strictly a part of the Constitution.*

trend in colonial thinking of the same ideas as those which emanated from Mason and his associates. Later on, when the substance of this Bill of Rights was incorporated in the Federal Constitution, this action by the various States was lost sight of except to the eye of the researching historian.

Nevertheless, it is a peculiar fact that it was one of the influences of the American Revolution upon that of France which left a definite trace for the historian. The Convention which was drawing up the Constitution of the French Republic ordered a translation to be made of the Constitution of Virginia, thus having at hand for comparison with the Declaration of the Rights of Man and the Citizen the Virginian Bill of Rights of George Mason. It is of much greater interest to us, however, to compare that document with the Declaration of Independence drafted by a different hand but drawn from the same creative source whose fountain-head was the College of William and Mary.

Mason's enumeration of "inherent natural rights" is longer but more precise. The great phrase of the Declaration, "Life, Liberty and the Pursuit of Happiness," has become so much a part of American history that we seldom pause to think of the swift sweep of the trilogy as needing any further definition. Yet, the longer phrase of Mason's text is a more careful statement, if less effective, than the headlining which Jefferson gave to it. The inherent "natural Rights" which Mason enumerated, are enjoyment of Life and Liberty, not Life itself, nor even Liberty. And parallel with this is the opportunity for acquiring and possessing property, enabling the citizen to pursue and obtain happiness and safety. Here we have Locke's Treatise on Government paraphrased in a single clause, but with a significant accent upon a phrase lacking in the Treatise on Government, "the pursuit of happiness." Locke was no Puritan to whom this world was merely a stern school fitting the soul for the life to come by an austere denial of present enjoyments. On the contrary, he emphasized the right which men have "to enjoy their goods and possessions" as a fundamental condition of organized society. But this ideal of the good life suffered a sea-change when Mason and Jefferson gave it voice in the New World; it was not the possession but the pursuit of happiness which was set before the American people as the thing to be desired. Never was prevision more justified, for it is surely the peculiar quality of American life

that it does find happiness in the pursuit of it. Forever following
its star, it is forever stirred with a sense of aspiration and endeavor.
Thus Jefferson, by the deft use of this single phrase, added a whole
new province to the field of natural law, carrying it over from the
static world of ancient times and the Middle Ages to that of the
tumultous pressures of today.

One wonders just what the New England Puritans thought of
this pursuit of happiness as an ideal for America. It must have
sounded strange in the ears of those for whom life in this world was
but a preparation for that in the world to come. It is certainly an
added reason for rejoicing that the Declaration of Independence
was turned over to be written by a Virginian, because otherwise it
is doubtful if it would ever have cheered, as it has, the prospect of
so many generations. Whether George Mason's Cavalier ancestry
predisposed him toward the acceptance of this genial idea of pursuing happiness while acquiring and possessing property, or whether
he was simply giving homely expression to the more sober thought
of Aristotle that the ultimate end of society was the furtherance of
the good life, is a point which can never be settled. It has been
surmised that perhaps the influences of the Swiss writer Burlamaqui, an author exceedingly popular in America at that time, was
responsible for the linking of the ideas of happiness with property.
Although almost forgotten now, he was the most widely read of
the political theorists of that time. His work was a textbook in the
classes of William and Mary, and was used by George Wythe, who
had so great an influence upon the intellectual development of Jefferson. The evidence of Jefferson's Commonplace Book, however,
seems to point to James Wilson as the medium through which the
influence of Burlamaqui's thought was transmited. However this
may be, the fact remains that Mason's reference to property disappeared from the Declaration of Independence.

We are now at last ready to turn to the announced subject of
this lecture, "The Constitution of the United States and the Safeguards of Freedom Contained in It." The history of the formation
of the Constitution is too well known for me to do more than point
to one or two of the more significant items in it. It was built on the
shifting sands of discord and discouragement. For a time, the winning of independence seemed to have burnt out men's enthusiasms
for the eternal verities. Divided north and south and in economic

interests, it appeared to many who had stood foremost in the fight against the external enemy that the fruits of victory were turning to ashes in their mouths. This is, of course, the situation which is almost sure to arise after any war in which the underlying differences of allied communities or states have been overcome or forgotten during the period of fighting but which come to the fore after the war is over. The critical period of American history, that which lay between the close of the War of Independence and the framing of the Constitution, was repeated in a sense in the years which followed after the First World War when partisanship and, then later, indifference in the American body politic frustrated the possibilities which lay in that first sketch of a Constitution for the world, Woodrow Wilson's Covenant of the League of Nations. Future historians will undoubtedly regard the years which lay between the two world wars as at least equally fateful for the liberties of this country as that critical period at the beginning of its history. It is to be hoped that the close of the present world war will find us better prepared, as we shall be more matured in political experience. And yet the problem of today is so much more difficult than that which confronted the Founding Fathers that we have at least no room for undue optimism at the present time.

There is nothing invidious in the fact, which Professor Beard was the first to emphasize, that it was primarily the concern for property rights which brought about the call for the Convention which met in Philadelphia in 1787. There was every reason for concern. Property was imperiled both by populist state legislation and the fear of widespread popular uprisings. But the only voice raised in the Convention in sincere concern for the rights of personal liberty was that of George Mason, who proposed that a bill enumerating the inalienable rights of the people, like that of his Virginia Declaration of Rights, should be inserted in the Constitution. When Gerry moved that a committee be appointed to draw up such a declaration, the Convention voted unanimously, ten to nothing, against it. Jefferson, who was absent as Minister to France, showed his concern over this drift of affairs. When Madison sent him a copy of the Constitution, he wrote back that "a Bill of Rights is what the people are entitled to against every government on earth, general or particular, and what no just government should refuse, or rest on inferences." The argument of the Federalists, on the other hand, was that a strong government would overcome the defect of a lack of specific guarantees of liberty by "that prompt and salutary execution of the laws which enters into the very definition of good government." It was not until the 84th number of the *Federalist*, however, that they came squarely upon the issue stating "that the Constitution is itself in every rational sense and to every useful purpose A BILL OF RIGHTS," in the same way as "the several bills of rights in Great Britain form its constitution." The heavy artillery of the Federalists, however, could not prevail against the deep feeling of the people that a formal guarantee was called for against the possible development of tyranny in the newly-formed government. This protest was not what Hamilton would have called "the voice of rabble." Its most powerful backer was still George Mason, to whom Jefferson in his old age paid tribute as one of the wisest among the statesmen of his time. Madison, apparently won over by the arguments of his Virginian friends, changed his Federalist standpoint for that of Mason, and finally on June 8, 1789, the Father of the Constitution rose in Congress to propose the first Ten Amendments to the great document which had been so largely his creation.

It is not my purpose to attempt to trace here the history of the Bill of Rights throughout the nineteenth century. That is a task for the specialist in the history of law. It is not a theme which has played any large part in American history as taught in the schools. Even in recent years the widely read volume on "The Rise of American Civilization," by Charles and Mary Beard, while giving a good account of the making of the Constitution itself, passes over the first Ten Amendments without any mention of the Bill of Rights contained in them. Indeed, the term "Bill of Rights" does not appear in the Index of that volume. The explanation for this is perhaps partly to be found in the fact that there was another safeguard of freedom, both of person and of property, in the Constitution, provided in the independence of the judiciary. This opens an entirely different prospect from that which we have been looking at hitherto. The architect of that tripartite edifice of government which rests upon a separation of the Powers was not John Locke, but Montesquieu. The manual of the French jurist which was destined to play so great a part in our history, "The Spirit of Laws," was primarily drawn from a study of the way in which the Romans of the Republican period had broken up the universal powers of Kingship into the appropriate divisions of government with especial reference to the evolution of Roman law. Later on Montesquieu thought he discovered in the English Constitution a similar separation of the powers. This was not Locke's point of view because he regarded the legislature as supreme. Nevertheless, the principle of the independence of the English judiciary as a bulwark against the extension of royal prerogative was one of the decisive gains of the English Revolution. There was therefore both French and English precedent behind the creation of a supreme court, the members of which were appointed for life, although it was left for John Marshall, by a broad interpretation of the Constitution, to give that court the place which it has come to occupy, not only in juristic theory but in the public opinion of the country. The extent to which the court had become "a palladium of liberty" in popular opinion was shown in the complete overthrow of a recent Executive effort to weaken it.

It was upon this independence of the judiciary that the great teacher of American Constitutional Law of the nineteenth century, Professor Burgess, based his test of government. A soldier of the Northern army in the war between the states and then a student of those German political philosophers who, following Hegel, exalted the state as the embodiment of absolute sovereignty, he yet found it essential to place a limitation upon the sphere of government so that it should not curtail the sphere of liberty. Time and again he emphasized both in his writings and in his lectures the peculiar merit of the American Constitution in having set up a judiciary which, because it was capable of checking both the other branches of government, exalted liberty above the processes of state action.

This explains why Professor Burgess never referred to the Bill of Rights by that name but always spoke of it as the First Ten Amendments to the Constitution. There was, however, another reason for this perspective. It was his extreme opposition to the doctrine of states' rights, an opposition which led him to interpret the middle period of American history, that preceding the War between the States, as a time when the fundamental principles of American unity, as they had been envisaged by Hamilton and applied even by Jefferson and Jackson, were lost sight of in the years following the Missouri Compromise. According to his theory of American history, the country recovered its title deeds only in the Fourteenth Amendment.

Through its application by the Supreme Court to limit the right of the States to engage in social experiments, this Amendment to the Constitution, originally conceived to embody the victory of the political theories of the north, became, by a strange turn in history, something quite different from what it was designed to be. Historically, the Fourteenth Amendment fits in between the Thirteenth and Fifteenth, emphasizing as it does the supremacy of the union. But the guarantee which it offers to all citizens is linked so definitely with the Federal system as to carry over into that system the elements of the Bill of Rights which were originally linked with states' rights theory. The Fourteenth Amendment does not put the limitation upon Congress, as was the case in the First Amendment, but upon the legislatures of the states. "No State shall make or enforce any law which shall abridge the privileges or immunities of citizens of the United States; nor shall any State deprive any person of life, liberty, or property, without due process of law; nor deny to any person within its jurisdiction the equal protection of the laws." The advantage of this text was that it linked the principles of the Bill of Rights with the Federal judiciary and thus, at last, seemed to have united the two currents which began with Mason and Jefferson, on the one hand, and Hamilton and his Federalist associates on the other.

The shape in which problems appear to each new generation is ever changing. The fundamental principles by which those problems must be tested remain the same but need to be restated from age to age in terms of the present. As this country filled up and its last frontiers were reached, new questions of social justice arose to challenge the conscience of men. The Bill of Rights, which had been a revolutionary product, now showed, in its new formulation in the Fourteenth Amendment, that it had also a conservative aspect. The question which arose therefore and which even yet is by no means settled was whether it would be possible to retain those liberties for which our ancestors had mutually pledged their lives, their fortunes and their sacred honor, and at the same time to provide for the economically submerged third of our nation the material basis without which, as George Mason may have meant to show in linking it with property, the pursuit of happiness is but an illusion.

And now finally we come to the issue of freedom in the world today. This is the supreme challenge of the Second World War. Never in all history has there been such a revolutionary movement as that which finds its chief and strongest champion in the country from which Professor Burgess drew his theory of government over half a century ago, Germany. Fascist Italy nurtures no such fanaticism as the Germans have shown themselves capable of. The other Axis power, however, Japan, outdoes Germany in its rigidity of thought, if not in the cruelty of its suppression of opposition. It was but natural that the United States should find it hard to believe the thoroughgoing denial of freedom which the forces of the Axis are fighting to impose upon the world, but now we have at last learned the truth of Wilson's noble phrase, and have realized that there is no safety for our freedom unless we have a whole world safe for democracy.

It was therefore but natural that occasion should have been taken to restablish the Bill of Rights in the public mind of this country. The more recent celebration of the 150th Anniversary of its adoption was referred to earlier. It is clear that this summary of the safeguards of freedom has now become more a political doctrine than a purely legal one. So far as its legal history is concerned, we know now how to apply it in our domestic life, conscious of the fact that eternal vigilance is the price which we must pay for its maintenance and strengthening. But in the political field we have not only to defeat the enemy that threatens our institutions and our way of life, but we have to create new institutions and adjust our way of life to a world-wide scene. This is the greatest task that has ever confronted the intelligence of mankind, for the New Federalism, as it has been called, which is destined some day to include the whole civilized world, is as yet only a dream and an inspiration, for which even the most matured in political experience are ill prepared.

Happily, the making of the Constitution of the United States provides a clue as to the basic thought which must underlie the new law of nations, for no one has yet devised any adequate substitute for that political philosophy which springs from the pioneering thought of the Greek philosophers, and which was the inspiration of Locke, of Mason, and of Jefferson. Natural law, or better still, the law of nature, is the only sound basis upon which to build the structure of government between nations as well as within a nation. The safeguard of freedom lies in the erection of those institutions which ensure justice. And justice is not what each sovereign claims for itself, but what is sound and healthful practice for society. The only way to ensure peace is to create the substitutes for war, without which there can be no guarantee of freedom anywhere in the world.

This, I venture to say, is the way in which the ultimate issue of the Second World War will have to be faced. It is fundamentally the same as that which was first formulated for the New World by gentlemen of Virginia, only a few steps away from where I stand.

NOTES

THE CONSTITUTION AND GUARANTEE OF FREEDOM

1. The text of this statute reads as follows: "que nul home ne soit oste de terre ne de tenement ne pris nemprisone ne desherite ne mis a mort saunz estre mesne en response par dues proces de lei." Behind this of course lies the classic phrase in Article 39 of Magna Carta: "No freeman shall be captured or imprisoned or disseised or outlawed or exiled or in any way destroyed, nor will we go against him or send against him, except by the lawful judgment of his peers or by the law of the land."
2. Those rights were limited as to treason, conspiracy, libel and slander; free speech was secured against those limitations by the privileged nature of communications made in the Confessional, to the physician, and between lawyer and client.

CHAPTER XIX

⚜

FRANKLIN D. ROOSEVELT,
CORDELL HULL, AND
THE BIRTH OF THE UNITED NATIONS

BY A HAPPY CHANCE I came to know Cordell Hull rather intimately, and have always treasured the memory of our friendship. I first met him at the 1932 Democratic Party National Convention in Chicago, which nominated Franklin Delano Roosevelt for the presidency. It was the only party convention I ever attended, and I went there for only one reason, to try to get a clause in the platform supporting United States entry into the World Court. The chairman of the Resolutions Committee was the senator from Tennessee, Cordell Hull, whom I found accessible and friendly, and we worked at the draft together, though the final text reflected his senatorial caution more than my eagerness for a full and frank commitment.

Shortly after the elections which had swept Roosevelt into power, I was in Washington and called on Senator Hull in the senatorial office building to discuss the outlook. I said that I supposed Norman Davis would be Secretary of State as he had held high office under Wilson. Senator Hull heartily agreed but said that for some reason which he couldn't make out, Roosevelt had been inaccessible to him, although he had been his strongest supporter in the

Reprinted from The Autobiography of James T. Shotwell (The Bobbs-Merrill Company, Inc., Indianapolis and New York, 1961), pp. 303-314.

South. He was much put out about it and said that evidently his services had been forgotten. Only a week or so later it was announced that he himself was to be Secretary of State. Instead of sending him a letter of congratulations, which would have been hard to write in view of our conversation, I called on him at his senate office. As the door was opened he got up from his desk at the back of the room and came over to me with a winning smile, and before I could say a word, said: "I still think Norman would have been a better choice!" It was all so disarming, so intuitive. He kept me on to talk of the problems ahead, the first of many such talks in the months and years which followed.

It was this intuition, this sense of what people were thinking that was the key to his success in both domestic politics and diplomacy. It was also the key to his cautious, almost conservative policy in foreign affairs. Once, in my campaign for the League of Nations I got the United States Chamber of Commerce to poll their local chambers on the question whether they would support an international sanction against an aggressor—the old issue of the League—and the response was over 60 per cent in the affirmative. But, when I took this vote to Secretary Hull, he refused to take it seriously, for he said that it couldn't be relied upon when challenged, and in any case Congress wouldn't act on it. The memory of Wilson's defeat was still too strong. The one point on which we wholly agreed was the need for lowering the tariff barriers, which had been raised to unprecedented heights by the Smoot-Hawley Tariff, passed after the crash of 1929 to make the nation "self-contained and self-containing," and signed with special gold pens by President Hoover, in spite of the fact that it had been denounced by a statement signed by a thousand members of the American Economic Association. Against this economic nationalism Hull had fought in the Senate, the low tariff traditions of the South strengthened by a study of Adam Smith. But he was too experienced in politics to be a doctrinaire freetrader and as Secretary of State proposed only reciprocal tariff reductions in treaties with nations meeting our terms, and with the possibility of extending their scope by the most favored nation clause. This proved to be a lasting contribution in statesmanship, for the reciprocal trade treaties are still the avenue for American tariff policy.

Fortunately I was in a position to do something in support of a lessening of trade barriers through my connection with the International Chamber of Commerce. In November 1935 this organization joined with the Carnegie Endowment for International Peace in holding an important conference of distinguished business leaders from all the European countries and the United States, among them a young monetary expert from Sweden, Dag Hammarskjold. It was my task to organize this conference, although I must confess that I got lost in the highly technical arguments of specialists on science and commerce. The keynote of the conference in the words of the American President of the International Chamber of Commerce, Thomas J. Watson, "World peace through world trade," was almost immediately seized upon by Hitler's two lieutenants Goering and Schacht to turn the conference into pro-German channels.

Mr. Watson was not the kind of man to let this falsification of his formula for international peace stand without rebuttal, and, securing funds from the Carnegie Endowment, he created an Advisory Economic Committee of the American Committee of the International Chamber of Commerce, of which I was Chairman and Professor John B. Condliffe of the University of California (an economist of high standing with whom I had worked in the Institute of Pacific Relations) was editor. We made an exhaustive study of the whole problem and published some twelve studies. Mr. Watson was not satisfied with academic monographs and he prepared a moving picture film for use both in Chambers of Commerce and in schools. The argument for freer international trade reached a wide audience, especially through women's organizations, and at least one state, Iowa, was won over from isolationist protection.

President Roosevelt had made it clear from the beginning that he intended to be his own foreign minister. That may have been one of his reasons for choosing Cordell Hull as Secretary of State; for, unlike Norman Davis, who was intimately acquainted with European statesmen, Mr. Hull had visited Europe only once, in 1925; but in the first great test he came out ahead of the President, so far ahead indeed that his position was assured from then on. This was the World Economic and Financial Conference, held in London in the summer of 1933 at the call of the League of Nations. Although the Secretary of State was the head of the limited States delegation, the President did not consult him on the choice of the

other members, and as an added slight sent Raymond Moley, of
his "brain trust" entourage, to London as his personal representative, to whom the European statesmen turned as though he were
another Colonel House. But that situation did not last long. The
Conference had not been prepared by experts beforehand, and
such conferences almost always fail. I was in Geneva at the time,
and found that its economic experts were much distressed over
President Roosevelt's failure to understand the point of view of the
Europeans. They were chiefly concerned with the problem of
worthless or unstable currencies—Great Britain had been finally
forced off gold in 1931—and wanted, above all, to get back to the
gold standard which had worked so well in the nineteenth century.

Tariff problems seemed secondary to them. But Roosevelt, who
had once lowered the gold in the dollar, took this as directed against
American freedom of action in the future and wrote a bitter and
abusive letter to the Conference, accusing them of having lost sight
of their purpose which was "to agree on permanent solutions of
world economics and not to discuss the economic policy of one
nation out of the sixty-six present." It was an insulting letter, and
the conference would have broken up but for the courage and persistence of Secretary Hull, who rescued it from immediate collapse.
Moley having been discredited, and the monetary problem out of
the way, the old champion of free trade made an eloquent appeal
to the Conference to turn to what to him was still the fundamental
problem. It was only a wreck of a conference, and nothing came of
it, but it was a personal triumph for the man whom Roosevelt now
hailed in a final cable: "Before you sail I want you to know once
more of my affectionate regard and confidence in you."

The contradiction between Roosevelt's action in wrecking the
Economic Conference and his kindly words to Hull can only be
explained—and only in part—by the fact, now generally forgotten,
that the President was as ardent a nationalist as Hoover had been.
His "first hundred days" in which he fought the battle for recovery
from the near bankruptcy of the nation, were based on the principle
that international trade was secondary to recovery at home; and
he shared a popular suspicion that international bankers in Europe
were undermining the dollar. As for the war debts, on which economists urged an international settlement, he refused to allow the
delegates in London to discuss them. His mind was wholly set upon

the domestic scene. Here he wrote one of the finest chapters in the history of the United States, but history will also have to place over against it the fact that he wrecked the last effort at international economic action in Europe, where the aftermath of the American crash had brought new financial disaster in countries already bled white by the war. The ominous rise of militant nationalism, symbolized by Hitler's advent to power in January, 1933, was still not fully understood. But if F.D.R. had seen the demonstrations which I watched in Berlin, he might have paused before disrupting the forces of liberalism in Europe.

I came back from Europe with Secretary Hull on the small, slow liner, *President Harding* (of all ships!), and for over a week, with our deck chairs side by side, we spent many hours together, reviewing the situation, both at home and abroad. As he had never specialized in finance, leaving that for the Treasury, he was less critical of the President's "bomb shell" than of the refusal of the European governments to give more than polite attention to his appeal for lessening the barriers to international trade. He was especially disappointed in the British, to whom imperial preference had become as much a fetish as protectionism in the United States. But if Secretary Hull was reluctant to blame the President for his letter, he had no kind words for Raymond Moley, whom he blamed—apparently in error—for having got himself appointed as a special envoy of F.D.R. to oversee the conference. Moley was certainly not to blame for the President's letter, which really hit him more than it did the Secretary; nor could he be blamed if the European governments treated him like another Colonel House. But the Secretary needed his Tennessee mountain vernacular to describe the incident with sufficient strength and color.

I have gone into the history of this conference in detail, not only because of its importance but also because it is now almost forgotten. My interest, however, was less in it than in the plans which I discussed with Secretary Hull on the voyage home. I had thought up what I hoped might offer him a new way for lessening international trade barriers, by the use of the International Labor Office, and I drafted a memorandum on it, which at least took our minds off the London Conference for several days. The main idea was simple—nations which raised the wages and standard of living in the production of goods should have favored tariff treatment in the country to which they were exported. The plan was directed against the argument for high tariffs because of low wage costs in other countries. It also aimed to increase the total volume of foreign trade by the increased prosperity of the workers, who make up the great body of consumers. I admitted that the problem of comparable wages would be difficult and sometimes impossible. But the International Labor Office, the scientific secretariat of the I.L.O., could at least furnish basic standards for nations to negotiate on.

Neither Mr. Hull nor his economic assistants liked the scheme, because of its lack of a fundamental free trade principle. I said it was the Trojan horse to get inside the protectionist walls. But I had to admit that it was at least premature, as we were not yet (until 1939) members of the International Labor Organization. This gave me a rare opportunity to explain the I.L.O.'s origin and method of working. The result was that, in 1934, at his request I drafted the document for Senator Pittman, chairman of the Senate Committee on Foreign Affairs, which, with the strong support of the Secretary of Labor, Frances Perkins, made the United States a member of the I.L.O.

The London Economic Conference has now passed into the limbo of forgotten things, but its failure was a blow to the League of Nations which had sponsored it, at a time when the League's prestige had already been shattered by Japan's conquest of Manchuria. That first chapter of World War II had been timed by the Japanese militarists to fit the calendar of economic disaster in Europe, the aftermath of the American economic collapse of 1929, when in 1931, one of the largest banking houses of the Continent, the Kreditanstalt of Austria, failed and the Bank of England had to go off gold. The tragic consequences of the abstention of the United States from the League of Nations were clearly revealed on that occasion. The British were unwilling to apply the League sanction against Japan unless supported by the United States and, as we have seen, all that Secretary of State Stimson could offer was "the Stimson Doctrine," that the United States would not recognize a change of status brought about by force.

By telephone to Norman Davis in Geneva, Secretary Stimson proposed an international conference called by the League of Nations, but the Japanese militarists would have none of it, and the League ceased to function in Asia. Now in the economic field its effort to build a European community was torpedoed by F.D.R. It had only a slight chance of success at best, in view of the rise of Fascism and Nazism, but the best economists of Europe were working for it, and liberal opinion was bitterly critical of Roosevelt.

The second chapter of World War II began in 1935 when Mussolini attacked Ethiopia. Again the Secretary of State was unable to work within the League of Nations, but he was willing to work alongside it. When the British Foreign Secretary, Sir Samuel Hoare, speaking at Geneva, made a veiled reference to the shipment of American oil to the Italian navy, he either did not know or preferred not to know that Secretary Hull was doing his best to get the United States oil companies to stop their increasing shipments in the interests of peace. The Secretary told me that he had got assurances from the great oil companies that they would comply with his request. But he said that by some failure in doplomacy the British Foreign Office seemed not to know of this and the Foreign Ministers of Great Britain and France, Sir Samuel Hoare and M. Laval, refused to take similar action for the League of Nations, on the pretext that United States oil would be available to Italy anyway.

As I was going to England at that time, Mr. Hull asked me to make clear to the Foreign Office what he had tried to do. It was a difficult and delicate mission, and all I could do was to talk informally with my friends in the Foreign Office. It was also too late, too vague, and unofficial, and both Sir Samuel Hoare and Laval were on Mussolini's side. The League of Nations never recovered from this blow, as both Hitler and Japan soon acted in utter disregard of it in their aggressions.

It was in this connection that at Secretary Hull's request I served on a joint committee of State Department and Pentagon. I mention this only because its secretary was a young officer, Major Dwight D. Eisenhower. We had only a few meetings and nothing much came of it. But years later when the General was President of Columbia University, I called on him at the request of General Telford Taylor to ask him to use his influence in cataloguing the German war documents which had been gathered up in baskets or crates, and remained unpacked in the Pentagon or in the Archive Building. He readily agreed and a month or so later the archival work was under way—to the great advantage of historians of World War II. But in the middle of my talk with General Eisenhower he looked over at me with a genial smile and said, "You don't seem to remember that we've met before." I said that I couldn't recall our meeting. Then, with that winning frankness, now so well known, he said "When you were sent over by the State Department on that security problem, I was the young major sitting across the table taking down what you said!" Only a great man is capable of that kind of self-effacement after he has reached the heights.

To return to Secretary Hull—I realize that these reminiscences are slight, and give no adequate picture of Cordell Hull as Secretary of State, of the quiet dignity of the man in his meditative mood or the flash of anger in the eye when confronted with what seemed deception or lack of good faith in those with whom he was dealing. But, I recall one little incident which reveals the inner tenderness of this old Tennessee mountaineer. One afternoon I was sitting with him and Robert Walton Moore, formerly Congressman from Virginia, Counselor to the Department, and the Secretary's closest friend, when a little mouse put its nose out of a hole in the wainscot just beside Secretary Hull's chair. He kept still and asked us not to move either. Then, after a reconnaisance the mouse came over beside Mr. Hull's shoes and curled up on one of them. It was the most incredible sight I have ever seen in Washington! Everyone kept absolutely still. Then as the mouse slipped back into its hole, the Secretary of State turned back to the affairs of the nation, with the casual remark, "I've been making a friend of it." I forget what we were talking about, but shall never forget the way everything stopped for Cordell Hull's mouse.

Throughout the years immediately preceding the outbreak of World War II as the ominous shadow of Japanese and Nazi aggression began to threaten international peace, there was a strong movement toward neutrality, especially in the Middle West. This resulted in a strengthening of the neutrality laws to prevent the involvement of the United States in foreign wars. Convinced that for the United States to remain neutral in a resort to war by an aggressor in violation of its pledge to settle its disputes by peaceful means would make it *particeps criminis* in the crime of such a war, I accepted the honorary presidency of a nation-wide organization for the revision of the neutrality laws to enable the United States to discriminate between aggressor and victim. With the actual outbreak of World War II this more or less academic body was merged into the Committee to Defend America by Aiding the Allies, under the leadership of the Kansas publicist William Allen White, which, according to the Secretary of State was largely influential in securing the passage of the Lend-Lease Act by the Congress. But more important than our work was the impact on the mind and conscience of the nation by the bombing of London, the heroic defense of its outnumbered air force, the ringing challenge of Churchill and the radio description of "England's greatest hour" by Edward Murrow, in the nightly message "This is London," reflecting courage by sharing in it.

World War II left nothing of the structure of peace, nothing but the faith in its ultimate restoration with all the lessons learned by catastrophe. So we began over again, in a Commission to Study the Organization of Peace, which I founded in 1939. Once a month a hundred of us would spend Sunday, generally all day long, in the frankest òf discussions, the results of which were set forth in a report, the first of an annual series, beginning with an analysis of war. These reports covered the problems of politics, economics, and international law. This work was naturally well known in the State Department. When it set up a small committee with Sumner Welles, the Under-Secretary of State, as chairman to draft a post-war policy, both Clark Eichelberger of the League of Nations Association and I were invited to serve on it. At first it was to be kept ultrasecret, for it would not do to give either our allies or our enemies the idea that we were thinking of peace terms in the very crisis of the fighting. But it was in this committee that the first blueprint was made of a charter for the United Nations.

After some months of work, Secretary Hull held several sessions under his own chairmanship, to which he invited the members of the Foreign Relations Committees of the Senate and the House. In these open sessions there was free discussion, and I found myself in the awkward position of having to oppose the proposition backed by Mr. Welles and Dr. Bowman, the eminent geographer, that Germany should be dismembered in order to ensure a lasting peace. I held, to the contrary, that it would make a lasting peace impossible.

More embarrassing, however, was the fact that Mr. Welles was in close touch with the President and it was evident that Secretary Hull was not. Still more important was the fact that every time Mr.

Welles came back from the White House he warned us against planning anything like a revival of the League of Nations. F.D.R. was determined not to repeat the failure of Woodrow Wilson and had been much disturbed over the isolationist uproar at his suggestion that an aggressor should be "quarantined." So, all he had in mind when we began work was an international Farm Bureau, perhaps at Des Moines, Iowa; a banking center, perhaps at London; a health center, perhaps at Paris; and other non-political bodies working on their own.

Mr. Welles asked the members of his committee on post-war planning not to refresh their memories of the League or even look at the Covenant, but to try to get something different. However, after a few months' work we found that our blueprint for an international organization was almost the same as the Covenant. It was simply a statement of fundamental realities. This document, revised at the Conference of Dumbarton Oaks, was then worked over into the Charter of the United Nations at San Francisco.

Looking back over our blueprinting, I am inclined to think that the major blunder was the proposal to limit the Council to problems of security. The Council of the League was a general executive, ready to deal with all kinds of disputes, such as the government of the Saar. It did not meet as potential enemies on the one issue of war and peace, but as an agent of constructive politics, using conciliation as its major technique. The lack of such a body in the United Nations is increasingly felt as the Assembly becomes so great in size as to be ineffective in action.

The work of the planning committee of the State Department was kept secret, until finally, at a conference of foreign ministers in Moscow in November, 1943, Secretary Hull secured the consent of Stalin to "establish a general organization, based on the principle of the sovereign equality of all peace-loving States . . . for the maintenance of international peace and security." The result was the San Francisco Conference in April, 1945, to draft a charter for the United Nations.

Recognizing the great popular interest in the success of this conference, the State Department invited "Consultants" to its delegation, consisting of representatives of business, labor, agriculture, education, law, and religion. This semi-official body met daily during the conference, and it is not too much to say that it was chiefly responsible for the economic and social provisions of the Charter, including the problem of human rights. The State Department was opposed to this extension of the work of the United Nations to cover such vast fields of an uncharted future. The Secretary of State, Edward R. Stettinius, Jr., showed obvious indifference to our proposals when they were laid before him at the session of the Consultants. But when my colleague Judge Joseph M. Proskauer reminded Stettinius that the members of the Consultants represented bodies that controlled four million votes, Mr. Stettinius suddenly woke to the political significance of this remark, and we had no further trouble with the State Department.

I was chairman of the Consultants for six weeks, until laid up by an attack of pneumonia which forced me to return home. I have never had a more inspiring experience than that of helping, at last, to weld the aspirations for peace into a world-wide organization. It seemed as if the long road which I had been traveling for years was at last reaching its goal. Yet such hopes were soon overcast.

Even during the conferences the attitude of the USSR was disquieting, as President Truman made clear to the dour Molotov in an outspoken demand that the Kremlin live up to its engagements. The way in which this divergence sharpened into a cold war lies outside the limits of this story, but it would be wholly wrong to end it there.

The Charter of the United Nations, drafted at San Francisco, provides an inspiring program for the organization of peace, which both sides of the great communist controversy invoke to justify their policies. This is not mere political hypocrisy; it marks the growth of new, if divergent, ideals coexistent in a world in which war had always been held to be the final and legitimate instrument of national policy. The full and adequate implementation of the revolutionary concept in the Charter may be long delayed. It took the English over four centuries to perfect representative government and the rule of law, and that was within a homogeneous nation. The United Nations is the most heterogeneous body in history, yet the forces of modern science are creating an interplay of interests, which is the way people will be living from now to the end of time. We are still only pioneering, but as Bergson, the philosopher, pointed out half a century ago, scientific invention and discovery hold promise of ever-increasing betterment and of man's release from unremitting toil, as well as from want and poverty. These, as well as the renunciation of war, are now the concern of the United Nations. The success or failure of that organization is, therefore, a measure of civilization itself. There can be no surer guarantee of its ultimate success.

CHAPTER XX

᙭

THE CONTROL OF ATOMIC ENERGY
AND A NEW INTERNATIONAL
WORLD

IN FEBRUARY, 1945, the League of Nations Association was transformed into the American Association for the United Nations,
with Mr. Sumner Welles, former Under Secretary of State, and I
as the two honorary presidents, and Clark Eichelberger continuing
his splendid service as director. My own work for the United Nations continued through the Commission to Study the Organization
of Peace, now under the chairmanship of Professor Arthur Hol-
combe.

But more pressing than these continuing problems were the two
problems directly due to the war, the control of atomic energy and
the recovery of Western Europe under the Marshall Plan.

The first and most obdurate of problems was the control of
atomic energy. In August, 1945, at Hiroshima and Nagasaki, the
conclusion which I had drawn in 1927 of the revolution in warfare
due to science was tragically fulfilled, and a new and terrible chapter in history was opened, that of thermonuclear warfare. Appalled
at the prospect, public opinion insisted that steps be taken to check
such a development, and in January, 1946, the United Nations
Commission on Atomic Energy was created. At its first meeting, in

*Reprinted from The Autobiography of James T. Shotwell (The Bobbs-Merrill
Company, Inc., Indianapolis and New York, 1961) pp. 315-317, 319-330.*

June, 1946, the United States delegation, headed by Mr. Bernard M. Baruch, called for an International Atomic Development Authority, exercising direct control of all atomic activities in all countries, a supra-national body, free from the veto of the Security Council of the United Nations, in short, an irresponsible body with the greatest power in the world.

While fully recognizing the sincerity of purpose which prompted Mr. Baruch and his associates, I could not accept their conclusion. The proposal to set up a world government primarily as a defense mechanism against the danger of atomic war would threaten the structure of democratic life throughout the world, in view of the fact that atomic power was also an ultimate power for peace-time economy. Therefore, in line with the discussions in such bodies as the Council on Foreign Relations and the Foreign Policy Association, in 1946 I organized a Committee on Atomic Energy under the auspices of the Carnegie Endowment for International Peace, composed of some fifty of the leading physical and political scientists and organizers of industry.

The report of our Committee differed from the official American proposal in that it did not provide for the ownership of all uranium and thorium in the world by an international commission which would also operate all atomic power plants. Instead, our report left such ownership in the hands of national bodies in each country, while an International Atomic Energy Commission vested with wide powers of control would be charged with the positive function of promoting the utilization of atomic energy for peaceful purposes. Each of the five states' permanent members of the Security Council would select one member of the International Commission, and the General Assembly would select four other members so that it would not be a mere organ of the Security Council, and its decisions would be taken by a simple majority vote. Thus, the veto of the Security Council would be at least partially overcome. The International Commission would have power in the course of its routine activities to take preventive measures against a nation shown by inspection to be planning atomic war. In the case of actual resort to atomic war, the Security Council would act under the Charter. The International Commission would have its own staff and maintain offices, laboratories and plants for its work. It would be assisted by an advisory board of scientific and technical experts, and monthly reports would be made to it by each national commission. It is perhaps unnecessary to add that neither the Baruch plan nor that of the Carnegie Endowment was ever realized, although the Endowment's subcommittee report on the *Feasibility of International Inspection of Raw Materials* was the first document which the Scientific and Technical Committee of the United Nations Commission was able to agree upon after their long stalemate in the summer of 1946.

The pioneering work of the United Nations Commission has not been sufficiently recognized. On July 5, almost six months after its creation, Mr. Baruch, as the American representative on it, offered a plan which would have brought the proposed Atomic Energy Authority within the Charter of the United Nations, by the provision that all serious offenses, constituting a threat to the peace, should fall within the jurisdiction of the Security Council. However, the opposition of the USSR to effective inspection left the whole problem unsolved.

In the summer of 1955 when I was eighty-one, I paid my last visit to Europe. Fateful years had passed since I had left it on the eve of World War II, when the structure of peace on which I had been working for the twenty years of the life of the League of Nations crashed under the blows of the Axis Powers. To restore that structure or erect one like it, in the United Nations, had been my chief interest during those trying years. But again the magnificence of the world organization—and it was magnificent in conception—was menaced by the rift between the Communist and the free nations; and the center of this conflict shifted from the United Nations to Western Europe, with the North Atlantic Treaty Organization (NATO) as the military shield for the free nations against Soviet aggression, and the Organization for European Economic Cooperation (OEEC), the creation of the Marshall Plan, as the expression of common economic interest. A new chapter was opening in the history of that part of Europe which had been the nursery of war in the past. It was to study this problem at first hand that I sailed for Europe the first week of June.

The European Movement, the term used to cover the whole effort to unify Western Europe, began with the pioneering work of

Count Coudenhove-Kalergi, whose book *Pan Europe*, published in Vienna in 1923, proposed a political federation like that of the United States. It was a bold challenge to the national state system and, indeed, to the whole history of Europe, but with courage and eloquence he held meetings in various countries and won support for the idea from statesmen as well as publicists. I always remained skeptical of it, however, for I did not believe that the parallel with the history of the United States was valid. Even there full sovereignty of the federal system was only won by a desperate civil war. The federation of the European nations would involve a much greater strain on ancient ties. I was, therefore, doubtful about the reality of this first phase of the European Movement, in spite of the fact that at first it had the backing of Briand and Churchill. My judgment was justified by Briand's vague generalities when he presented the idea to the League of Nations and by Churchill's subsequent withdrawal from support for the Movement, of which he had been the most eloquent advocate. In his speech at Zurich University in 1946 Churchill proposed as a "sovereign remedy" for the tragedy of European wars, a United States of Europe, which would "provide a structure under which it could dwell in peace, in safety and freedom. . . ." But this was one time when Churchill spoke irresponsibly, for he never followed up this dream of a federated Europe. My doubt as to the reality of a political union seemed justified.

Then the incredible happened when six western nations—France, West Germany, Italy, Belgium, the Netherlands, and Luxembourg —created a supra-national body, the Coal and Steel Community, to deal, independent of any governmental interference, with the heavy industries—coal, steel, and transportation—which are the indispensable munition industries of modern war. The purely businesslike name of the Community was misleading, for it had a government of its own—legislature, court, and executive offices. The Movement for European Union was being realized not by working from the top, but from the practical needs of an interdependent economy.

It was, however, the implied guarantee of peace which the French Foreign Minister Robert Schuman emphasized when he presented the plan to the French Chamber of Deputies. But, once launched on its career, the success of the Coal and Steel Community led its brilliant founder, Jean Monnet, to mobilize popular support for an attack on the whole war system by a proposal to create a European Defense Community (EDC), which would internationalize the armies themselves. The rejection of this plan by the Chamber of Deputies showed that the old nationalism was by no means dead. But if internationalizing the armies was going too far—and to the distress of some of my friends I said that I thought it was—there still remained the question which interested me most: what were the possibilities of the Western European Union (WEU), the political body which had begun as a consultative body at Strasbourg, composed of members of parliaments and governments?

Stirred by new hope, but sobered by past experiences, I sailed for Europe to study this new chapter in the history of freedom. (Happily my daughter Helen went along with me. She was already an established painter, with canvases in museums, and while I spent my time in interviews, she set up her easel in London, Paris, Chartres, Strasbourg, or Luxembourg; and while my memory of our journey grows dim, I have only to look at her canvases, glowing with light and color, to recall those scenes of my last visit to Europe. Happily, too, the European offices of International Business Machines, following instructions from New York, looked after us in London and drove us from city to city in luxurious cars, so I was able to study the problem, not only from foreign offices but on the spot.) To get my bearings, I went first to London. Somehow it seemed the natural place to start, but I soon found from intimate talks with officials at the Foreign Office and members of parliament that there was little to be gained from this second-hand way of studying the problem of continental politics. The British still remained isolationist at heart, almost as distrustful of the French as of the Germans. In diplomatic circles there was complete skepticism, except for a few "back benchers" in Parliament who had attended sessions of the European Assembly at Strasbourg.

Fortunately, just as I arrived in Europe a conference of Foreign Ministers held at Messina had greatly cleared the situation by recognizing the Strasbourg meeting as the Council of Europe, and by setting up a working office in London. But the British, who had never joined the Steel and Coal Community, still held back. Foreign Secretary Eden had been only an observer at Messina, and when

I tried to find out more about the London office of the Council, I found that it had been set up in an ordinary house at 2 Eaton Place, a purely residential section. The Belgian in charge of it told me I was the first visitor who had ever found his way to it. My friends at the Foreign Office seemed even a little taken aback by my having discovered it.

However, on June 8 the *Times* spilled the beans by a news item from Paris from which I quote, because it stated the program for European union with the clarity of French diplomacy at its best. In a press conference at the Quai d'Orsay, M. Pinet, the Foreign Minister, summarizing the results of the Messina conference, stated that:

> It had been decided to set up a new organization which would finance and direct atomic research in all six countries of the European Coal and Steel Community. Cooperation in the fields of transport, gas and electricity would also be developed, by giving wider powers to organizations already existing.
>
> A European common market was still the aim of all six governments, but this could only be brought about progressively. At Messina France had secured the recognition by her partners of the prior need for: (1) a common tariff policy; (2) the equalization of social and wage rates; (3) a fund for the reconversion of local industries affected by international competition; (4) general agreement between all members before the adoption of convertibility by any one of them.

There were no comments in the *Times*. Evidently it was time to leave London for Paris and the countries of the Coal and Steel communities.

Before leaving, however, I had the chance to state my point of view in an address at the Royal Institute of International Affairs. I made two points which seemed to me vital for the future of the free world. First of all, European union would not develop into a federation like the United States, as some idealists seemed to think. It would develop functionally, where common interest impelled unity of action and policy, rather than by the acceptance of a new federal state system. The European Coal and Steel Community had been the first to realize this unity of interest in its own field. Now it was proposing to take over the vast potentialities of atomic energy. No one could tell how far this movement would go, but it was no longer merely a dream.

I ended my address with a prophecy which has now been fulfilled, five years later. I pointed out that the control of atomic energy would become the major problem of all nations when the process for making the A bomb was cheapened, and I said that the history of applied science showed that such a cheapening was inevitable, because it was a problem of engineering. The progress of steam power had depended not on the power in the steam, but on the inventors of Bessemer steel, which made the engines safe. The same dependence on engineering was true of electricity as Edison had shown.

I pointed out that the cheapening of the thermonuclear process would be a political fact of the first importance because it would mean that the smaller nations would have a different place in the power structure of nations. From this point of view little Belgium, I implied, with its access to African uranium, could rank as a great power. It would not need to accumulate the vast supply of atomic weapons that the great powers could bring together. It would need only half a dozen bombs to acquire a new influence on the political decisions of its neighbors. Half a dozen such bombs as were then available would be enough. This possibility of the small nations acquiring new power can make it either a nuisance on the pathway of progress or an aid to progress itself; but it raises international problems of an entirely new nature and recasts the old ones in a completely different setting from that of the national state system of history. This is an entirely different situation from what has existed until now. We have not sufficiently awakened to the problem which this revolutionary fact implies.

A few weeks later I had the chance to state my theory before one of the leading atomic scientists, then visiting Europe, and found him convinced that nothing like that could happen. The thermonuclear process would always be the monopoly of the great powers. He and his colleagues on the Atomic Energy Commission were wrong, for all the time, a cheaper process had been known and had been discarded for the gaseous diffusion plants such as those on which the United States had spent over three billion dollars.

It was not until October 11, 1960, that the *New York Times* published an account of a cheaper process and pointed out that this was creating an entirely new problem in the control of atomic energy. My address at the Royal Institute of International Affairs, five years before, was finally and fully justified. Today, in fact, the possibilities have become even more extraordinary, for the new, undeveloped nation of the Congo, for example, with the world's largest known supply of uranium could soon become a major power, given time to utilize the capital and skill offered from abroad. The cheaper thermonuclear process will, of course, cut the time required to a minimum.

My two weeks in London had been sobering in more ways than one. The city itself still bore the wounds of war. Although the wreckage of the blitz had been removed everywhere, there were hundreds of acres of gaunt cellar walls, mute reminders of the hours when England remained the one last hope of freedom in Europe. But Britain's "greatest hour" was for the defense of its heritage, not for the untried experiment of the structure of peace, which was taking new shape on the Continent.

On my arrival in Paris there was a telephone call from the Director General of policy at the Ministry of Foreign Affairs, M. Danridan, inviting me to come to the Quai d'Orsay. It was almost thirty years since I had been there, in the days of the Briand peace offer, and I was puzzled at the interest in my visit to Europe. Evidently the young men at the Foreign Office were concerned that I should give a good report on the French attitude on European union. I was told that arrangements would be made for me to keep closely in touch with the French delegation at Strasbourg, and I was taken over to see the specialist working on disarmament. He had no new ideas, but the incident recalled my work on Herriot's plans for a disarmament conference on which I had worked with M. Cassin in the last days of the League of Nations. I always found it somewhat strange that I could work more closely with the French Foreign Office than with the British, but I left the Quai d'Orsay convinced that it was more forward looking than at least the British Civil Service, whose chief service was to keep the machinery of empire—or commonwealth—going.

More important than these contacts with the Quai d'Orsay was my visit with M. Robert Schuman, who, as Minister of Foreign Affairs, had piloted the Coal and Steel Community—known then as the Schuman Plan—through the Chamber of Deputies. I had long talks with him at his new office in the Ministry of Justice. He had not lost any of his optimism. He was particularly happy that M. Spaak was chairman of the committee to "study" the plans of the Messina Conference for European Union. To M. Schuman that, alone, was a guarantee that the program was real. He also paid a warm tribute to his colleagues in the cabinet for their continued support and co-operation.

This confidence in the sincerity of French policy was strongly insisted upon in the Ministry of Public Works, which was responsible for the detailed plans for enlarging the Coal and Steel Community to include transportation. On the invitation of the Chef de Cabinet of this ministry, M. René Servoise, I went over these plans with the minister, M. Corniglion Molinier. He said that the plan was nowhere near so revolutionary as people thought, for already 40 per cent of the railway rates were under the Coal and Steel Community. The Swiss and the British were the only opponents to the plan, but it could be set in operation by a common fund for financing, modeled somewhat on the Bank and Fund in Washington.

This was the bright side of the picture. But I found that the friends of Jean Monnet, including my old friend M. Henri Bonnet, former ambassador at Washington, were still distrustful of the fine promises of the government. Evidently Paris was little better than London for studying the new Europe. So we left for Strasbourg, to be at the center of action.

The city of Strasbourg—a crossroads of the old and new—was an ideal site for the shadow parliament of Europe, reaching out from the old city with its timbered houses, along broad boulevards, to the new buildings of the Council of Europe.

The Consultative Assembly of the Council of Europe was in session when we arrived. At this meeting, composed of one hundred and thirty-five members from sixteen countries, it got a shot in the arm from the presence of practically all the Foreign Ministers of Western Europe, fifteen in all, including Harold Macmillan, later Prime Minister of Great Britain. The sessions which I attended lasted from 10 A.M. to 1 P.M. and from 3 P.M. to 7 P.M., I was frankly exhausted at the end of a week of listening to so many debates. Most of them were based on the steps which each government had taken or was planning to take in fulfillment of the Messina program. It was at once clear that the Council of Europe was facing up to realities, beginning to co-ordinate policies instead of merely talking in generalities. It dealt with all the phases of functional international action along the lines laid down by the Benelux Powers at Messina: international transport control, extension of postal and telegraph facilities, lessening of barriers to trade, and, finally, the control of atomic energy.

This was as much as could be done without a revolutionary change in the European state system. The Council of Europe was for consultation and agreement among sovereign powers. It was a convention, not a parliament with authority to act independently of its members. It was merely applying and extending, as far as it could, the revolution that had already taken place in the creation of the Coal and Steel Community. So, at the end of a week in Strasbourg, we left for Luxembourg, where I had engagements with the Prime Minister of the Duchy, M. Joseph Bech, and M. René Mayer, former Prime Minister of France, who had succeeded M. Monnet as head of the Coal and Steel Community. They surprised me by telling me that they had read some of my books, and we talked at length about the impact of the Coal and Steel Community on the political problems of European unity. M. Mayer brought up the point which the Quai d'Orsay had made to me in Paris, that the agreement on atomic energy raw materials between the United States and Belgium was a real obstacle to Europeanizing atomic energy production. When I tried to tell him that the United States would not want to be "a dog in the manger," we found there was no parallel expression in French. Sir Cecil Weir, the "observer" of British industry at the Coal and Steel Community, felt sure that M. Spaak would find a way out.

M. Bech had been on the committee of three—himself, M. Spaak and M. Beyen from Holland—which had been meeting in Brussels to "study" the way to enlarge the Coal and Steel Community to include transportation, electricity and atomic energy. They had been surprised to have support of the German representative as well, although he had come merely as an observer.

From Luxembourg we went on to Brussels, which, as I had learned both in Paris and Strasbourg, was the power house which was transforming the European Movement—which Churchill had hailed and then left in the lurch—into a working organism.

I spent three busy days in Brussels, ending with the talk with M.

Spaak. He was having conferences with Benelux statesmen until 6:30, but showed no sign of fatigue and kept me for an hour in which we went into the heart of things. In these complicated political situations, he said, personalities and personal relationships count. But when I suggested that what the European union needed most was forceful, eloquent, imaginative leadership, his reply showed his own very winning personality. He said that not long ago he was addressing a political meeting in a country town, and his theme, as always for the last twenty years, was the unity of Europe and the criminal folly of nationalism. After he finished, an old farmer came up to him and said that it was splendid, but why hadn't M. Spaak been saying it before? He laughed gaily over it.

Then I turned to the problem of atomic energy, especially the plans for the control and development through the Coal and Steel Community. He had not had time to follow the blueprints of Paris and Strasbourg, but the one time when I saw intense concentration in his eyes was when I opened up on the cheapening of the thermonuclear process and the revolutionary effect this would have on the power structure of the European States, offering a new place to smaller nations, not now but in the future. As we parted it was agreed that the interview would continue by letters and documents. But that was not to be.

There was one more capital to visit, Bonn. At Bonn the head of the IBM office met the train, and we arranged to visit the American Embassy in the morning. Dr. Conant, our ambassador, had had to go to Geneva, but he had left a message for me and instructions to his staff. I found that the first secretary of the embassy, Raymond Lisle, had been a student of mine, and he took pride in recalling to me portions of some of my Columbia lectures from as long ago as 1938. He brought in other members of the staff, and we spent over two hours going over the whole German situation.

I had known that there was no chance of meeting the one man I was most anxious to see, Dr. Hallstein, who had made a great impression on both Prime Minister Bech and M. Spaak by his firm adherence to their plans for extending the Messina program. He was back in Brussels, while Chancellor Adenauer was in Switzerland. The visit to Bonn was rescued from complete failure, however, by Mr. Lisle who got me in touch with the official of the Foreign Office who was actually in charge of the negotiations. This was Frau

Putkammer, the only woman official with whom I had talked in
my whole journey. She was thoroughly conversant with every
phase of the movement for European unity, but was strongly in
favor of solving the problems of the six nation group before dealing with the larger issue of the free trade national group led by
London. It should be union, not merely co-operation. Her point of
view was shared by Dr. Caspari, who was to represent West Germany at the United Nations in the fall. It was also strongly en-
dorsed by the German ambassador in London, to which I returned
by plane from Dusseldorf.

There were a few days left for London before leaving for home.
I at once got in touch with my friends at the Foreign Office. They
were still skeptical of the six nation supra-national approach to
Europe. This was becoming more than a difference of opinion; it
was beginning to look like a fundamental split between the British
and the Continental nations, the difference between a willingness
to co-operate and a willingness to unite. To trained British civil
servants—and to British opinion generally—international bodies were
simply instruments for getting things done rather than the initial
stage of a new undeveloped organ of international government.
Here, in another setting, was the same kind of distrust of commit-
ments for the future which had led the British to reject the Protocol
of Geneva thirty years before. But this time, the Continental nations were going ahead in disregard of British failure to join.

The last journey to Europe had come to an end. What were the
conclusions to be drawn from it? My answer to this question was
set forth in the closing section of the diary which I had kept, and
from which this narrative is drawn.

There is no doubt that Western Europe is undergoing a revolutionary change in which the old state system of absolute sovereignties is giving way to a new international complex; but it is equally
clear that history determines the way the different nations look at
it. Continental nations, inheritors of Roman tradition, built their
political institutions like architects, mindful of form and structure;
to the British, politics is more like engineering, the test being
whether it works. Its motive power is adjustment to practical needs.
As a matter of fact, this same pragmatic process is at work in the
reshaping of the Continental nations. The supra-nationalism of Jean
Monnet was, after all, a way to get things done—in other words the

practical method which the British so strongly emphasize. The solution of their differences lies in opening the doors of the Union to wider avenues of trade, and inviting not only Great Britain, but America and all the free world to associate itself with the Union. Some such idea, as we have already seen, lay in the grand design of General De Gaulle, but obscured and falsified by his insistence on French nationalism. It was also the slogan of the movement Union Now, led in the United States by Clarence Streit. Fortunately that movement, which began as a movement for political federation, has now put the accent on co-operation in an economic Atlantic union.

Finally, on September 7, 1960, President Eisenhower signed a bill, passed by Congress, which offers a new approach to the whole question. It sets up a "United States Citizens Commission on NATO," comprised of twenty private citizens appointed by Vice-President Nixon and Speaker Rayburn to organize and take part in a convention composed of similar commissions from other NATO countries "to explore means by which greater co-operation and unity of purpose can be developed to the end that democratic freedom may be promoted by economic and political means." In the election campaign both candidates gave assurance of their interest in this participation by the United States in the movement for union of the free world. After the elections no time was lost to make good this promise. Vice President-Elect Lyndon B. Johnson, accompanied by Senator J. W. Fulbright, Chairman of the Foreign Affairs Committee of the Senate, and Senator John Sherman Cooper, Republican of Kentucky, attended a meeting of the parliamentary conference of NATO, strongly urging the enlargement of its program to include international economic relations. To make good on this will mean action by the Congress, but Mr. Johnson sought to reassure his European listeners:

> Our recent elections have resulted in the choice of new leadership. In no sense is that a repudiation of President Eisenhower's support for the instruments of mutual strength in Western Europe.
>
> A new generation of Americans—who came to early maturity fighting for freedom on the fields of Europe and the islands of the Pacific—is coming to power in the leadership of our land.
>
> In their hearts is a determination to make the most vigorous use of America's resources and capacities to assure their children, your

children, and the children of all nations a life without war—a future of peace.

The Vice President further pledged that the United States would do "everything in its power" to strengthen the North Atlantic Treaty Organization with the long term objective of "a true Atlantic community with common institutions." The pledge was also a challenge not only to American isolation but the structure of sovereign national states, which had been the heritage of centuries of historical development. It was a recognition of the reality of a new international world.

Since these last words were written, the world has been shocked by the tragic death of President John F. Kennedy. Anguish overcast the earth, and out of the shadows of our sadness we emerged—as we did in the past crises in our history—with a greater sense of unity and continuity.

END

Date Due

PRINTED IN U.S.A.　　CAT. NO. 23231

908
S559   61897

AUTHOR
Shotwell, James Thomas
TITLE
The faith of an historian

61897

908
S559

Shotwell, James Thomas
The faith of an historian...

LIBRARY
OHIO DOMINICAN COLLEGE
COLUMBUS, OHIO 43219